Routledge Philosop

Husserl and the Cartesian
Meditations

'This is an excellent introduction to Husserl's difficult introduction to phenomenology, providing a comprehensive background to the work and detailed explanations of Husserl's idiosyncratic terminology while relating the work to issues in contemporary Anglophone philosophy.'   Jonathan Webber, *University of Sheffield*

'A timely book which provides an excellent introduction to the *Cartesian Meditations* and thus to phenomenology as such. Smith displays a gift in making accessible a text that is mostly regarded as highly complex and ridden with philosophical jargon . . . it will most likely become an essential introduction to any student wishing to become acquainted with Husserl's work.'
Lilian Alweiss, *Trinity College Dublin*

Husserl is one of the most important philosophers of the twentieth century and his contribution to the phenomenology movement is widely recognized. The *Cartesian Meditations* is his most famous and most widely studied work.

This book, in conjunction with the text itself, will serve as a proper introduction to Husserlian phenomenology – a philosophy that is attracting increasing interest within the analytical tradition, as well as being regarded as one of the most important developments in philosophy from within the continental tradition. A.D. Smith introduces and assesses the key concepts that arise in the book in a clear and engaging way. His style is accessible and suitable for anyone coming to the *Cartesian Meditations* for the first time.

A. D. Smith is Lecturer in Philosophy at the University of Essex.

IN THE SAME SERIES

Routledge Philosophy GuideBook to

Husserl and the
Cartesian Meditations

A. D.
Smith

 Routledge
Taylor & Francis Group

LONDON AND NEW YORK

First published 2003 by Routledge
2 Park Square, Milton Park, Abingdon, Oxon, OX14 4RN

Simultaneously published in the USA and Canada
by Routledge
270 Madison Ave, New York, NY 10016

Transferred to Digital Printing 2006

Routledge is an imprint of the Taylor & Francis Group, an informa business

Typeset in Aldus by RefineCatch Limited, Bungay, Suffolk
Printed and bound in Great Britain by
TJI Digital, Padstow, Cornwall

British Library Cataloguing in Publication Data
A catalogue record for this book is available from the British Library

Library of Congress Cataloging in Publication Data
Smith, A. D. (Arthur David)
    Routledge philosophy guidebook to Husserl and the Cartesian
    meditations/A.D. Smith.
        p. cm.—(Routledge philosophy guidebooks)
    Includes bibliographical references and index.
    1. Husserl, Edmund, 1859–1938. Cartesianische Meditationen.
    2. Phenomenology. I. Title. II. Series.

    B3279.H93 C3738 2003
    193—dc21

                                                2002033311

ISBN 10: 0-415-28757-X (hbk)   ISBN 13: 978-0-415-28757-9 (hbk)
ISBN 10: 0-415-28758-8 (pbk)   ISBN 13: 978-0-415-28758-6 (pbk)

CONTENTS

PREFACE

That Husserl's *Cartesian Meditations* is his most widely read work
is not surprising. It is short, available in paperback, and its subtitle –
'An Introduction to Phenomenology' – promises accessibility. As
such an introduction, however, the work must be judged a dismal
failure. Most strikingly, although Husserl by the time he wrote this
work had developed a battery of technical terms to express his
philosophy – terms that he employs repeatedly in the *Meditations* –
he usually doesn't bother to explain their meanings to the reader.
Furthermore, the work's very brevity actually works against its
accessibility. For Husserl's philosophy was complex and wide-
ranging, its various parts being multiply related to one another.
The result is that, even though he focuses on just a few fundamental issues in the text, he is repeatedly forced to allude to
various other aspects of his thought that do not get properly
treated. This is particularly sad in the case of Husserl, because
one of the most significant and impressive aspects of his philosophy is the depth with which he pursues his analysis of particular topics. It is only in the final meditation, one that deals
exclusively with a single topic, that the reader gets a glimpse of
the penetration characteristic of Husserl's work in general. Even
setting aside these factors, the *Cartesian Meditations* is far from

ideal. Throughout his life Husserl was worried by the problem of effectively presenting phenomenology to the public. For he was convinced, not only that phenomenology is the one true way of philosophizing, but that engaging in phenomenology requires a decision on the part of the philosopher – a decision that, as he says at one point, is analogous to a religious conversion (*Crisis*, 140 [137]).[1] Husserl therefore repeatedly worried over the best way to induce the reader to make such a decision. It cannot be said that the presentation in the first of the *Cartesian Meditations* is one of his best. For these reasons at least, a companion to the work may prove useful. Because of the shortcomings of the *Cartesian Meditations* itself, I have been obliged, in writing this companion, to refer repeatedly to Husserl's other writings so as to fill out the frequently unsatisfactory presentations in the target text. Only in this way can the present introduction to the *Cartesian Meditations* be what Husserl had wished for that work itself: that it be a decent introduction to transcendental phenomenology in general.

An additional reason for writing an introduction to the *Cartesian Meditations* is that it is a work of Husserl's maturity. It was written in 1929, less than ten years before Husserl's death at the age of 79. This constitutes a reason, at least in relation to readers within the English-speaking world, because the majority of discussions of Husserl's work within the so-called 'analytical tradition' of philosophy, which dominates that world, focus on his earlier philosophy. The principal reason for this is that, as we shall see, in the early years of the twentieth century Husserl became an idealist – a philosophical position with which the overwhelming majority of 'analytical philosophers' have no sympathy at all. Husserl's work dating from after this period tends, therefore, to be shunned. This is both unfortunate and silly. It is silly because much of what Husserl has to say in his middle and late periods can be assessed independently of that metaphysical issue. And it is unfortunate because Husserl is one of those philosophers whose thought quite simply got more profound as the years passed. Although I shall sometimes refer to Husserl's earlier writings on issues where his position did not substantially change, the present work is definitely meant as an introduction to his mature philosophy: to *transcendental* phenomenology, as he called it.

The *Cartesian Meditations* is an expanded version of two lectures that Husserl gave (in German) in Paris, appropriately enough in the Sorbonne's *Amphithéâtre Descartes*. Although a French translation of Husserl's expanded version of those lectures was published in 1931, no German version appeared during his lifetime. This is because, as Husserl continued to work over the lectures, he conceived the project of expanding them even further, in collaboration with his assistant Eugen Fink, into a large-scale work that would give a comprehensive account of his philosophy. It is to this projected work that he is referring when he says, in 1930, that it 'will be the principal work of my life', upon the completion of which he will be able to 'die in peace' (Schuhmann 1977, p. 361).[2] It was not long, however, before he gave up on this project, and turned his attention to composing another large-scale work that would give a different sort of introduction to his philosophy. Husserl died, in 1938, before this latter work could be brought to completion, though the extensive extant manuscripts were edited and published after his death as *The Crisis of the European Sciences and Transcendental Phenomenology* – commonly known as '*The Crisis*', for short. This was the last fruit of an intensely active philosophical career that lasted over half a century.

Edmund Husserl was born into a Jewish family on 8 April 1859 in Prossnitz, Moravia (now Prostejov, in the Czech Republic). At school he excelled in mathematics, the subject that he would pursue at university (after three terms studying astronomy). He first went to the University of Leipzig, where attendance at some philosophy lectures brought him into brief contact with Wilhelm Wundt. While in Leipzig he became a close friend of Thomas Masaryk, who later became the first president of the Republic of Czechoslovakia, but who at the time was a philosophy student of Franz Brentano's in Vienna. In 1878 Husserl moved to the University of Berlin, where he studied under the mathematicians Weierstrass and Kronecker. It was the former, Husserl attested, who 'awoke in me an interest in a radical grounding of mathematics', and from whom he got 'the ethos of my scientific endeavour' (Schuhmann 1977, 7).

In 1881 Husserl moved to Vienna, where his friend Masaryk was still living. Although he at first continued his mathematical studies, submitting a dissertation in the subject, he also attended philosophy lectures given by Brentano, who first convinced him that philosophy could also be conducted in the spirit of 'most rigorous science' (Schuhmann 1977, 13). This led Husserl to face the decision whether to devote his life to mathematics or to philosophy. He says that the impulse that finally led him to the latter 'lay in overwhelming religious experiences' (*ibid.*). Husserl now attended many more lectures by Brentano; and the two of them finally became sufficiently close that Husserl could spend a three-month summer vacation with Brentano and his wife. While in Vienna, and under Masaryk's influence, Husserl closely studied the New Testament. In 1886 he was baptized and received into the Evangelical (i.e., Lutheran) Church. He finally left Vienna as a result of Brentano's recommendation that he move to Halle to study under the philosophical psychologist Karl Stumpf, who himself now began to exercise a considerable influence on Husserl. It was in Halle that Husserl gained his first university appointment. His philosophical work at this time was focused on the philosophy of mathematics and logic, and his first book, *Philosophy of Arithmetic*, appeared in 1891. Husserl's philosophical horizons were broadening rapidly, however, and at the end of the decade he published the massive *Logical Investigations* – his first indisputable masterpiece, a work that ranges far more widely than its title would suggest, and one in which Husserl himself saw the 'breakthrough' to phenomenology (as he put it in the foreword to the second edition of this work). Soon after its publication Husserl moved to Göttingen to take up a chair of philosophy.

In the early years of the new century Husserl entered a deep philosophical crisis, in which he despaired – the *Logical Investigations* notwithstanding – of being able to give any sound justification for human claims to knowledge. The result of his working his way out of this epistemological impasse was the most decisive philosophical turning point in Husserl's career: he became an idealist, and embraced what he would call the 'transcendental' viewpoint. It is with the philosophy that Husserl began to work out after this point in his career, and of which the *Cartesian Meditations* is a mature expression, that we are primarily concerned in this book. Husserl published nothing during the first decade of the twentieth century, but his new-found philosophical outlook received expression in his lecture courses from this time – most notably, perhaps, in the 'Five Lectures' of 1907, now published under the title *The Idea of Phenomenology*, together with a companion series of lectures now published as *Thing and Space*. From this period also come Husserl's first sustained investigations into the nature of our consciousness of time – a topic that would preoccupy him throughout his life. In 1911 he published an article entitled 'Philosophy as Rigorous Science' in the journal *Logos* – an article that has something of the character of a manifesto. The first full-length publication to express what he now called 'transcendental phenomenology' appeared, however, in 1913: a book with the somewhat forbidding title *Ideas Pertaining to a Pure Phenomenology and to a Phenomenological Psychology, Book One* – commonly known as '*Ideas I*'. This is the first major expression of Husserl's mature philosophy. From now on, until the end of his life, there will be no more radical changes of direction, but simply an ever deeper pursuit of what he had come to regard as the true path of philosophy. Books Two and Three of *Ideas* were both projected and largely written around this time, but they did not appear during Husserl's lifetime. Indeed, apart from one or two articles, nothing more was published by Husserl until the late 1920s. As his manuscripts show, however, this period (indeed, the period until shortly before his death) was one of intense philosophical activity. In fact, the work to be found in Husserl's manuscripts is arguably the most important that he ever produced. Fortunately, these works are gradually seeing the light of day in the series *Husserliana*. We should all be grateful to the dedicated Husserl scholars who are responsible for this on-going work.

In 1916 Husserl moved to take up the chair of philosophy at Freiburg, where, despite an invitation in 1923 to take up Germany's most prestigious chair in philosophy at Berlin, he remained until his death, retiring in 1928 to become Emeritus Professor. During his teaching career at Freiburg Husserl attracted a large number of outstanding students, among whom he himself placed his greatest hopes in Martin Heidegger. In 1927 the two of them collaborated on several drafts of an article entitled 'Phenomenology' for the *Encyclopaedia Britannica*, though the final version shows little, if any, of Heidegger's influence. Heidegger succeeded Husserl in the chair of philosophy the following year, and he also brought out a selection of Husserl's writings on time-consciousness from the previous two decades – Husserl's first book for fifteen years. Only the next year, however, yet another book appeared – *Formal and Transcendental Logic* – which Husserl had written in a matter of months. At this time, also, Husserl's assistant, Ludwig Landgrebe, had been charged with the task of preparing several of Husserl's manuscripts dealing with 'transcendental logic' for publication. This project involved Landgrebe, in consultation with Husserl, up-dating and expanding the manuscripts in the light of *Formal and Transcendental Logic* – a project that lasted until Husserl's death. The book was finally published in Prague in 1939 with the title *Experience and Judgement*, though the publishing house in question was then immediately shut down as a result of Germany's annexation of Czechoslovakia.

Although Husserl had converted to Christianity in the previous century, life as a born Jew became difficult for him after the rise to power of the Nazis. As a result of a local decree, Husserl was given an enforced leave of absence from the university on 14 April 1933. Although this was soon rescinded, Husserl, a true German patriot, regarded it as the greatest affront of his life (Schuhmann 1977, 428). After this time he was effectively excluded from university life. In particular, Martin Heidegger, now the University Rector, cut off all contacts with him. And a few years later the German government refused Husserl permission to take up an invitation to give a keynote address at an International Descartes Conference in Paris. In August 1937 Husserl fell seriously ill with a form of pleuritis. 'I have lived as a philosopher,' he said to the nurse tending him during his last days, 'and I will try to die as a philosopher' (Schuhmann 1977, 488). He did so at 5.45 on 27 April 1938. Only one member of the Freiburg philosophy faculty, Gerhard Ritter, attended his cremation two days later. After his death, his manuscripts were smuggled out of Germany by Fr H. L. van Breda, who established the first Husserl Archive in Leuven, Belgium, where the work of sorting out Husserl's huge philosophical legacy continues to this day. I wish to thank the Archive, and its director Prof. Rudolf Bernet, for permission to consult as yet unpublished material by Husserl held there, and to quote from it in the present work.

NOTES

1 For an explanation of the abbreviations of the titles of Husserl's works used in this book, see the List of Abbreviations, pp. xvii–xix. Page references without any such preceding abbreviation are always to the *Cartesian Meditations* itself. For an explanation of the page references, see the 'Note on Translations and Citations'.

2 Some indication of how this 'principal work' might have shaped up is given in Eugen Fink's so-called *Sixth Cartesian Meditation* (Fink, 1988). This work, however, contains far more of Fink's contribution to the collaborative project than of Husserl's. And so, despite its great intrinsic interest, I shall not be discussing it further.

NOTE ON TRANSLATIONS AND CITATIONS

I quote from Dorion Cairns's English translation of the *Cartesian Meditations*, though the references I give follow the pagination of the standard German edition, which is given in the margins of the Cairns translation. Indeed, I follow the pagination of the German editions whenever reference is made to any of Husserl's works, although I quote from their English translations where these exist. In almost all cases such pagination is indicated in the translations. In cases where it is not, I give two page references, the first to the German edition, the second to the English translation.

Cairns's is not at all a bad translation of the *Cartesian Meditations*. He typically manages to render Husserl's frequently tortuous German prose into reasonable English. I have felt free, however, to modify his translation where I see fit. Since this happens so frequently, I have not cluttered up the text with indications of the fact. There are, however, three issues of translation over which I have departed from Cairns that are of sufficient note to warrant a warning and an explanation to the reader. The first concerns Cairns's use of italics and inverted commas, which is very confusing. More often than not sets of inverted commas correspond to italicization in Husserl's original text. German editions of Husserl's works frequently employ wide spacing to signify emphasis, though this is often unrepresented in Cairns's translation. Conversely, Cairns's own italics often correspond to nothing in Husserl. I advise the reader as far as possible simply to ignore all these aspects of the Cairns translation. I have myself employed inverted commas to represent inverted commas in Husserl, and italicization for both of the other two devices of emphasis, though I have sometimes cut down on Husserl's somewhat excessive use of them (as I have, also, when quoting from translations of other texts by Husserl).

Second, throughout his translation Cairns renders 'wirklich' as 'actual'. I almost always translate it as 'real'. There is reason for Cairns's choice, since Husserl also employs the German word 'real', which also needs to be translated somehow; and Cairns uses the English word 'real' for this purpose. There are two disadvantages to this policy, however. The first is that, although 'wirklich' does sometimes need to be translated by 'actual', most of the time, and especially in the crucially important Third Meditation, where it bulks so large, the English word 'real' is precisely what we want. By contrast, Husserl's German term 'real' has a highly technical meaning. Something is 'real' in this sense if it is spatio-temporal (or at least temporal) in nature, and subject to causality. It contrasts, not with things that are illusory or otherwise unreal, but with things that are 'ideal' – such as numbers, propositions and essences. Since this term is far less prominent in Husserl's text than 'wirklich', I also render it as 'real', but explicitly indicate the fact that the technical meaning is in question. The second disadvantage to Cairns's policy is that Husserl sometimes employs the German word 'aktuell', which Cairns also translates as 'actual' (as I do). It is not clear from Cairns's translation that the 'actuality' that features in the heading of §19 of the *Cartesian Meditations* is different from that which dominates the Third Meditation. What is 'aktuell' contrasts not with what is unreal, illusory and so forth, but with what is *potential*. This notion will receive some discussion in Chapter 2.

The third significant departure from Cairns's translation policy concerns the German words 'Gegenstand' and 'Objekt', and their associated adjectives. In a footnote to p. 45, Cairns indicates that there are two Husserlian terms that need to be rendered by 'object', which he will distinguish by using capitalization. He employs 'object' with a small 'o' to express '*Gegenstand*', and 'Object' with a large 'O' to stand for '*Objekt*'. This is a policy that Cairns also advocated in his influential book *Guide for Translating Husserl*. Although Cairns does not himself claim this in that work, the idea has grown up among certain scholars that Husserl uses the term '*Objekt*' only to refer to something that is objective in the ordinary sense: i.e. that is not 'subjective' but, rather, 'public' or intersubjectively determinable. '*Gegenstand*', by contrast, is held to refer to any object of consciousness at all – even one, like an object in a dream, that is not 'objective'. In fact, although very occasionally – as on p. 153 of the *Cartesian Meditations* – Husserl can indeed use the term '*Objekt*' with a connotation of objectivity, usually he does not, and the two terms '*Objekt*' and '*Gegenstand*' are standardly used interchangeably by him. Indeed, on p. 128 of the *Meditations*, it is essential that the term '*Objekt*' *not* be given the 'objective' reading. I, therefore, dispense with capitalization, and render both of these terms as 'object'. On the rare occasions where '*Objekt*' does carry a connotation of objectivity, I make this clear by writing of 'something objective' or of an 'objective thing'. By contrast, there *is* commonly (though not always) such a difference in meaning where the two related adjectives are concerned. The term '*objektiv*' (always capitalized as 'Objective' by Cairns) does often mean *objective* in the everyday sense, and '*gegenständlich*' ('objective' with a small 'o' in Cairns) does not, but has the technical meaning of 'pertaining to an object' (whether objective or not) rather than pertaining to our *awareness* of the object. For example, if you dream of a large dragon, its size is something '*gegenständlich*', since it attaches to the object of your dream, to *what* you dreamt – unlike, say, the vividness with which you dreamt it, which pertains to you the subject; but the large size is not something objective, since we are dealing with but a dream object. I again dispense with capitalization, since we shall not have much call to refer to what is technically *gegenständlich*. On the rare occasions where the technical notion of what is *gegenständlich* is at issue, I employ some construction involving the noun 'object': as in 'object-sense' for '*gegenständlicher Sinn*'.

ABBREVIATIONS

Almost all the works by Husserl published in German are in the *Husserliana* series, now published by Kluwer Academic Publishers, Dordrecht, and formerly by Martinus Nijhoff, The Hague. In the list below, volumes from this series are referred to simply by the number of the volume in the *Husserliana* series ('Hua I', etc.) and the date of publication.

APS   *Analysen zur passiven Synthesis*, Hua XI (1966).

Bernau   *Die Bernauer Manuskripte über das Zeitbewusstsein (1917/18)*, Hua XXXIII.

CM   *Cartesian Meditations*, tr. Dorion Cairns (The Hague: Martinus Nijhoff, 1973).
          Cartesianische Meditationen und Pariser Vorträge, Hua I (1973).

Crisis   *The Crisis of European Sciences and Transcendental Phenomenology*, tr. David Carr (Evanston: Northwestern University Press, 1970).
          Die Krisis der europäischen Wissenschaften und die transzendentale Phänomenologie, Hua VI (1954).

EB   Various drafts of the *Encyclopaedia Britannica* article 'Phenomenology' in *Psychological and Transcendental*

Phenomenology and the Confrontation with Heidegger (1927–1931), trs Thomas Sheehan and Richard E. Palmer (Dordrecht: Kluwer, 1997), 83–194. German versions in *PP*, 237–301.

EJ   *Experience and Judgment*, trs James S. Churchill and Karl Ameriks (Evanston: Northwestern University Press, 1973).
Erfahrung und Urteil (Hamburg: Claasen & Goverts, 1948).

Epilogue   'Epilogue' in *Ideas I* (see below), 405–430.
'Nachwort', in *Ideen zu einer reinen Phänomenologie und phänomenologischen Philosophie. Drittes Buch*, Hua V, 138–162.

EP I   *Erste Philosophie (1923–1924): 1. Teil*, Hua VII (1956).

EP II   *Erste Philosophie (1923–1924): 2. Teil*, Hua VIII (1959).

FTL   *Formal and Transcendental Logic*, tr. Dorion Cairns (The Hague: Nijhoff, 1969).
Formale und Transzendentale Logik, Hua XVII (1974).

Ideas I   *Ideas Pertaining to a Pure Phenomenology and to a Phenomenological Philosophy. First Book*, tr. Fred Kersten (Dordrecht: Kluwer, 1982).
Ideen zu einer reinen Phänomenologie und phänomenologischen Philosophie. Erstes Buch, Hua III (1984).

Ideas II   *Ideas Pertaining to a Pure Phenomenology and to a Phenomenological Philosophy. Second Book*, trs R. Rojcewicz and A. Schuwer (Dordrecht: Kluwer, 1989).
Ideen zu einer reinen Phänomenologie und phänomenologischen Philosophie. Zweites Buch, Hua III (1984).

Int I   *Zur Phänomenologie der Intersubjektivität. Erster Teil: 1905–1920*, Hua XIII (1973).

Int II   *Zur Phänomenologie der Intersubjektivität. Zweiter Teil: 1921–1928*, Hua XIV (1973).

Int III   *Zur Phänomenologie der Intersubjektivität. Dritter Teil: 1929–1935*, Hua XV (1973).

IP   *The Idea of Phenomenology*, tr. Lee Hardy (Dordrecht: Kluwer, 1999).

Die Idee der Phänomenologie. Fünf Vorlesungen, Hua II (1973).

LI   *Logical Investigations*, tr. J. N. Findlay, 2 vols (London: Routledge & Kegan Paul, 1970).

Logische Untersuchungen. Erster Band, Hua XVIII (1975).

Logische Untersuchungen. Zweiter Band, 2 vols, Hua XIX (1984).

PA   *Philosophie der Arithmetik*, Hua XII (1970).

P&A   'Phenomenology and Anthropology', in the Sheehan and Palmer volume (see under '*EB*' above), 485–500.

'Phänomenologie und Anthropologie' in *Aufsätzte und Vorträge* (1922–1937), Hua XXVII (1989).

PP   *Phenomenological Psychology*, tr. J. Scanlon (The Hague: Nijhoff, 1977). This translation omits much supplementary material published in the Husserliana edition.

Phänomenologische Psychologie, Hua IX (1962).

Time   *On the Phenomenology of the Consciousness of Internal Time (1893–1917)*, tr. J. B. Brough (Dordrecht: Kluwer, 1990).

Zur Phänomenologie des inneren Zeitbewusstseins (1893–1917), Hua X (1969).

TS   *Thing and Space: Lectures of 1907*, tr. Richard Rojcewicz (Dordrecht: Kluwer, 1997).

Ding und Raum, Hua XVI (1973).

'A II 1, 25' and suchlike are references to still unpublished manuscripts.

INTRODUCTION

(§§1–2)

Husserl would wish to be remembered for one thing: the discovery of *transcendental phenomenology* as the one true path of philosophy. In fact, for many of us the unforgettable achievement of Husserl is to be found in the detailed analyses at which he toiled throughout his life – analyses of a profundity rarely seen. Husserl himself did not, however, regard many of his findings as definitive. He repeatedly speaks of how difficult it is properly to carry out detailed phenomenological work, and his manuscripts clearly testify to a constant reworking of his accounts of a range of phenomena that, to judge by his published works, one might think he had 'settled'. Moreover, Husserl always saw in phenomenology a *communal* enterprise. It would proceed by a critical interchange of views; and he looked to others to lead forward philosophical (i.e., phenomenological) enquiry after his death. In fact, as §2 of the Introduction to the *Cartesian Meditations* indicates, his own time (and equally, he would no doubt think, our own) calls for phenomenology because of the irreconcilable divisions within philosophy itself. Transcendental phenomenology would *communalize* philosophy, fashion it into a community of mutually respectful co-workers: an *ethical* community, moreover, because, as we shall soon see, the ethical demand is inseparable, for Husserl, from the very drive to philosophize itself. No; despite the ground-breaking profundity of many of his treatments of specific philosophical topics, Husserl would not have wished to be remembered primarily for his 'results', but for his discovery of transcendental phenomenology as such.

THE 'IDEA' OF PHILOSOPHY

I write of a discovery, rather than an invention, of phenomenology because, although Husserl can freely speak of such a phenomenology as something new, he saw it not as some replacement for traditional philosophy, but, to use a Hegelian turn of phrase, as a matter of the (Western) philosophical tradition 'coming to its own truth'. Transcendental phenomenology is, as Husserl himself put it, the 'secret longing' of all genuine earlier philosophy. It constitutes the final breakthrough to a realization of the *idea* that has governed philosophy from its inception among the ancient Greeks. The word 'idea' (*Idee*) is one that occurs frequently in the *Cartesian Meditations* (indeed in Husserl's writings generally), and it is short for what Husserl will sometimes spell out as 'an idea in the Kantian sense'. It is a *regulative* idea: one that points us forward in an enterprise that can have no final, finite completion, though we have a definite recognition of progress. It is most simply thought of as an ideal. Philosophy is in its present divided state because the directive idea of philosophy, which, according to Husserl, was born in ancient Greece and was revivified by Descartes, has lost its vital force. The 'newness' of transcendental phenomenology is but that of the unprecedented radicality with which we decide to be led by this fundamental idea, the one and only idea that could, according to Husserl, govern a life that deserves to be called philosophical.

The sub-title of Husserl's *Cartesian Meditations* is 'An Introduction to Phenomenology'; the sub-title to Husserl's first major work after his move to idealism (mentioned in the Preface) was 'General Introduction to a Pure Phenomenology'; that of his last, unfinished, major work, the *Crisis*, was 'An Introduction to Phenomenological Philosophy'; and he also referred to his *Formal and Transcendental Logic* as an introduction. These repeated attempts to introduce transcendental phenomenology to the world not only bespeak a dissatisfaction with his earlier efforts; more importantly, they indicate an essential characteristic of transcendental phenomenology itself. For equally balanced with the difficulty of carrying out detailed phenomenological work is the difficulty of attaining the transcendental phenomenological perspective in the first place. True philosophizing is, as Husserl repeatedly states, an unnatural activity. In all our non-philosophical life – not only in all our 'everyday' activities, but also in all scientific endeavours – we are concerned with *objects in the world*, determining their properties and their reality (or lack of it). In such a life we are, as Husserl puts it, 'given over' or 'dedicated' to the world. All our concerns and activities are 'objectively' directed. As we shall see in our examination of the First Meditation, transcendental phenomenology involves a *switch of interest* – away from the world, and towards our own conscious life in which such a world presents itself to us. Such a redirection of mental focus is not a matter of engaging in psychology, since psychology, too, is concerned with what exists in the world: it is just that it is selectively interested in one domain or stratum of it – the 'mental', or the 'psychological'. The radical newness of transcendental phenomenology consists in its claim to have discovered an entirely new realm of being – one 'never before delimited', as he says in *Ideas I* – together with a new method of dealing with this new subject-matter. Much of the difficulty in introducing transcendental phenomenology consists precisely in getting someone even to discern this new field of enquiry – especially as it is so easy to misconstrue it as simply the familiar domain of the psychological. At a number of points throughout the *Cartesian Meditations* the reader will notice Husserl speaking of 'beginning philosophers'. This is not a reflection of the nature of his audience. On the contrary, the work was originally delivered to a gathering of some of the leading intellectuals in France. The point is that we are *all*, Husserl included, beginners at coming to grips with this new field of enquiry – an enquiry into what he will call 'transcendental consciousness' or 'transcendental subjectivity'.

In fact, according to Husserl, the notion of a beginning, of making a start, is central to understanding the very nature of philosophy itself. In his most extended treatment of the history of philosophy, developed in lectures given a few years before the composition of the *Cartesian Meditations* and now collected in Part One of *Erste Philosophie* ('First Philosophy'), Husserl says that three figures stand out for him in their significance: the 'binary star' Socrates/Plato and Descartes. What is significant in the present context is that he singles them out as 'the greatest beginners' in philosophy. Husserl regarded transcendental phenomenology as 'a first breakthrough of a true and genuine first philosophy'; and 'first philosophy' is 'a philosophy of beginnings', a 'scientific discipline of the beginning' of philosophy (*EP I*, 6–8). We cannot dissociate ourselves from the beginning of philosophy, because philosophy cannot be identified with any set of results or doctrines, but only with how it begins – with the spirit of its beginning – and how that beginning is sustained as a 'living force' (compare *CM*, 44). Philosophy is not a set of doctrines, because it is at root a certain form of *ethical life*. To understand such a life we need to see how it is motivated, how it begins.

What Husserl calls the 'primal establishment' or 'primal institution' (*Urstiftung*) of philosophy is to be found among the Greeks, specifically Socrates and Plato. It begins with the 'idea' mentioned above – an idea that is, specifically, the ideal conception of *genuine science* as *universal knowledge*. The universality that is in question here has two senses: such knowledge concerns reality as a totality, and it can be accepted as binding by any rational person whatever. This second feature implies, furthermore, that such science should be both grounded in, and developed through, *absolute insight*, and hence be *absolutely justified*. The 'idea' of philosophy is the idea of 'rigorous science', as Husserl put it in the *Logos* article that was his first published proclamation of his philosophy after his 'transcendental turn'. The commitment to this idea, which defines the philosopher, is a commitment to a life of *reason*, for 'philosophy is nothing other than [rationalism] through and through' (*Crisis*, 273

[338]).[1] In a sense, philosophy proper would be – not the complete realization of such universal, absolutely justified knowledge through insight (for that, since it encompasses infinite tasks, is impossible), but – a secure method leading to absolute success in each of its steps. This would be the 'final establishment' (*Endstiftung*) of philosophy (*ibid.*, 73 [72]), in relation to which Husserl can refer even to transcendental phenomenology as but destined to *become* philosophy (*CM*, 67). To exist as a philosopher between these two points is to strive for a 're-establishment' (*Nachstiftung*) in one's intellectual life of that desire for universal insight found in Socrates/Plato – becoming with them, as he says elsewhere, 'joint beginners' of philosophy (*EP I*, 5). So even philosophical beginners in the everyday sense must be led to reproduce previously discovered truths through their own insight, and therefore to *reproduce a true beginner of philosophy in themselves.*

Philosophy, being a methodologically clarified attempt to progress towards the ideal of absolute knowledge, must of course be systematic. But Husserl refuses to separate the 'systematic' Plato from the 'ethical' Socrates in philosophy's origin. For the ideal of absolute knowledge is the goal that a certain sort of life sets for itself. We can, therefore, characterize philosophy as much by the nature of its motives as by the nature of its goal. And what above all characterizes the philosophic life is *self-responsibility*. 'Philosophy', as Husserl says in the very first section of the *Cartesian Meditations*, 'is the philosophizer's quite personal affair. It must arise as *his* wisdom, as his self-acquired knowledge tending towards universality, a knowledge for which he can answer from the beginning, and at each step, by virtue of his own absolute insights' (44). In fact, the reader will find references to responsibility scattered throughout the *Cartesian Meditations*. And at one point he speaks of the need for the philosopher's radicality to become 'an actual deed' (50). The responsibility in question is initially, of course, an intellectual responsibility to settle for nothing less than 'insight' in all matters. Socrates' method was that of 'tireless self-reflection and radical appraisal', a method of 'complete clarification' which leads to a knowledge that is 'originally produced through complete self-evidence' (*EP I*, 9–10). The self-responsibility that is philosophy is the responsibility to accept nothing as knowledge that you have not validated for yourself. It is nothing but the demand for 'universal self reflection', for 'a resolve of the will to shape one's whole personal life into the synthetic unity of a life of universal self-responsibility and, correlatively, to shape oneself into the true "I", the free, autonomous "I" which seeks to realise his innate reason, the striving to be true to himself' (*Crisis* 272 [338]). Such reason, as he goes on to say, is '*ratio* in the constant movement of self-elucidation'. Indeed, transcendental phenomenology is characterized by Husserl as ultimately nothing but absolute self-explication (*CM*, 97). Philosophy is nothing other than absolute honesty.

The notion of *insight* has already started to emerge as being at the very heart of Husserl's vision of philosophy, and he will spell it out in his own fashion in a way we shall investigate later. Preliminarily we can contrast it with '*doxa*' – mere opinion, what we take on trust, what we have not interrogated and brought to clarity in our own minds: in short, *prejudice*. Despite the fact that such *doxa* is indispensable for ordinary life, it is, because of its typical unclarity and its necessary relativity to a given culture, open to question. In fact, Husserl saw epistemological naïveté as giving way to philosophy as a result of the 'prick of scepticism' (*EP II*, 27). He presents Socrates and Plato as reacting against the Sophists (whom Husserl construes as sceptics); he presents Descartes as attempting to answer various later sceptical schools of thought; and his own move towards transcendental phenomenology in the first decade of the twentieth century was itself motivated by sceptical worries about the very possibility of knowledge – as the 'Five Lectures' of 1907 make plain. Scepticism rots the human spirit, corroding not only the life of the intellect but all moral and spiritual values. Nevertheless, by bringing all claims to knowledge into doubt, scepticism fulfils its destiny by making possible a truly philosophical perspective, one oriented to the possibility of knowledge as such and its implicit goal of universality. Once the human spirit has been goaded into philosophy, has decided in favour of a life of reason guided by the idea of science, a new level of human existence is achieved. As Husserl says in a late text, 'Philosophical reason represents a new stage of human nature and its reason. But the stage of human existence under ideal norms for infinite tasks, the stage of existence *sub specie aeterni*, is possible only through absolute universality, precisely the universality contained from the start in the idea of philosophy' (*Crisis*, 337–8 [290]).

The idea of philosophy – and its implied idea of mankind as beings capable of philosophy, capable of following the absolute demands of reason – was not engendered in an abstract humanity: it had a specific historical origination, and it is kept alive (or dormant) only through a specific tradition. The idea of philosophy should be of interest to us because that tradition is *our* tradition. The birth of philosophy determines 'the essential character and destiny of the development of European culture' (*EP I*, 17); it is the *'teleological beginning* . . . of the European spirit as such' (*Crisis*, 72 [71]). Philosophy does not confine itself to the groves of academe. As a transformation of the human spirit, as the raising of humanity to a higher level of existence, it will resonate through, indeed transform, the culture in which it is genuinely alive. 'Science spreads itself across all areas of life and everywhere that it flourishes, or is believed to, claims for itself the significance of being an ultimately normative authority' (*EP I*, 17). Philosophy has so changed humanity, at least European humanity, that any subsequent stage of its culture will be whole and hale only where the life of reason flourishes as a unifying and directive force, transforming mankind into 'a new humanity made capable of an absolute self-responsibility on the basis of absolute theoretical insights' (*Crisis*, 329 [283]). Needless to say, the history of European humanity has hardly been that of the clear-sighted unfolding of reason. Philosophy begins with insight; but as it is handed on in a tradition, it can and does become doctrine. Truths that were attained through original clarity become 'sedimented': they are passed along, like so many possessions, without our reliving the experience of insight which brought them into being as truth, and in which their 'proper' meaning is alone to be found.[2] And so philosophy itself can turn into the very kind of 'prejudice' against which it originally arose. This, however, is the death of philosophy. And when philosophy dies, the whole civilization which it once

informed grows sick. Husserl established transcendental phenomenology, as a rebirth of the original vital spirit of philosophy,
in opposition to what he saw as the malaise of Western culture.
This malaise was, he believed, directly attributable to philosophy
having lost its way by having lost touch with its vital origin or
'primal establishment'. He saw a clear manifestation of this, as the
Introduction to the *Cartesian Meditations* itself indicates, in the
'splintering of present-day philosophy', in an absence among
philosophers of a 'commonness of their underlying convictions',
and in a 'pseudo-reporting and pseudo-criticizing, a mere sem-
blance of philosophizing seriously with and for one another . . .
[which] hardly attests a mutual study carried on with a consciousness of responsibility' (46).

One thing that Husserl sees as an immediate consequence of this
philosophical decadence is the supposed independence from philosophy of the so-called 'positive sciences'. The reader will have
noticed that when discussing the 'primal establishment', Husserl
speaks indifferently of 'philosophy' and of 'science'. On the very
first page of the *Cartesian Meditations* Husserl attributes to
Descartes the view that all the various sciences 'are only non-self-
sufficient members of the one all-inclusive science, and this is
philosophy. Only within the systematic unity of philosophy can
they develop into genuine sciences' (43). This is, however, not just
Descartes's view; it is also Husserl's, because it is part and parcel of
philosophy's 'primal establishment' – this time, specifically at the
hands of Plato. The 'idea' of a systematic enquiry into universally
valid truth comes first; any 'positive' science is but a 'regional'
application of this philosophical perspective to a particular domain
of reality. During the course of the nineteenth century, however,
the positive sciences separated themselves off from philosophy as
supposedly autonomous disciplines. One thing that results from
this is that such 'sciences' lose 'that scientific genuineness which
would consist in their complete and ultimate grounding on the
basis of absolute insights, insights behind which one cannot go back
any further' (44). That is left as a philosopher's pipe-dream. But
this means that they are no longer expressions of genuine *science* –
a failing that is actually manifest, as Husserl repeatedly points out,

in the unclarities and controversies concerning the 'foundations' of the various sciences, even such 'hard' sciences as physics and mathematics (e.g. 179). An even more important result is that 'science' ceases to have any human meaning. 'Merely fact-minded sciences make merely fact-minded people.' Such positive science, Husserl goes on to say,

> excludes in principle precisely the questions which man . . . finds the most burning: questions about the meaning or meaninglessness of the whole of this human existence. Do not these questions, universal and necessary for all men, demand universal reflections and answers based on rational insight? In the final analysis they concern man as a free, self-determining being in his behaviour towards the human and extrahuman surrounding world and free in regard to his capacities for rationally shaping himself and his surrounding world. What does science have to say about reason and unreason or about us men as subjects of this freedom?
>
> (*Crisis* 4 [6])

Husserl saw the role of transcendental phenomenology as being nothing less than the saving of a lost European civilization through the 'final establishment' of genuine philosophy, one that would 'infuse our times with living forces' (45) through a reassertion of that 'radicalness of philosophical responsibility [which] has been lost' (47). If he were alive today, more than half a century after his life's work ended, he would weep.

HUSSERL AND DESCARTES

The foregoing exposition of Husserl's views – featuring as it does an origin of true philosophical thinking among the ancient Greeks, one which has become sedimented and 'inauthentic' in our tradition, one which, therefore, we must revitalize by attempting to think it through originally – may remind some readers of Martin Heidegger. Some, indeed, have suggested that Husserl *derived* such a perspective from Heidegger himself, importing it, unacknowledged, into (only) his late work the *Crisis*, which postdates

Heidegger's first major published work, *Being and Time*. When readers bear in mind that the above exposition has drawn principally on lectures delivered before the publication of *Being and Time*, they may well, however, draw the conclusion of the present author that the substantial (and largely unacknowledged) influence is in precisely the opposite direction.[3] Be this as it may, Husserl's reading of philosophy's history is in fact significantly different from Heidegger's in two respects. First, he traces philosophy's 'primal establishment' primarily to Plato, whereas for Heidegger Plato represents already a falling away from the truly original thinkers Anaximander, Heraclitus and Parmenides. Second, Husserl points to Descartes as the second major landmark in philosophical history, whereas for Heidegger he is where things go about as badly awry as can be. The reasons behind this divergence run deep, as we shall see later. That said, let us turn our attention to Descartes.

In the first two introductory sections of the *Cartesian Meditations* Husserl attributes everything I have expounded as involved in the 'idea' of philosophy to Descartes. My earlier exposition has focused on Plato (and Socrates) for two reasons. First, that is how Husserl himself saw matters, as I have indicated. So, when he attributes to Descartes a concern for 'ultimate grounding on the basis of absolute insights' (44), he is not implying that this originated with Descartes as a philosophical concern. Second, there is an issue discussed by Husserlian scholars under the title 'the Cartesian way' into phenomenology. The *Cartesian Meditations*, together with *Ideas I* and certain other writings, are held to provide just one possible route towards transcendental phenomenology, to which there are non-'Cartesian' alternatives. In fact, even the *Cartesian Meditations* themselves, which as a whole follow 'the Cartesian way', speak of '*one* of the ways that has led to transcendental phenomenology' (48, my emphasis), and two other ways are concretely, if briefly, indicated. We shall explore this matter later; but we are already in a position to see that a concern with absolute insight, unconditional justification, universal and absolute truth – in short a concern with 'rigorous science' – cannot constitute the 'Cartesian way' into phenomenology. For one thing, it is not peculiarly Cartesian: at one point Husserl refers to it as 'the Platonic and Cartesian idea' (*EP II*, 5). For another, Husserl himself, as we shall see, does explicitly speak of 'the Cartesian way' into phenomenology and contrasts it with others. But there is no *alternative* to the Platonic–Cartesian perspective for Husserl: that is just what true philosophy is! One eminent Husserlian, Ludwig Landgrebe, who actually worked as Husserl's assistant towards the end of the latter's life, has supposed otherwise (Landgrebe 1981, Ch. 3), citing a late text in which Husserl writes, 'Philosophy as science, as serious, rigorous, indeed apodictically rigorous science – *the dream is over*' (*Crisis*, 508 [389]). But although Husserl did indeed pen these words, they are not in his own voice. This sentiment is expressed by an imaginary objector – 'such is the generally reigning opinion of such people' (*ibid.* [390]) – and the whole thrust of the piece from which the quotation comes is, consistently with Husserl's entire project, to reject it. Such a view is precisely what is 'inundating European humanity' (*ibid.*).

But if 'philosophy as rigorous science' does not serve to distinguish Descartes as making a radical new step in philosophy, what does? According to Husserl, Descartes, in contrast to Plato, takes mathematics as a paradigm for philosophical knowledge 'in a particular sense' (see *Crisis*, §§8, 16). But that, as he says in our own text, is a 'fateful prejudice' (48–9), not something that redounds to his glory. In certain passages Husserl seems to suggest that one thing that is both new and valuable in Descartes is the emphasis on 'insight' being *apodictic* – i.e., so absolutely justified that the negation of what is thought is unintelligible. As a matter of fact, however, although Husserl does speak of apodicticity more frequently in relation to Descartes and post-Cartesian philosophy, his own included, this concept is not wholly absent from his discussions of Socrates and Plato. Socrates' method, for example, is characterized as that of 'clarificatory self-reflection that is brought to completion in apodictic self-evidence' (*EP I*, 11). Still, at least the difference of emphasis is unmistakable; and Husserl doubtless thought that although Socrates (and Plato) may have *sought* for apodicticity, and that it was part of their 'idea' of philosophy, only with Descartes do we have a radicalization of philosophy that actually promises to deliver the goods. For Husserl sees the original Greek establishment of philosophy as involving a certain 'naïveté'. And one thing that for Husserl is indisputably novel in Descartes was the necessary step to overcome this naïveté – a step which changes the fundamental character of philosophy as such. This distinctive achievement of Descartes was the fashioning of 'a philosophy turned toward the subject himself' (44) – towards the subject of consciousness, the 'ego', the 'I'. Descartes managed 'to uncover . . . for the first time the genuine sense of the necessary regress to the ego, and consequently to overcome the hidden but already felt naïveté of earlier philosophizing' (48). More precisely, it was the recognition of the subject, of one's own conscious self, as the one indubitable, apodictically certain being – in short, the famous Cartesian *Cogito* – that was Descartes's historical achievement. In fact, as Husserl mentions elsewhere, Descartes was not the first person to have recognized the absolute indubitability of the conscious subject's own existence for himself. As critics pointed out even in Descartes's own day, we already find it in St Augustine. What even more precisely, therefore, is distinctive of Descartes is his 'regression' to the indubitable ego *as the only possible way of combating scepticism*. It was scepticism that 'had the great historic mission of forcing philosophy on to the way toward a transcendental philosophy' (*EP I*, 62). Since, for Husserl, scepticism provided the goad that led the Greeks to the primal establishment of philosophy, such a regression to the ego now emerges for the first time with Descartes as the necessary first step in philosophy. *This* is the 'eternal significance' of Descartes's *Meditations*. They 'indicate, or attempt to indicate, the necessary style of the philosophical beginning' (*ibid.*, 63). Or, as he says in the *Cartesian Meditations*, 'they draw the prototype for any beginning philosopher's necessary meditations' (44).

In fact, the *Cogito* is the *only* thing in Descartes that is, according to Husserl, of any philosophical significance at all. Almost every time he refers to Descartes's *Meditations* in his other writings (e.g., *EP I*, 63; *Crisis* 76 [75]), it is the *first two* meditations that he refers to: those that solely concern the regression to the indubitability of the ego and its 'thoughts' through the offices of methodical doubt. Descartes's last four meditations do not even get a look in. So the reader should not be surprised that there are only five Husserlian meditations, in contrast to Descartes's six. The *Cartesian Meditations* are in no sense a commentary on, or companion to, Descartes's work. They are so called, rather, because 'France's greatest thinker, René Descartes, gave transcendental phenomenology new impulses through his *Meditations*' (43). This does not mean, of course, that Descartes gave such impulses to transcendental phenomenology in the seventeenth century. At that time there was no such thing – it being Husserl's own discovery. What Husserl means is that reading and reflecting on Descartes's work gave new impulses to Husserl's own move towards such phenomenology, in the first decade of the twentieth century. The *Cartesian Meditations* is an acknowledgement of this influence, and of an essential relationship between Descartes's work and transcendental phenomenology. But it is not a work about Descartes; it is itself a work of transcendental phenomenology; and only one move that Descartes ever made is relevant to this.

Although Husserl speaks of this regression to the ego in Descartes's writings as *radically new* – indeed as an epochal, world-historical event – Husserl sees it, as the reader should by now be in a position to appreciate, as but a radicalization of the philosophical life that first emerged as a possibility for mankind with Socrates and Plato. It is such a radicalization because, in the first place, the original demand for self-responsibility is made an unavoidable characteristic of philosophical *method* once the philosopher begins with his or her own conscious life alone and must philosophize *solely from that perspective*. Any 'findings' must then necessarily 'arise as *his* wisdom, as his self-acquired knowledge' (44). In the second place, the existence of the self for itself now provides a concrete benchmark – that of apodicticity, the inconceivability of error – which any subsequent gains in philosophical knowledge must match. Such factors do not, however, constitute what was truly world-historical about Descartes's step to subjectivity. What makes the step of such moment, for Husserl, is that in it Descartes, though not clearly aware of what he had achieved, had stumbled across *transcendental* subjectivity and had made *transcendental* philosophy possible. Coming to understand what it is for philosophy to be transcendental, why this is of such moment, and why and how Descartes stumbled on this path to an ultimate radicalization of philosophy, is the principal task of Chapter 1.

NOTES

1 Husserl is therefore happy to refer to himself as a 'rationalist' – albeit, for sure, not a representative of that 'misguided' rationalism that grew up in the Enlightenment (as he puts it in the 'Vienna Lecture' published together with the *Crisis*). In relation to such misguidedness, see Husserl's remark in the *Cartesian Meditations* about the 'fateful prejudice' in favour of a *mathematical* conception of ideal science (48–9). As we shall see later, however, Husserl was also happy to call himself an 'empiricist', at least 'in the true sense'.

2 'Proper' is *'eigentlich'* – also commonly translated as 'authentic'. This term is as important for Husserl as it became, more famously, for Heidegger.

3 Indeed, germs of the general scheme are already to be found in the *Logos* article of 1910. I shall not discuss this general issue of influence further in this work. I cannot, however, forgo pointing out the striking parallels between Heidegger's famous 'analytic' of *Dasein* in *Being and Time* and Husserl's account of the 'person' in *Ideas II*. The latter even includes a brief discussion of what Heidegger will famously term *'das Man'* – the 'they' (*Ideas II*, 269).

1

FIRST MEDITATION

§§3–11

One thing makes us philosophers: the 'idea' of philosophy itself: a conception of knowledge that would be absolutely grounded in insight, and hence, in principle, universally acceptable. We philosophize only when, in complete self-responsibility, our intellectual life is wholly dedicated to this ideal. This idea comes alive for us originally through a certain contrast: with the relative and unclarified opinions of our everyday life. And if we are in a historical period where various 'positive sciences' have separated themselves from their philosophical origin, they too will appear questionable, indeed positively lacking, in relation to this guiding idea of absolute truth. This idea is our sole possession *qua* philosophers. As philosophers we are *indigent* in contrast to the 'wisdom of the world'. But such poverty, seen from a philosophical perspective, is a freedom from prejudice – from the 'pre-judgements' that we find ourselves lumbered with prior to a validation through insight. As philosophers we must become intellectual beginners. Because of the need to overcome prejudice, the philosopher is one who has become 'a nonparticipating spectator, surveyor of the world' (*Crisis*, 331 [285]), one who, through radical reflection, stands above his or her own life and its 'prejudiced', flowing contingency, and attempts to understand it. In the passage from which I have just quoted, Husserl relates this to the classical Greek thought that philosophy begins with wonder. What is distinctive of Husserl, as we shall see, is that this wonder is not one that is naïvely directed at the world as such, but is a wonder at a world *appearing to consciousness*. Philosophy is a matter of making such wonder habitual and fruitful.

This involves a decision, 'the decision of philosophers who begin radically: that at first we shall put out of action all the convictions we have been accepting up to now, including our sciences' (48). For this 'putting out of action' Husserl employs a term of the ancient sceptics: 'epoché' – literally a 'stoppage', but most commonly glossed by Husserl as a 'bracketing'. To 'bracket' something is not to reject it. It is not even, as we shall see in more detail shortly, to doubt it. Even in my purest philosophical moments I do not cease to be of the opinion – i.e., to believe – that cats chase mice, that the first-order predicate calculus is complete, and so forth. It is simply that in my philosophical endeavours I *make no use* of these beliefs of mine. I take none of them, as Husserl sometimes puts it, as *premises* for my philosophical thinking; and such thinking does not concern itself with the reality or truth of the objects of such beliefs. In the *Cartesian Meditations* Husserl begins, as did Descartes in his own meditations, with the most superficial form of such bracketing: the putting out of play of preconceived opinions, whether they be those of everyday life, of the positive sciences, or of philosophy itself. We might term this the 'philosophical epoché'. Such a decision means that we do not even assume any 'normative ideal of science'. All we begin with, as radical philosophers, is 'the general aim of grounding science absolutely'. We do not even assume that this aim is capable of realization. At first this idea, 'the genuine concept of science', merely 'floats before us' in a state of 'indeterminate fluid generality', as a mere 'precursory presumption'. And yet we have this idea, we cleave to it as our 'guiding idea', one that will 'continually motivate the course of our meditations' (49–50).

Although, as we saw in the Introduction, philosophy, according to Husserl, precedes the positive sciences both historically and by virtue of essence – indeed precisely *because* these sciences are thus informed by the ideal of absolute, universal knowledge – we can, as the historically situated beings that we are, turn to such sciences, and ' "immersing ourselves" in the scientific striving and doing that pertain to them . . . see clearly and distinctly what is really being aimed at' (50). The idea of science, after all, is not something lodged in a Platonic heaven. It is a *human* ideal: indeed, a specific-ally European one. It is to be found nowhere else than in relation to a certain form of human striving – the striving for ultimate responsibility in our quest for knowledge. And this is actually to be found in the lives of practising scientists. Even if critical reflection leads us to conclude that the idea of science is but imperfectly realized in such activity, this very recognition implies some grasp of the perfection which that activity shows itself as failing to attain. Indeed, the perfection and the imperfection only emerge as thinkable for us in relation to such striving. So we must 'immerse ourselves' in it. This resolve is but a particular application of a fundamental conviction that informs the whole of Husserl's philosophy from first to last. We might say that it is his one 'pre-supposition', except that he sees in it the principled exclusion of all presuppositions, of all 'prejudices'. In §5 he lays it down as his 'first methodological principle': 'I . . . must neither make nor go on accepting any judgment as scientific that I have not derived from self-evidence, from *experiences* in which the relevant things and states of affairs are present to me as *they themselves*' (54). We shall turn our attention to Husserl's account of 'self-evidence' later in this chapter, but the basic idea is easy enough to understand. It is that we should not, as self-responsible philosophers, accept as absolutely binding mere second-hand opinions or things of which we have some vague intelligence, but only those things which we have *directly experienced for ourselves*. So, in relation to the idea of science, it is not enough for us merely to bear in mind that there are scientists around and that they are concerned with dis-covering truth, corroborating hypotheses and so forth. We need concretely to think ourselves into such activity, making the scientists' concerns our own. Only then will the 'idea' of science have any real meaning for us, and cease to be a mere abstract ideal. Only then shall we really know what we are talking about. When we do so, we come to realize the fundamental role that 'evidence' plays in the scientific life. Unearthing the full significance of the notion of evidence will help to clarify our initially vague conception of the scientific ideal, that which motivates and ultimately makes sense of the life of the true scientist – i.e., of the philosopher. Our first faltering steps as beginning philosophers are directed towards trying to understand what it is to philosophize.

THE EPOCHÉ AND THE TRANSCENDENTAL REDUCTION

I wish, however, briefly to postpone discussion of Husserl's account of evidence, because it is very easy, when reading through this First Meditation, to think that its overall argument is really very simple, and that Husserl's disquisition on evidence just slows the proceedings down somewhat. For at the end of that discussion he seems simply to say that *apodicticity* is demanded by the scientist, so that we, as beginning philosophers in search of true science, should settle for nothing less. Something is apodictic if its non-being, its non-existence, is inconceivable (56). Now, it doesn't take long, with Descartes before us, to realize that even the existence of an 'external' world, of anything other than one's own conscious life, is not apodictic in this sense. Therefore we should not rely, in our philosophizing, even on the 'prejudice' that there is such a real world. This is (one aspect of) the second, and more radical, bracketing which Husserl introduces in §7, and which he eventually refers to as the 'phenomenological epoché' (60). By contrast, your own existence as a conscious being is absolutely indubitable (for you). Moreover, what emerges as thus indubitable is not a bare, featureless entity, but a being with a *field* of consciousness. Not only can you not doubt that you exist, you cannot doubt that you have various kinds of 'thoughts', *'cogitationes'* – a term that Husserl, like Descartes, understands in a broader sense than the everyday one, so as to include perceptual experiences, and, indeed, everything that involves us being attentively directed towards some object or

other. Since you, as a beginning scientific philosopher, are restrict-
ing what you accept *as* a philosopher to what is apodictic, you are,
at least initially, now restricted to your conscious self and its
'thoughts': to your 'pure' self and your 'pure' thoughts, as Husserl
puts it, since they are untainted by any 'prejudice' concerning the
reality of a non-apodictic world. He then for some reason calls this
field of consciousness 'transcendental consciousness', and the
restriction of your concerns as a philosopher to this field of
research he terms the 'transcendental reduction'. At the very end
of the First Meditation Husserl then seems to make some rather
dubious idealist-sounding moves.

This, as I say, can easily appear to be the basic thrust of the First
Meditation. But although not *completely* awry, such a reading
misses what is novel and of primary importance in this meditation.
It should also leave the reader extremely puzzled – and the more so,
the more he or she reads on. For if this is what is achieved by the
First Meditation, then, given that our motivation is a quest for
absolutely certain knowledge in the face of scepticism, we should
expect Husserl to attempt to confute the sceptic by going on to
prove the reality of the world, and to demonstrate how we can have
genuinely 'scientific' knowledge of it – as did Descartes. But this is
precisely what we do not find in the remaining meditations. Recall
that Husserl was consistently interested only in the first two of
Descartes's meditations. This is not simply because he thought that
most of the arguments in Descartes's other meditations were
invalid and based on unquestioned, mostly Scholastic, prejudices
(though he did think this), but because he thought that the whole
attempt to go beyond what Descartes had attained in the first two
meditations was misguided in principle. In particular, Husserl
thought that the very idea of trying to prove the existence of an
'external' world on the basis of the contents of 'inner' experience
was, as he liked to put it, using the French term, a *nonsens*. According to Husserl, Descartes discovered a *transcendental* perspective in
his first two meditations, *but then abandoned it* in busying himself
with such a nonsensical proof. In Husserl's view, Descartes should
have *stayed* with his initial discovery and explored it further; for
such an exploration of pure consciousness from the transcendental

viewpoint *is the sole concern of the true philosopher*. This and this alone is the field of 'rigorous science' that will answer to the longing for absolute knowledge that was bequeathed to us by Socrates and Plato. But this may seem like a capitulation to the sceptic. Even without the resultant disappointment of the subsequent meditations, the above construal of the first is intrinsically puzzling. For the above is what you get, more or less, in Descartes himself. So what is supposed to be so radically *new* here? Where is Husserl's supposedly epoch-making discovery of phenomenology? For this is not to be found in the later meditations. They rather explore the breadth and depths of the field of pure consciousness; whereas it is the discovery of the field itself, as the sole philosophical domain, that inaugurates transcendental phenomenology. So it ought already to be visible in the First Meditation. On the above reading, however, we get little that is not to be found already in Descartes. In particular, it doesn't capture the emergence in Husserl's pages of the notion of the *transcendental* – a most un-Cartesian term, far more suggestive of Kant.

A less superficial reading of the First Meditation can be motivated by paying attention to the strongly qualified praise that Husserl bestows on Descartes as the second great 'beginner' in philosophy. Descartes 'could not himself take possession of the proper meaning of his discovery'; he 'let slip away the great discovery he had in his hands' (*EP I*, 63; *Crisis*, 76 [75]). That Descartes went astray, in Husserl's eyes, into a nonsensical enterprise in his last four meditations is already determined by the precise nature of the first two. He had stumbled across something, but did not know what to do with it *because he did not recognize the true nature of his discovery*. Hence the importance of the following words from the beginning of §8: 'At this point, following Descartes, we make the great reversal that, *if made in the right manner*, leads to transcendental subjectivity' (my emphasis). Descartes did not make it 'in the right manner', and so failed to become a transcendental philosopher – the only true sort of philosopher. Understanding the distinction between what Descartes himself set out to achieve in his first two meditations and Husserl's interpretation of what Descartes actually did achieve, albeit in a way unappreciated by

Descartes himself, is therefore essential for understanding how transcendental phenomenology is supposed to emerge in the present work. There is, to be sure, a close structural similarity between the movement of thought in Descartes and in Husserl. Starting with the idea of science, Descartes, through methodical doubt, regresses to the apodictic *'mens sive animus'* – mind or soul – and its 'thoughts'. Starting with the same idea, Husserl, through the phenomenological epoché, regresses to the apodictic 'transcendental ego' and its 'thoughts'. What, however, is regressed to is different in the two cases. Husserl calls Descartes's indubitable self 'a little *tag-end of the world*' (63), a 'piece of the world' (64). It is not a *transcendental* self. In order to understand what Husserl means by this, we need to examine the two respective paths to the Cartesian and the Husserlian 'reductions', since the radically different destinations are determined by the radically different procedures for arriving there. The phenomenological epoché is not, and does not involve, any process of doubt.

In his first published systematic presentation of the epoché, in *Ideas I*, Husserl relates the epoché, not to doubt, but to the *attempt* to doubt something; and he says even of this that it 'shall serve us only as a *methodic expedient* for picking out certain points which, as included in its essence, can be brought to light and made evident by means of it' (*Ideas I*, 54). The important thing that is included in the essence of attempting to doubt something is what Husserl calls 'bracketing' (or, almost as often, 'disconnecting' or 'putting out of play'). This is not restricted to the phenomenon of attempting to doubt, and can 'make its appearance *also in other combinations* and, equally well, *alone*'; it is just that it is 'particularly easy' to analyse it out of the phenomenon of attempting to doubt (*ibid.*, 55). In the phenomenological epoché we have this operation in its purity, not as a mere ingredient in an attempt to doubt something, let alone as an ingredient in any actual doubt. Indeed, doubt *excludes* the operation in question. For doubt is a certain 'position', as Husserl puts it, *vis-à-vis* the existence of something, other positions being certainty (the positive limit), disbelief (the negative limit), regarding as likely, etc. 'Bracketing' is a matter of putting *all* such positions out of play, it is not a matter of cleaving universally to one of them – namely, doubt or uncertainty. Since doubt is precisely a matter of holding a position on the reality of something, it is a particular way in which bracketing, disconnection, has *not* been effected. Hence, Husserl insists over and over again that if we initially believe something, such belief *remains* when we effect the bracketing. The epoché is, he says, a certain 'refraining' from belief *'which is compatible with the unshaken conviction of truth, even with the unshakeable conviction of evident truth'* (*Ideas I*, 55, incorporating a marginal correction of Husserl's). As he says in the *Cartesian Meditations* itself, although we no longer 'ratify' or 'accomplish' the natural belief in the world, 'that believing too is still there and grasped by my noticing regard' (59). He is even more emphatic in the *Crisis*, where he says that 'there can be no stronger realism' than the position we find ourselves in after the epoché, if by realism 'nothing more is meant than: "I am certain of being a human being who lives in this world, etc., and I doubt it not in the least"' (*Crisis*, 190–1 [187]). Indeed, if the epoché were a form of doubt, it would be both impossible to execute and also nonsensical as a gateway to transcendental phenomenology. It would be impossible, because effecting the epoché, like the *attempt* to doubt, 'belongs to the realm of our *perfect freedom*', whereas doubt, like any other 'position', does not (*Ideas I*, 54). Doubt, like belief, is not under our control, but is necessarily 'motivated' by the course of our experience:

> One cannot arbitrarily and without further ado modalize something that holds good for us, convert certainty into doubt or negation . . . But one can without further ado abstain from any holding-good; that is, one can put its performance out of play for certain particular purposes.
>
> (*Crisis*, 240 [237], translation modified)

In the present circumstances, for example, it is, according to Husserl, impossible for you to doubt that you really are reading this book. Abstract sceptical worries about 'the external world' simply have no force here, as Hume's quip – about seeing whether the sceptic, who has just been pontificating on the uncertainty of the 'external world', leaves the room by the door or leaps out of the window – nicely illustrates. We begin, in our experience of the world, with *full conviction* concerning the reality of what we experience. Husserl calls it the *Urdoxa*: that certainty which is the primary and primal 'position' of our cognitive lives, which can only be *modified*, or 'modalized', and that only in one way – by some *disharmony* or *conflict* entering our experience. If you were to reach out to touch this book you seem to see, and your hand went straight through it; or if the book started to move around as you shifted your gaze, fixed in the centre of your visual field; then your certainty in its reality would indeed be shaken – but *only* as a result of some such discrepancy. Failing that, the reality of the objects of your experience is indubitable. Even when the reality of a particular object is questioned – perhaps even rejected: it was mere illusion, or downright hallucination – it is so only against the background of a continuing certainty concerning the reality of the world in general. In practice, all such 'cancellings' are *local*. The book may be put down to a mere delusive 'appearance' when your hand goes through it or when it tracks your gaze, but only in contrast to the reality of your hand, of the rest of your visual surroundings, indeed of the rest of the world. Short of a *radical* discontinuity in your experience as a whole, the reality of the world as such, as opposed to particular, local elements in it, is indubitable. Indeed, Husserl can even say that if your experience continues to unfold in its typically harmonious way, the reality of the world has a relative *apodictic* certainty for you (*EP II*, 397–8).[1]

Second, if the epoché involved doubt, it would make nonsense of the science of transcendental phenomenology, since this, as we shall see later, involves *faithful description* of the accomplishments of consciousness – a faithfulness that is achieved by pure reflection on the processes of conscious life. Now, one thing of which we shall expect a faithful phenomenological description is belief in a real world. But this would be impossible if all such beliefs had been eradicated, or in any way altered, by the epoché. It is, therefore, absolutely vital that, as far as the content of our natural experience is concerned, *the epoché leaves everything exactly as it is*. This, however, may seem to make even more obscure what is supposed to be achieved in this First Meditation. We may also now wonder what Husserl's project has to do with Descartes's at all. Surely some sort of search for certainty is in question? Indeed it is; but in order to see precisely what this amounts to, we need, after having seen what the epoché does not involve, to see what it does require of us.

Let us, therefore, return to the phenomenon of attempting to doubt, since Husserl suggests that the epoché can be 'easily abstracted' from it. How does attempting to doubt differ from simply doubting something? One difference is this: that although the latter must be motivated, it need not be explicitly reflective, whereas the former must be. In *attempting* to doubt something, indeed in attempting to determine the 'validity', the epistemological worth, of anything in any degree, you must in a certain way hold the presumed state of affairs 'in abeyance', regard it as being 'in question'. For if belief in its existence wholly ruled your reflections, these would make no sense. This reference to the level of *reflection* is what is critical for understanding the First Meditation. For although our natural experiencing of the world is not under our control, our possible reflections upon it are. Here we are free. In particular, we are free both as to the subject-matter we shall reflect upon, and what we choose to motivate or guide us in our reflections. For example, one thing I could decide to reflect on is how my life would be emotionally for me if I were twice as tall as I am and everyone else were his or her normal size. In such a reflection I never cease to believe that I am of normal size, but I simply do not let that fact influence me in my reflections. I 'bracket' it. Transcendental phenomenology involves but a radicalization of this freedom from position that attaches to reflection as such. *The epoché is nothing but reflection, or reflexivity, carried through with true philosophical radicality*. This radicality consists in the fact that through the epoché we disregard *all* our 'positions', all of our beliefs about any matters of fact – except for the unavoidable and absolute certainty that we have of our conscious life itself while we reflect. The epoché does not nullify, or weaken, our natural beliefs about the world. Rather, as Husserl says at one point, it *adds* something to the original belief. What is added is a 'specifically peculiar mode of consciousness' (*Ideas I*, 55): a higher-level,

reflective consciousness which proceeds in its enquiries unin-
fluenced by the beliefs that it clearly sees persisting. In attaining
this 'disconnected', spectator view of ourselves and our experiences,
we abandon what Husserl calls the 'natural attitude' – that pre-
reflective certainty in the reality of the world that thoroughly
informs not only our everyday lives, but also all 'positive' sciences.

The epoché is intelligible as an operation only in relation to a
certain theoretical concern, to a certain direction in which reflective
thought can move. As Husserl says in a passage already quoted,
'One can without further ado abstain from any validity, that is, one
can put its performance out of play *for certain particular purposes*'
(*Crisis*, 240 [237], emphasis now added). In the absence of such
purposes, although we may grant the theoretical possibility of
effecting the epoché – as lying generally within the free power of
reflection – there will seem little *point* to the exercise. The point
of Descartes's methodic doubt is straightforward: it is to find an
Archimedean point of apodictic certainty on the basis of which such
doubt can be reversed, so that the objects of our earlier beliefs can
be reaffirmed against the sceptic, albeit perhaps in a clearer and
more distinct form. But there can be no reversal of the epoché: 'The
"transcendental" epoché is . . . a habitual attitude which we resolve
to take up once and for all' (*Crisis*, 153 [150]). To 'reverse' the
epoché would simply be to return to the 'natural attitude', and
hence to cease to be a philosopher in what we are discovering to be
the one true sense. So even if Husserl does succeed in finding an
apodictically certain entity, thereby achieving an 'absolute' knowledge that surpasses the empirical indubitability of the world, the
significance of this fact may still seem obscure.

As a matter of fact, Husserl does not even claim apodicticity for
the field of consciousness that is opened up by the epoché. In §9 he
admits that although the present existence of his conscious self is
apodictically certain, nothing else, even within the sphere of 'pure'
consciousness, may seem to be. Memory, for example, certainly
does not give apodictic testimony, as Husserl himself points out
(61–2); and yet it would seem that we shall have to have recourse to
it in order to assure ourselves of the whole range of conscious
phenomena that is required for transcendental phenomenology to

be the omnicompetent fundamental enquiry that it pretends to be.[2] Hence, Husserl can speak of the need of a 'critique' of phenomenological knowledge. Such a critique would address such questions as 'How far can the transcendental ego be deceived about himself?' and 'How far do those components extend that are absolutely indubitable, in spite of such possible deception?' (62). However, although this issue is raised in the First Meditation, it is not squarely addressed. It is taken up at the start of the following meditation; but, as we shall see in the next chapter, its working out is then again deferred. Indeed, it is never fully addressed in the present work. Despite this, despite failing to demonstrate the apodicticity of the field of transcendental subjectivity in contrast with the merely empirical indubitability of the world, Husserl feels that he can push the present meditation through to an important conclusion concerning transcendental subjectivity. He believes that he can reach such a conclusion because transcendental experience has a privilege over mundane, natural experience even if the issue of apodicticity is left in the wings. This privilege derives from a certain *priority* that attaches to transcendental experience.

Although Husserl does indeed accord great weight to apodicticity in the *Cartesian Meditations*, the careful reader of the first few sections of the First Meditation will discern that Husserl is even more concerned about some notion of evidential priority. He is intent upon a philosophy 'that begins with what is intrinsically first' (49); one that involves 'an order of cognition, proceeding from intrinsically earlier to intrinsically later cognitions' (53). What he is in search of are 'evidences that . . . are recognizable as preceding all other imaginable evidences' (55), ones that are 'absolutely first' (58) or 'first in themselves' (54). Indeed, after having underlined the necessity of apodictic certainty for truly philosophical knowledge, his *first* employment of this notion is in the requirement that we should have apodictic insight that certain types of evidence are 'first in themselves' in relation to all other imaginable types of evidence (56). Only then does he say that such evidences should also themselves be apodictically certain. And when he finally charges natural experience with a lack of apodicticity, he is not content to let matters rest there, but immediately observes that 'it becomes manifest that it also cannot claim the privilege of being the absolutely first evidence' (57). It is this *second* lack that then drives the argument through to the 'great reversal'. But precisely what sort of priority is in question here? At the beginning of the Second Meditation, Husserl speaks of a priority 'in the order of knowledge' (66); but surely Husserl cannot be proposing that we come to know things about transcendental subjectivity before we know things about the world – if only because transcendental subjectivity itself emerges for us only with the unnatural, reflective turn away from the natural attitude, which is where we all start. As he says clearly in the *Crisis*, 'We perform the epoché . . . as a transformation of the attitude which precedes it not accidentally but essentially, namely, the attitude of natural human existence' (*Crisis*, 154 [151]). And in the *Cartesian Meditations* itself, Husserl, by implication, rejects the idea that the priority that is at issue allows transcendental subjectivity to be 'in the usual sense, the knowledge on which all objective knowledge is grounded'. What we are concerned with, rather, is *'a new idea of the grounding of knowledge'* (66).

In order to understand the kind of priority that is in question here, we need to see that the point of the epoché is that it gives us a new, unnatural *perspective* – the transcendental perspective, from which for the first time we can survey 'transcendental subjectivity' as an entirely new field of facts and problems. *This* is what is entirely missing from Descartes's own Meditations, and what, according to Husserl himself, is – aside from a few halting premonitions in Berkeley, Hume and Kant – new in Husserl. The *point* of the epoché is the 'transcendental reduction'. These two terms do not mean the same thing. 'Epoché', as we have seen, means the bracketing or putting out of play of our entire belief in the reality of the world, whereas 'transcendental reduction' means the restriction of our philosophical enquiries to the field of 'subjectivity'. Yet the two are intimately related (though not, as we shall see in Chapter 3, mutually entailing). The epoché, as a refusal to use any of our natural beliefs as 'premises', only makes sense in relation to a novel, unnatural concern. Rather than being interested in the world and the things it contains, we must be interested in *something else*, something that is such that the question about the truth or falsity of our natural beliefs is simply *out of place*. That something else is our experiencing self – the one thing of which we are guaranteed even if all our natural beliefs are false. Only if we are concerned *solely* with this domain does the epoché, as introduced in the context of the present meditation, make any sense. Conversely, if we are concerned purely with our own subjective lives, the epoché *must* be effected, since to use the content of any natural belief as a 'premise' would be to concern ourselves about the reality of some worldly object, and so to transgress the limit imposed on our future enquiry as one related solely to our subjectivity. This is why Husserl can sometimes say that bringing in any natural belief would simply be *absurd*, for it would be inconsistent with our newly established intellectual concern (e.g., *Crisis*, 157 [154]). Why, however, does Husserl refer to the exploration of consciousness as a *transcendental* enquiry? And why does he credit it with so much importance?

In order to understand this, we need to focus on a claim that Husserl makes over and over again in his writings in slightly different formulations. At one point he refers to it as 'the chief thought' (*EP II*, 139). It is to be found, for example, in a passage towards the end of the First Meditation: 'The world that exists for me, that always has and always will exist for me, the only world that ever can exist for me – this world, with all its objects . . . derives its whole sense and existential validity which it has for me from me myself' (65). I shall refer to this as the 'transcendental insight'. Another statement of it is to be found in the Fourth Meditation: 'Whatever exists for me, exists for me thanks to my knowing consciousness; it is for me the experienced of my experiencing, the thought of my thinking, the theorized of my theorizing, the intellectually seen of my insight' (115). What it is for consciousness to be 'transcendental' is, as Husserl standardly puts it, for it to *constitute* all of its objects. It is the gaining of this insight that is the climax of the First Meditation. It is precisely because Descartes did not clearly attain to this insight, whereas Husserl has, that Husserl can see in transcendental phenomenology the *third* great 'beginning' in philosophy. In order to see why Descartes missed his way here and how Husserl's own procedure therefore differs *essentially* from Descartes's, we need to pay especial attention to §6 of the present meditation.

Husserl frequently contrasts Descartes's interest with his own by saying that whereas Descartes was concerned with the dubitability of the world, he is interested in its possible non-existence (e.g., *EP II*, 80 and 264). Although this may seem a 'nice' distinction, it is crucial, since it is in play at the very place in the First Meditation where Husserl speaks of 'the great reversal', the one that 'if made in the right manner, leads to transcendental subjectivity' (58). The point from which the reversal is made is, of course, the Cartesian recognition that, whereas the existence of the world is not apodictic, you can have apodictic certainty of your own conscious existence. What Husserl focuses on in particular at this juncture is that the non-existence of the world is *thinkable*. Everything hinges on the significance of this fact. You are to think concretely for yourself the following thought, which I shall term the 'Cartesian thought': *Although I exist and am experiencing in this present manner, this world I seem to be experiencing does not exist. It has no reality.* This is not something you can believe; it is not even something to which you can attach the slightest probability; but you can coherently think it. In case you are having difficulty, Husserl frequently offers a train of thought to bring alive the possibility in question. You are to entertain the thought that your future course of experience ceases to have that coherence (or 'harmoniousness', as Husserl liked to put it) which it has embodied up to now. For it is precisely *because* of such coherence that you have a belief in a world in the first place. If we entertain the possibility of a subject whose conscious life is either but a tumult of chaotic experiences, or one with but temporary stabilities in which nothing confirms anything else and in which almost all the subject's anticipations and expectations are frustrated, we must surely grant that such a subject would have no sense of dealing with a real world. You are to entertain the thought that this should happen to you. There are certain such courses of experience in the face of which the thought 'None of this is real, and never has been' would become tenable. This, in fact, is the only way in which Husserl ever attempts to make the vital thought in question concrete. It is not, however, one that he himself held to be beyond question (*EP II,* 391–3). Would not an equally rational response to such a future course of experience be that you had gone mad? Or that the world had gone out of existence, but that it (or *a* world) might come into existence again? Nevertheless, although the fact that Husserl chooses to fill out the Cartesian thought in such a manner is not, as we shall see later, without significance, we need not dwell at this point over such difficulties, since the thinkability of some such thought is entailed by the admission that belief in the world is not possessed of apodictic certainty – a point which, with Descartes before us, Husserl feels it unnecessary to labour.

The importance of the 'Cartesian thought' is that Husserl regards it as motivating the 'transcendental insight'. To determine whether this is indeed the case we need to see what precisely the repeated statements of the 'insight' are saying. For there are two things they might be taken as saying, which I shall contrast as the 'strong' and the 'weak' readings. According to the strong reading, such statements are statements of idealism: everything other than consciousness itself is but a construction thrown up by consciousness, and its existence is dependent upon consciousness. This would be a great insight indeed; it would go far beyond Descartes; and it would warrant the restriction of any ultimately grounded and grounding science to the domain of consciousness itself. And, in fact, Husserl was such an idealist.[3] But does he really think that he can establish such a position already at this early stage of his enquiries? This is an important question to ask, because the claim that the Cartesian thought entails any form of idealism at all is widely held to be a gross fallacy. For the argument would have to run along something like the following lines: It is apodictically certain that I exist and that I at least seem to be experiencing various real objects in a real world; it is not apodictically certain that any worldly object, anything other than my own conscious self, exists at all; therefore my present experiences, and all that I am indubitably aware of, can exist whether or not there is a world at all over and above my consciousness; therefore the objects of my experiences are independent of the existence of anything other than myself and depend entirely on me for their existence. Such an argument would seem to involve an invalid move from what is merely 'epistemically' possible – i.e., what is imaginable, or conceivable – to what is 'metaphysically' or genuinely possible – i.e., how things might have been.[4] The question is whether Husserl endorsed such an invalid form of argument. In fact, it is far from clear that he didn't. He can, for example, state, *as an immediate consequence* of the Cartesian thought, that his consciousness is a sphere of being 'neatly separable' from the world (*EP II*, 76). Moreover, the grammatical moods he employs in expressing the Cartesian thought are significant. He says, for example, that 'This experiencing life exists and is my life even if nothing real *were to exist* or does exist' (*EP II*, 81, my emphasis). The use of the subjunctive here seems to indicate that Husserl is going beyond the merely 'epistemic' claim that his own consciousness certainly exists even if (perchance) the real world *doesn't*, and embracing the 'metaphysical' claim that his consciousness would exist even if the real world *didn't*. Moreover, he can gloss 'transcendental subjectivity' as 'that which would remain even if there were no world' (*EP II*, 128). So it may well be solely on the basis of the Cartesian thought that he can say of consciousness that '*Nulla "re" indiget ad existendum*' – it requires no 'reality' (in the sense of spatio-temporal reality) in order to exist – and that 'the existence of nature *cannot* be the condition for the existence of consciousness' (*Ideas I*, 92, 96). In fact, Husserl frequently makes use of inferences from epistemic to metaphysical issues in a way that can seem outrageous. He seems to infer, for example, from the impossibility of doubting my own existence, that I am therefore a *necessary existent*. He can write that

> it is self-evident to me not only that I am, but that I am necessarily. It is unthinkable for me that I should not exist . . . I am always contingent only with respect to the being of how I am, not with respect to my being as such . . . I am an absolute, uncancellable fact.
>
> (*Int II*, 154–5)

Indeed, Husserl not infrequently employs turns of phrase in relation to his own conscious self that traditionally have been reserved for God. Here essence is inseparable from existence; the self '*in se et per se concipitur*' ('is conceived in and through itself' – an echo of Spinoza); and it is '*causa sui*' ('self-caused') (*Int II* 159; 257; 292). I shall be leaving this deeply problematic aspect of Husserl's thought largely out of account in these pages; and in the present context, I shall set aside the distinct possibility that Husserl moved directly from the Cartesian thought to idealism. For Husserl in fact has a much better argument for idealism than the above fallacious train of thought (if that is what it is), and we shall be considering it in Chapter 4. So, as far as the present context is concerned, we need to see if Husserl succeeds in establishing something of importance concerning the 'transcendental' nature of subjectivity in the First Meditation that is not simply idealism.

This is where the weaker reading of the 'transcendental insight' comes in. Such a reading can be motivated by introducing some judicious emphasis into expressions of the insight: 'The world that exists *for me*, that always has and always will exist *for me*, the only world that ever can exist *for me* – this world, with all its objects . . . derives its whole sense and existential validity *which it has for me* from me myself' (65). Or, to take yet another example: 'All the world, and therefore whatever exists naturally, exists *for me* only as it holds good *with the sense it has for me at the time*, as the cogitatum of my changing . . . cogitationes' (75). Rather than amounting to idealism, the 'insight' may now, however, appear to be the merest platitude, and not the world-historical revelation that Husserl clearly takes it to be – especially when he tells us that talk of objects existing 'for me' amounts to saying 'only that they hold good for me – in other words, they are for me consciously as cogitata that on each occasion we are conscious of in the positional mode of certain believing' (95). Obviously, something can exist 'for me', in this sense, only if I am around. And perhaps the claim that the world 'derives its whole sense and its existential status' – i.e., what significance it has for me, and how it 'holds good' for me – is to be given a similarly platitudinous reading. In fact, Husserl *did* regard the insight as a platitude, or at least as manifestly true. Sometimes he is content simply to assert it, without argument, and to claim that it is just obviously true: for example, 'And is it not self-evident that I have a world only through certain kinds of experiences and subjective habitualities ... ?' (*EP II*, 448). And again: 'That all knowledge is the accomplishment of knowing subjectivity is something that is simply self-evident' (*ibid.*, 38). We need, therefore, to explore what significance Husserl could find in such an obvious truth.

THE CONSTITUTION OF OBJECTS

Although Husserl will eventually be particularly concerned with 'existential holding-good', with our taking things to be *real*, his first concern is with how there are any objects 'for us' at all – a topic that he discusses in terms of consciousness 'constituting' objects. In order not to misunderstand Husserl on this issue, it is important to appreciate quite what the term 'object' is to signify in this context. In the current analytical tradition in philosophy the term 'object' is standardly used interchangeably with 'entity'. A good way towards understanding the nature of Husserl's transcendentalism, however, is to read the term 'object' as having its original sense: an 'ob-ject', and similarly a *'Gegen-stand'* in German, connotes being *over against* – specifically, over against a cognizing subject. Under this interpretation, not any old entity is an 'object'; rather, it *becomes* an object when it is 'cognized' – i.e., perceived, thought about, imagined, referred to, etc. Before that, it was but a *possible* object (though an actual 'entity'). An object is always an object *for a subject*. Now, a 'transcendental realist', as Husserl calls him, is someone who believes that at least many of these entities that may become objects for a subject have an existence 'in themselves', wholly independently of becoming, or even being able to become, objects of consciousness. Calling them 'objects', or even 'possible objects', is a 'merely extrinsic denomination'. In themselves they have an existence 'outside consciousness', but can come to stand in some external relation (usually conceived of in causal terms) to conscious subjects, in virtue of which they become 'objects' in the present sense – the only one that will be employed in these pages. Now, Husserl will eventually declare this position to be a *'nonsens'*; but the immediate point to note is that the sheer existence of such a realm of 'beings-in-themselves' in no way accounts for there being any *objects* at all, let alone for the possibility of any of these entities themselves becoming objects. For even given such a realm, if there were no conscious beings at all, there would be no objects. Even if there were conscious beings, but their mental lives were but a tumult of experiences, there would still be no objects. And even if their mental lives were somewhat less chaotic, so that evanescent objects did emerge, they might not be identifiable with the realist's 'entities', since they might be but elements in a wholly subjective stream of consciousness wholly out of touch with reality. What Husserl is primarily concerned with is how objects, and the variety of objects with which we know we have dealings, are possible at all. In particular, what Husserl wants to discover is what the conscious life of a subject must intrinsically be like if that subject is to be consciously related to any objects, whether these be real or not.

Not only is the sheer existence of the realist's 'entities in themselves' wholly insufficient for accounting for our awareness of objects, increasingly complex types of object require increasingly complex processes of consciousness. Consider yourself and a five-year-old child. Certain things – such as atoms, the decimal expansion of π, the state of the nation – are possible objects for you, but are simply unavailable to the child. There must be something about the configuration of your mind that differs from the child's, something which allows you to have such objects. Or compare the child and a horse in relation to such objects as words, or utensils. Or consider all of these in contrast to a subject whose life is nothing more than a tumult of experiences, one who is not even aware of coherent objects persisting in a space around itself. At each level we come across various mental processes which are presupposed by having, or even being in a position to have, various sorts of objects. Now, no one, I think, would disagree with this claim that conscious processes are *necessary* if there are to be objects 'for us', and certain specific forms of conscious process if we are to be aware of certain specific sorts of object. But although this is certainly part of what Husserl intends by the 'insight', it is not all. For Husserl is clearly of the opinion that certain conscious processes *suffice* for objects to be present to us. If certain subjective processes occur in you, then – *ipso facto* – an object of a certain sort is present to your consciousness. Objects *supervene* on such subjective processes. In the Second Meditation, for example, Husserl writes of how 'consciousness in itself, and thanks to its current intentional structure, *makes it necessary* that in it we become conscious of . . . an object' (85, my emphasis). The detailed tasks of phenomenology as 'constitutional research' are concerned with specifying what sorts of mental accomplishments are *required* to *constitute* various types of object: i.e., what sorts of processes are *necessary and sufficient* for various types of object to be given to consciousness. Is there, however, a way of construing this claim that is not simply the strong, idealist reading of the 'transcendental insight'?

Many transcendental realists would accept that being aware of an object *as such* may be supervenient upon various subjective processes – since such an object may be completely hallucinatory. In the case of hallucination, in the total absence of a relevant object in the real world, subjective processes can be all that are involved. But, such realists will insist, some objects – namely, *real* ones – do not so supervene, but require the existence of independently existing entities. Indeed, such objects just *are*, according to them, certain real entities, and calling them 'objects' only brings in some external, contingent relation to some cognizing subject. To deny this at this stage would be simply to assume idealism. A weaker claim, however, is that a conscious subject *could* exist even if none of its apparently worldly objects were real. So as not initially to prejudice the question of whether physicalism might be true, we had better exclude this possible subject's own brain (if the subject turns its attention to it, so that it becomes an object) from the range of objects that may be unreal. All that is being countenanced on this weaker reading, therefore, is a possible consciousness for whom the Cartesian thought is true, and where the latter is restricted to objects external to the subject's physical seat of consciousness, if it has one. We are, that is to say, to conceive of a subject all of whose sensory life consists in a more or less coherent hallucination – or a 'coherent dream', as Husserl puts it (57) – in which a real world merely *seems* to be there. Here, the suggestion goes, we have a possible case of an experiencing subject, and objects of experience, for which nothing external to the subject is required.

Until recently, there would have been very few who would have denied this possibility. Today, however, there are many advocates of various varieties of 'externalism' who do precisely this. One form of such externalism is the so-called 'object-dependency' view of consciousness. (See, for example, McDowell, 1986.) According to this view, a hallucinating subject is aware of precisely nothing. Perceptual experience presents itself as giving us immediate awareness of an entity ontologically distinct from us. When such an entity is absent, as in hallucination, there is no perceptual awareness at all. Now, Husserl himself would have regarded such a view as plainly absurd. Indubitability attaches not only to your conscious existence, but also to the *objects* of your consciousness. The only issue is whether they are real or not. Indeed, it is precisely the certainty of our being aware of objects that Husserl points to *first* when making 'the great reversal':

> In short, not just corporeal Nature but the whole concrete surround-
> ing life-world is for me, from now on, only a phenomenon of being,
> instead of something that is. But, no matter what the status of this
> phenomenon's claim to reality and no matter whether, at some future
> time, I decide critically that the world exists or that it is an illusion, *still
> this phenomenon itself, as mine, is not nothing* but is precisely what
> makes such critical decisions at all possible.
>
> (59, my emphasis)

Even if, re-entering the Cartesian thought, you entertain the idea that the world does not exist, you know that you are yet presented with a variety of sensory objects, that you can turn your attention to different objects of thought, and so forth. To deny this seems preposterous, to deny the very character of the conscious life that you are living. Indeed, the term 'phenomenology' itself simply means the truly scientific study of such 'phenomena' (and, as we shall increasingly come to see, of their preconditions). Abstracting from the reality of the world, we are to take nothing more than such phenomena, and our experience of them, as our 'basis'.

It is possible, however, to provide a less impatient response to the externalist. We should note, first, that from a Husserlian point of view the term 'object-dependence' is wholly inappropriate to the externalist position in question – one that expresses the typical 'analytical' conflation of 'object' and 'entity'. For Husserl himself *agrees* that there can be no experience – or, more generally, consciousness – without *objects*. Consciousness is *essentially* of objects, it is essentially characterized by 'intentionality' – a claim that is a cornerstone of Husserl's entire philosophy, and one we shall be investigating in the next chapter. The view in question would more aptly be termed an 'entity-dependence' view, since it claims that, in the absence of a suitable object *in the real world*, various 'mental' states and processes are unavailable. Now, there is disagreement among upholders of this position over how radical a denial is in question here. Some appear to hold that in the absence of a suitable real-world object – as in hallucination – no conscious state can be attributed to the subject at all: 'all is dark within', as it is sometimes put. Others are more concessive. What, however, they all agree upon, is that in such a 'defective' situation, there is no *entity* of which the subject is conscious. But Husserl agrees with this too. For, as we shall see in the next chapter, whereas many philosophers who have allowed that a hallucinating subject is aware of some object have felt obliged to introduce certain peculiarly subjective entities to fill this role – sense-data, sensations, sense-impressions, and so forth – Husserl does not. Even within the Cartesian thought we are aware of the *same kind* of objects that we usually take ourselves to be conversant with: natural, 'worldly' objects. The Cartesian thought should not convince us, according to Husserl, that in the 'defective' situation, where a real worldly object is absent, we are aware of a peculiarly subjective set of entities; it should convince us, rather, that we are not aware of any *entities* at all, but that the objects we are aware of are *unreal* or *non-existent*. Given the analytical tradition's conflation of object and entity, this position is hardly even considered in its recent debates. A more indulgent response to the 'entity-dependence' theorists is, therefore, to ask them to await the descriptions and analyses of consciousness that are to be found in the following meditation. For it surely *is* absurd to suppose that 'all is dark within' for a hallucinating subject: to deny that it is subjectively 'like anything' to hallucinate. And what Husserl will be primarily intent upon demonstrating is that a distinction between object and subjective processes must be made even in such cases. Descriptive adequacy to psychological life, in all its possible forms, *forces* talk of 'objects' upon us.

That said, the next point to realize is that there is no restriction on the *kind* of world in the face of which you can yet think the Cartesian thought. In other words, there is no limit on the richness and variety of the 'world' that may merely appear to our postulated hallucinating subject. Any kind of experience that we have is one that a possible hallucinating subject could have – so long as we do not specify the kind in a question-begging way that entails the reality of what one is aware of. In short, there is no *type* of wordly object that cannot merely appear to be there – for it is but an implication of the Kantian thesis that existence is not a 'real predicate' that 'existent' and 'non-existent', 'real' and 'unreal', are not types of object in the sense relevant here. Transcendental phenomenology, in other words, has a *universal* field of enquiry. Its aim is to tell the 'constitutional' story for *any possible* object of consciousness: i.e., to give an account of the subjective processes that suffice for any such object to be an object for one. The subsequent meditations will give us a glimpse of the breadth and depth of the problems of 'constitutional analysis' that open up when we adopt this phenomenological attitude, one that ignores any question concerning the reality of the objects in the world and is solely concerned with what is required of consciousness if objects of any sort are to be possible for us *whether they are real or not*. To say that consciousness is 'transcendental' is simply to attribute to it this 'constituting' function in relation to all types of object.

At this point, yet another sort of externalist will raise an objection. For many have claimed that certain *types* of conscious state are unavailable if certain *kinds* of object are not actually instantiated in the real world. Is it, for example, possible to think about water if there is not, and has not ever been, any water in the world (at least for a subject ignorant of chemical theory, and who therefore cannot think of water as H_2O)? What, in the absence of some real water in the world to tie down the content of a thought to that determinate natural kind, would make any possible thought that our purely hallucinating subject could have a 'water thought'? Such a subject could, perhaps, think of something as being a colourless, odourless liquid and so forth. But that, it is claimed, does not amount to thinking of something as water; for something could fit this conception of water and yet not be water. There could, so the idea goes, be two subjects who are 'phenomenologically' identical, but whose 'mental contents' are different simply in virtue of their relatedness to different physical environments. Therefore Husserl's attempt to spell out, apparently in purely internal, psychological terms, what suffices even for certain *kinds* of conscious accomplishment, independently of how the subjects are located in a real world, is destined to fail. An adequate reply to this objection must again await our examination of how Husserlian phenomenology unfolds. But, by way of an initial response, the following may be said. First, Husserl need not, of course, assume that just *any* way of characterizing a psychological state is independent of whether the subject of that state is related to a real world or not. To take an obvious example, 'having a visual experience of a real physical object' is not thus independent. And perhaps 'is thinking of water' is another. Husserl requires only that there be *some* level of description – phenomenological description – that has the required independency. Second, if it is allowed, in response to the first 'externalist' objection above, that it is indeed 'like something' to be a hallucinating subject, then there must be ways of dividing such purely 'subjective' states into kinds in a way that is dependent only on 'how it is' for the experiencing subject. These two points do not, however, fully address the externalist's worry, which properly concerns not the theoretical possibility of classifying mental states in some purely subjective way, but the issue of whether any such classification could possibly do justice to our *actual* mental lives – lives which feature thoughts about water, and experiences of real things. A more important initial point to make, therefore, is that, third, Husserl is far from leaving questions of reality and objectivity wholly to one side, as we shall see in Chapters 4 and 5. These topics, too, he holds, are amenable to phenomenological analysis. So it is not out of the question that the kinds of classifications of mental states that the present sort of externalist wants to defend, as actually applicable to us, may be sustained on a phenomenological basis. Indeed, finally, and anticipating a *great* deal in what will follow, although phenomenology is in some sense a 'subjectivistic' philosophy, it is not *individualistic*, or, as Husserl standardly puts it, 'solipsistic'. Husserl will frequently say that the kind of individualistic descriptions with which, given the epoché, the beginning phenomenologist must perforce start, are *abstractions* from our actual subjective lives. Indeed, it is far from clear, as we shall see, that Husserl thought that a truly individualistic mental life, a stream of consciousness in the absence of a real world, was, ultimately, a genuine possibility. All he requires, for his phenomenological project to start, is that such a consciousness be *thinkable*. In short, externalist objections to the very conception of phenomenology that one can find in the literature do not take the full sweep of Husserl's thought properly into consideration. Once again, therefore, we have to await the unfolding of Husserl's project. The relationship between externalism and Husserlian phenomenology is, in fact, *far* from straightforward. Perhaps there are certain extreme forms of externalism that simply are incompatible with the phenomenological project. If so, such an externalist should be able to pinpoint places where purely phenomenological analysis is inadequate to some given type of object. I shall, therefore, because of the complexity of the present issue, leave the externalist objector to make up his or her mind as to the adequacy of Husserl's project as we see it unfold in detail. This is a procedure of which Husserl himself would have approved. For he says on many occasions that the proof of his transcendental philosophy is the concrete working out of the phenomenological analyses themselves.

In fact, even if certain externalists eventually turn away from Husserl's work dissatisfied, that work can still be regarded by them as of philosophical value. For even if Husserl should fail in providing a *complete* constitutional account of consciousness of any possible object – an account, purely in terms of mental processes, that *suffices* for consciousness of such an object – if his analyses unearth an increasingly rich set of conditions that are *necessary* for such forms of consciousness, conditions that had not been fully appreciated by any previous philosopher, his achievement would be significant indeed. Hence my remark, at the beginning of the Introduction, that Husserl's greatness resides, for many of us, precisely in the depth and originality of the detailed phenomenological analyses he offers. They are of such an unparalleled acuity that no one who has a pretension to be a self-responsible philosopher can afford to ignore them. Nevertheless, the reader should not be under the illusion that Husserl himself set his sights no higher. He was in search of nothing less than *sufficient* constitutional accounts of all possible objects. Indeed, as we shall see in Chapter 4, he was in search of nothing less than an absolute idealism that can justify itself by reference to such accounts.

We have found a reading of the 'transcendental insight' that is weak enough not to be rejected outright, and which at the very least promises to sustain an investigation that will be of philosophical interest. It is, to repeat, the claim that, for any type of object, specified independently of questions of reality, a certain configuration of conscious life suffices for an awareness of an object of that type. *This* is (at least part of) what Husserl can, on occasion, regard as 'self-evident'. As we have seen, it is not self-evident at all: not for certain present-day 'externalists', for example. But if Husserl himself thought it was obvious, why did he feel the necessity, not only in the present text but elsewhere, of building up to this 'insight' through a critique of everyday knowledge that employs the extremely strong criterion of apodicticity? The answer to this, I think, is that Husserl felt that in the absence of the Cartesian thought one might fail to realize that a real-world object is not necessary in order for one to be in any form of conscious state. And there may well be something to this idea. Who, after all, are those for whom the 'transcendental insight' is obvious? Is it not those who have come across sceptical arguments and have some knowledge of Descartes's search for an 'Archimedean point'? Is it really obvious to just *anybody* that a certain configuration of the mind suffices for awareness of any given type of object? Someone who found the Cartesian thought *unthinkable* would hardly be able to appreciate the 'insight'.

We can now see the sense in which the field of transcendental subjectivity has a priority over 'natural experience'. For, given any kind of perceptual experience at all, and any finitely extended sequence of such experiences, we can conceive of a coherent hallucination that subjectively matches it. When we investigate such a hallucination, we shall discover something that is present, yet unacknowledged, in all everyday perceptions of the real world. A certain epistemic privilege therefore attaches to the internal character of subjective life itself in virtue of its being, at least, a *necessary part* of any natural experience. For whatever 'entities' there may be in the world, and however they may stimulate our sensory surfaces, without a certain functioning of subjective life we should not be aware of any objects whatever. The natural attitude, including that of the most sophisticated 'positive' sciences, is, as Husserl puts it, '*naïve*', because, being wholly given over to a concern with entities within the world, with objects presumed to be real, it simply *overlooks* the functioning subjectivity in which alone such objects can arise, or in which they are constituted. In the natural attitude, such subjective accomplishments remain, as Husserl often puts it, 'anonymous' (e.g., 179). Whenever we treat an object as real, whenever we assume that the world as a whole is real and pursue our everyday or 'scientific' concerns, transcendental (i.e., constituting) subjectivity *has already accomplished something*. Such subjectivity is always presupposed whenever we have any dealings with anything at all. Furthermore – though this claim is as yet to be justified by reference to Husserl's actual analyses – certain processes of consciousness *suffice* as an account of what various types of object mean *for us*. At least what we *take* an object to be, and whether we *regard* its existence as certain, dubious, and so forth, is surely a matter *solely* concerning our subjective lives. A genuine science, which demands insight in all matters, must therefore turn to transcendental subjectivity as a matter of *primary* concern – primary, because harbouring 'the ultimate sources of meaning' (*Crisis*, 197 [194]). Even mathematical and logical knowledge, which is certain enough for most of us, implicitly refers back

to the consciousness in which it is accomplished, and so it too, prior
to a transcendental investigation, is afflicted with a naïve 'positiv-
ity'. (See, for example, *EP II*, 31 and *FTL*, *passim*.) The absolute
clarity demanded by our guiding philosophical 'idea' must take the
form of 'transcendental clarity' (*EP II*, 22). Recognizing that consciousness has a constituting function in relation to all types of
object, and that such 'transcendental' consciousness is to be the sole
concern of the radical philosopher, is the real (and most un-
Cartesian) conclusion to the First Meditation.

TRANSCENDENTAL PHENOMENOLOGY
AND PSYCHOLOGY

We have not yet reached a full understanding of the transcendental
viewpoint. We now know that to say that consciousness is transcendental is to say that it is constituting in relation to all types of
object; but it is easy to fail to appreciate the full universality of this
claim as it is intended by Husserl. For Husserl's project, as I have
outlined it, may sound like (a certain kind of) *psychology*. We are
to turn our attention away from objects in the 'external world', and
focus, rather, on those mental accomplishments in virtue of which a
world appears to us. In fact, Husserl freely admitted that psychology is far closer to transcendental phenomenology than any
other discipline. Indeed, when properly conducted, psychology
would constitute 'a precise parallel to transcendental phenomenology'; and the difference between the two is, as he says towards
the beginning of the Second Meditation, a seemingly trivial
'nuance' (70). On the other hand, as he says later, the move from
psychology to transcendental phenomenology is nothing less than
a 'Copernican revolution' (171). Consequently, Husserl was particularly concerned to distinguish transcendental phenomenology
from psychology – especially from that kind of psychology which
agrees with Husserl over the correct way to analyse psychological
phenomena: 'phenomenological psychology' as he usually called it
(or 'purely descriptive' psychology, as on p. 70). In order to
appreciate why Husserl is not engaged in 'mere' psychology, we

need to recognize that the 'constitutional' approach to objects *extends even to your own mind.*

Psychology aims at being a 'positive science' in parallel with the physical sciences. The latter abstract away from many aspects under which the world presents itself to us – aesthetic aspects, for example, social, political and psychological aspects – so as to focus on a bare 'nature' conceived simply in terms of physicality. Analogously, psychology abstracts away from this physical stratum of reality and focuses purely on consciousness. At least that is what Husserl thinks it should do; this is the kind of psychology Husserl himself is interested in. In attempting to follow through such an interest, the psychologist could indeed come to recognize the kinds of constituting accomplishments that Husserl himself will describe in the following meditations. Such an attempt might begin as follows:

> Every experience and every other way we are consciously involved with objects clearly allows of a 'phenomenological turn' . . . In simple perception we are directed toward perceived matters, in memory toward remembered matters, . . . and so on. Thus every such pursuit has its own *theme*. But at any given time we can effect a change of focus that shifts our thematic gaze away from the current matters . . . and directs our gaze instead toward the manifoldly changing 'subjective ways' in which they 'appear,' the ways they are consciously known.
>
> (*EB*, 237)

In pursuing this change of focus, we give up the 'natural attitude' for a 'phenomenological' one, and Husserl can speak in this connection of a 'psychological reduction', and even of a 'phenomenological reduction'.[5] Yet all of this, however much it may sound like the instigation of Husserl's project, is merely the province of psychology. Still, Husserl thought it extremely important that psychology should be refashioned in this kind of way under the guidance of his own philosophy: 'Phenomenology signifies indeed a fundamental refashioning of psychology too' (170). The result would be 'phenomenological psychology', which he regarded also as his own achievement. It is not, however, *transcendental* phenomenology; nor is it genuine philosophy. The reason for this is that such a psychology has merely made an *abstraction* from one aspect of the real world (*i.e.,* materiality), and is therefore left focusing on *another aspect of the real world* (*i.e.,* the 'mental' or the 'psychological'). Psychologists are, somewhat like Descartes, left with a 'tag-end of the world'. They have not, therefore, totally abandoned the natural perspective that simply presupposes the reality of the world (see §11). In particular, psychologists continue to think of themselves as really embodied. At the very least, they will continue to think of their own experiences as being on the same level as material things, so that it makes sense to suppose that various worldly relations (such as causality) could subsist between them. Thinking of oneself in such a way is itself, however, an achievement of constituting consciousness, which cannot, for the radical philosopher, simply be taken for granted. It is the achievement of *self-mundanization,* or *self-objectification,* as Husserl terms it: 'The transcendental I is purely in itself; however it brings about in itself a self-objectification, it gives itself the sense-form "human soul" and "objective reality"' (*EP II,* 77). One of the things that a radical philosopher will want to know is *what is involved in regarding oneself as a part of the world.* The transcendental self not only constitutes 'external' objects, but its very own self as worldly. Only when this has been realized, when the reduction and its epoché have been *universally* applied, will the transcendental perspective have been truly attained. With its attainment, the domain of the 'psychological' will have been left behind. The fundamental distinction, for Husserl, is not between the 'outer' and the 'inner', between the material and the mental, as it is for so much traditional philosophy, but between what is constituted and what is constituting.

EVIDENZ AND INTUITION

By now the reader may well be wondering what has happened to the epistemological concerns with which this whole enterprise got off the ground. Where in all this is the absolute grounding of human knowledge, or even the promise of it? This is, in fact, a question that cannot be properly addressed until we have seen the kind of thing that transcendental phenomenology turns out to be in practice. I shall, indeed, defer discussion of it to our Conclusion. But before moving on to investigate the phenomenological analyses in the subsequent meditations, we do need to have a look at the way in which Husserl generally approaches epistemological matters. In particular, we need to examine the account of 'evidence' given at the start of the present meditation, which we have skipped over. In the course of this examination I shall explain a number of technical terms that Husserl employs throughout these meditations, but which he does not bother to explain.

What I have termed the 'philosophical reduction' is the expression of the conviction that a mere trafficking in handed-down ideas and theories, however venerable and pertinacious, is inconsistent with that self-responsibility that is definitive of the philosopher. The true phenomenological method, by contrast, is summed up in a phrase that became something of a slogan of the phenomenological movement: *To the things themselves!* At one point Husserl proclaims himself to be an empiricist in the true sense of this term, and defines empiricism as amounting to the following claim: 'To judge rationally or scientifically about things means to direct oneself *to the things themselves*, or to return from words and opinions to the things themselves, to consult them in their self-givenness and to set aside all prejudices alien to them' (*Ideas I*, 35, translation modified). This same determination to hold 'prejudice' in abeyance and to see for oneself is expressed towards the end of the *Cartesian Meditations* when Husserl declares that what he has written is drawn 'directly from concrete intuition' (165). Phenomenology is grounded on intuition – and especially on a pre-eminent type of intuition that Husserl calls an *originally giving intuition* (*originär gebende Anschauung*).[6] In *Ideas I* he dignifies with the title 'The Principle of All Principles' the claim that 'every originally giving intuition is a legitimating source of cognition'; and calls 'the principle of the original right of everything that is given' the *'most universal principle of all methods'* (*Ideas I*, 43; 48, translation modified). And in the *Cartesian Meditations* he says that 'every genuine intuition has its place in the constitutional nexus' (165). It is clearly of considerable importance that we should understand precisely what Husserl means by these notions. Let us start with an 'originary' or 'self-giving' intuition. In such an intuition an object is 'self-given' or given 'in person'; and where the object in question is a concrete individual – as opposed to something 'abstract', such as a number, or a universal – this amounts to its being given 'bodily'. Husserl standardly spells out these ideas in terms of *seeing*. Something is self-given, he says at one point, when it '*itself stands before our eyes*' (*EP II*, 32), though he certainly does not wish to restrict the phenomenon to the sense of sight. The sound of a violin that you are now hearing would be standing 'before your eyes' in this sense. (Indeed, we shall later find Husserl speaking of 'seeing' essences, though for now I shall focus on our awareness of concrete objects). Such 'seeing' is 'the ultimate legitimating source of all rational assertions'. It is this that alone gives us the 'things themselves'. Conversely, 'not to assign any value to "I see it" as an answer to the question, "Why?" would be a counter-sense' (*Ideas I*, 36). In relation to individual objects originary intuition is *perception*. For in perceiving something, the thing itself 'stands before our eyes'. At least that is the attestation of 'straightforward consciousness', before it has been bewitched by philosophical or psychological theory.

The range of what is intuitional, or of acts that 'give' us something, is greater than these 'originary' cases, however. Acts of concretely imagining something, for example, are also cases of intuition, as are cases of concretely recollecting something. The contrast for the general class of what is intuitive, or 'giving', is with acts which are *empty*. One common type of empty act is the comprehension of speech. When you speak to me and I understand you, my mind is not focused on the mere sounds that you utter. Rather, through grasping their meaning, I am directed to the 'theme' of your speech – i.e., what it is you are speaking about. I can, however, follow what you are saying without at all having to *imagine* the various things you are referring to; and even less do I have to perceive them (except in the special case of demonstrative reference, where language is not self-sufficient). Nevertheless, I typically *can* imagine, concretely bring to mind, the things you are speaking of. Should I do so, my formerly empty directedness to the topic of your conversation would be *intuitively illustrated*. Another possibility is that I should come actually to perceive what it was that I understood you to be talking about. Suppose, for example, that you ask me for an ashtray. I wander into the next room and I espy the very thing I understood you to be referring to, and recognize it as such. No imagining of ashtrays need bridge the understanding and such a perceptual recognition. There occurs here a 'synthesis of identification', and Husserl speaks of the perceptual experience in question as 'covering' the content of the empty 'meaning intention', by virtue of which the latter is 'fulfilled' by the 'bodily presence' given by the former. It is this that Husserl has in mind when he writes:

> A merely supposing judging becomes adjusted to the things or the states of affairs themselves by conscious conversion into the corresponding evidence. This conversion is inherently characterized as the fulfilling of what was merely meant, as a synthesis in which what was meant coincides with and is 'covered' by what is itself given; it is an evident possessing of the correctness of what previously was meant at a distance from the things.
>
> (51)

Husserl will in fact claim that it is in such fulfilments of mere thought by perception that we find the origin of all ideas of truth and correctness; and he can characterize the 'striving for knowledge' as a striving 'for fulfilment of one's meaning intention' (52).[7] The comprehension of language, or, more generally, of signs, is not the only instance of being emptily directed to objects. Indeed, as we shall see in the following chapter, Husserl believes that *every* form of mental directedness to objects features some empty component. It is, however, perhaps the clearest example, and the one from which Husserl's own thinking in this area arose. Husserl's most general account of what is intuitional is given by reference to *clarity*; and since the latter comes in degrees, so does the former. A memory of a certain face, for example, may be so clear and stable that, if you had the gift, you could paint a reasonable portrait.

Sometimes, however, we have difficulty in visualizing a face: there is a particular face we are intent upon, but the image just won't 'come', or does so only fleetingly and in part. Since intuition as such, and not just originary intuition, 'gives' us an object, and since in the case just mentioned the face is not properly given – it will not 'come', or come properly – it has a low degree of intuitiveness. As Husserl says,

> In the case of *complete unclarity*, the polar opposite to complete clarity, nothing at all has become given; the consciousness is 'blind,' is *no longer in the least intuitive*, is not at all a 'giving' consciousness in the proper sense. As a consequence we have to say: *A giving consciousness in the pregnant sense* and an *intuitional* consciousness in contradistinction to an *unclear* one: these coincide. The same holds for *degrees of givenness*, of *intuitedness*, and of *clarity*.
>
> (*Ideas I*, 126, translation modified)

That clarity should be an essential aspect of that self-responsibility in thinking to which philosophy calls us is a point that I trust does not need to be laboured.

There is another distinction, which cuts across the previous one, that Husserl also employs in the *Cartesian Meditations*. This is the distinction between the *presentation* of something and its mere 'presentification', or 'presentiation', as Husserl's term 'Vergegenwärtigung' is commonly rendered. (The word in German is not as unusual as these English terms: it means having something in mind, or bringing something to mind.) Imagining something, recalling something, anticipating something's arrival, and merely having something in mind in a wholly 'empty' way are all forms of presentification: in none of these are we, even apparently, *confronted* by the thing itself. It is not, however, that in such cases we are intentionally directed to something *other* than the thing itself. When, for example, I concretely recall the last time I saw my mother, it is my mother herself I 'mean', it is towards her that I am mentally directed – not towards some image of her. (Thinking of an image would be a *very* sophisticated and unusual mental operation.) But such acts are simply not directed to their objects as present and manifest. Nevertheless, such presentifications can themselves be intuitive (see, e.g., 78–9). They will not themselves involve straightforward sensory perception of their objects, of course, since that would be a case of 'presentation'. They can, however, involve the intuitive 'illustration' of their objects, as when we imagine or concretely recollect objects. So intuitions can either present or merely presentify their objects; and presentifications can be either intuitive or not. The only necessity here is that a presentation be intuitive, indeed originarily so.

Husserl's understanding of 'Evidenz' is to be understood in the light of the above distinctions and claims. This German word is both imperfectly and misleadingly translated as 'evidence'. A fingerprint is (very good) evidence that someone had been at a scene; for Husserl such a fingerprint is not 'evidence' at all. For it is not simply to objects as such that this term applies, but rather to states of consciousness, or our apprehension of objects. 'Evidenz' is to be understood as that in virtue of which something is *evident* to you. Indeed, Husserl demands nothing less than that it be 'a mental seeing of something itself' (52), an *experience* of things 'as *they themselves*' (54). I shall, therefore, following certain translators of Husserl's works other than Cairns, from now on render 'Evidenz' as 'self-evidence'. ('Evidentness' is another reasonable rendering, but leads to some ungainly turns of phrase.) In short, as we can now say, something is 'self-evident' if and only if it is *originarily presented* to you in a self-giving intuition. As we shall increasingly see as we proceed, the notion of an originary intuition is absolutely central to Husserl's methodology. Phenomenology is chiefly a matter of 'sense-explication' – spelling out precisely the content, or 'sense', of our various conscious states and processes – and empty, non-intuitional states are intrinsically objects of suspicion for Husserl. Prior to an explication of their sense they might well be irremediably confused or ultimately senseless. They always need to prove their cognitive credentials, for it is they above all that fail to give us the 'things themselves'. What Husserl claims is that it is only by tracing such empty acts to those intuitive (and, ideally, originary) acts in which the empty acts find their 'fulfilment' that we shall come plainly to see their real meaning. Phenomenology 'proceeds within the limits of pure intuition, or rather of pure sense-explication based on a fulfilling givenness' (177).

Returning to the topic of 'self-evidence', the reader may well now be puzzled over how Husserl can regard scepticism as a serious issue at all. If physical objects are 'self-given' in perception, if such perceptions possess 'self-evidence' that intrinsically has a right to ground judgements, where's the problem? The problem arises from the fact that something's being self-given is compatible with its being given *incompletely*, and from the related fact that one self-givenness can conflict with another. As we shall see in more detail in the next chapter, Husserl employs the concept of 'emptiness', originally introduced in connection with linguistic meaning, in his account of how we can mentally be directed to objects at all. For example, and staying with the perceptual case, any physical object is necessarily perceived by a subject only from one side at a time. As a three-dimensional body, there is something that such an object essentially withholds from you at any given time. Any visually perceived opaque body, for example, has a rear side that is, at any one time, occluded from view by the part of the object that is directly seen. And yet you take such a body to have such a hidden part, even though this does not typically involve your imagining it. So taking it is, indeed, necessary if you are to have an object of consciousness of the type 'physical body' at all – as opposed, say, to the type 'shadow' or 'after-image'. But not being sensorily given or imagined is the hallmark of 'emptiness'. Therefore there are 'unfulfilled components', 'expectant and attendant meanings' (55), even in perceptions that 'give' such an object, and give it 'bodily'. (These components, as we can now say, are technically 'non-intuitional presentifications'.) The object is self-given, but only in part, through what Husserl calls 'adumbrations' – in effect, 'profiles'. Now, precisely because empty meanings point towards a possible sensory fulfilment that takes the form of a *synthesis of identification* ('this is what I formerly had in mind'), there is in principle the possibility of such attendant meanings being *frustrated*. Because there is always more to such objects than is manifest to perception at any time, it is always possible that this 'more' – which is demanded by the very 'sense' of the perception –

will fail to materialize. So, as you move round to view, say, the far side of a vase you see before you, you may discover that the 'vase' was really but a cardboard cut-out, or, more dramatically, a hologram. The original perception, as Husserl memorably puts it, then 'explodes' (*Ideas I*, 287). You now recognize that your perception *of a vase* (and in the second case, *of a material object*) was illusory. Such discordancy is the origin of our sense of illusion – which is why Husserl always points to it in order to motivate the 'Cartesian thought'.

Husserl now introduces the term 'adequate' to refer to any self-evidence in which there are *no* unfulfilled components. In such cases an object is not merely self-given but *completely* given. Everything that pertains to it would be given together all at once. We have just seen that no *physical* thing or phenomenon can be adequately given in this sense – even to God, as Husserl sometimes adds (e.g., *Ideas I*, 315). Adequacy, here, can signify only an 'idea of perfection' (55) – i.e., an 'idea in the Kantian sense', or an ideal. If, however, adequacy could be attained in any domain, it might seem to follow that this adequate self-evidence would amount to *apodictic certainty*, the utter unthinkability of the object's non-existence or unreality, because nothing that pertains to the object's existence would fail to be given to us. There may seem to be an intelligible possibility of doubt only when something of the object is absent from our 'sight'. Conversely, how could anything that was not given to us adequately be known apodictically, since something of it would escape our sight? Indeed, just a few years before the *Cartesian Meditations* Husserl explicitly says that the terms 'apodictic' and 'adequate' are coextensive (*EP II*, 35). Earlier in his career Husserl had taken the traditional view that subjective experiences are adequately given – because they have no hidden sides, and because we cannot take up different perspectives on them: we just live through them, completely. By the time of the *Cartesian Meditations*, however, he had come to reject this view – a move that is reflected in the present meditation in the expression of the worry 'whether adequate self-evidence does not necessarily lie at infinity' (55).[8] Conversely, he had come to believe that apodicticity 'can occur even in relation to self-evidences that are inadequate'

(55). In another text Husserl says that the grasp we have on a present experience flowing into the past is 'uncancellable', but not properly adequate (*APS*, 369); and in yet another he says that the 'I think' is knowable apodictically but not adequately (*EP II*, 397). Even given these changes to his erstwhile position, however, even given that apodicticity may be attainable and adequacy not, Husserl's account of apodicticity in the present meditation cannot but appear puzzling. For how, it may be wondered, could anything more possibly be asked of self-evidence than that it be 'adequate'? For even if this is an ideal lying at 'infinity', Husserl claims that 'this idea continuously guides the scientist's intent' (55). And yet he immediately goes on to say that scientists confer on apodicticity a 'higher' epistemological dignity. In fact, nothing that Husserl says in the present context warrants any such judgement. Indeed, when he goes on to focus on the value of apodicticity, he contrasts it with self-evidence as such, not with *adequate* self-evidence. A solution to this problem perhaps lies in a passage in which Husserl suggests that in order for something to be apodictic its non-existence must not only be inconceivable at the time the thing is experienced, but inconceivable at any time: 'An apodictic cognition is completely reproducible with an identical validity. What is at one time apodictically self-evident gives rise not only to possible recollections of having had this self-evidence, but to the necessity of its validity also for the present, and so for ever: definitiveness' (*EP II*, 380). Hence Husserl can say (in contradiction to the passages quoted above from *APS* and *EP II*) that no temporal being, even within the phenomenological attitude, is knowable apodictically (*EP II*, 398). The reason for this is, presumably, that even though the non-existence of a current, phenomenologically purified experience of mine is now unthinkable by me, this indubitability is not 'completely reproducible'. I cannot be absolutely certain of the existence of that experience at any future time when I am no longer living through it. In accordance with this approach it would be natural to infer that only general, essential truths would, because of their non-temporal subject-matter, be possible objects of apodictic knowledge – which perhaps explains why, in the present passage, Husserl links the 'higher dignity' of apodicticity with the scientist's quest for *principles*.[9] However this matter is to be resolved, at the beginning of the next meditation Husserl will repeat the doubts already noted to the effect that the field of transcendental experience may not be apodictically ascertainable. Indeed, he says there that, for the rest of the present work, he will set to one side concern with the apodictic status of his phenomenological findings.

'THE CARTESIAN WAY'

The way into phenomenology offered by this first meditation therefore emerges as somewhat problematic. We are led along by the 'carrot' of apodictic knowledge, which is then indefinitely deferred. And from the early 1920s we can find Husserl sketching alternative 'ways' into phenomenology. The *Cartesian Meditations*, together with *Ideas I* and the early *Idea of Phenomenology* follow what Husserl came to call the 'Cartesian way' – one that proceeds via epistemological critique. Not only this, but Husserl on occasion can express reservations about how convincing the Cartesian way is (e.g., *EP II*, §46). Indeed, in the *Crisis*, the work that was left uncompleted at Husserl's death, he not only renews this criticism, but seems to offer two alternative ways into phenomenology in distinct preference to the Cartesian way. This has led certain commentators to suggest that Husserl came to abandon the approach to phenomenology represented by the *Cartesian Meditations*.[10] Although this introductory work is not the place for a substantial discussion of this somewhat tangled exegetical issue, since the reader may now worry that he or she is not being offered a proper introduction to phenomenology through the *Cartesian Meditations* at all, but one that Husserl came to abandon, I should like briefly to say something by way of reassurance concerning the value of this work as a representation of Husserl's considered philosophical position.

The first point to understand in this connection is that what are in question here are not different ways of doing transcendental phenomenology, but merely different ways *into* such phenomenology, different ways that Husserl tried out to get his readers to understand and accept the transcendental perspective. We are, in fact, here dealing with nothing more than Husserl's perennial worry over how best to *introduce* transcendental phenomenology as the one, true philosophical perspective. Most importantly, the reader should not be in any doubt as to whether the transcendental reduction and its epoché, which bulk so large in this initial meditation, were ever regarded by Husserl as less than absolutely essential components of phenomenology: they were not. Although in a sense the gateway to phenomenology, they are not a 'way' into it in the present sense. The alternative ways that Husserl himself mentions are different ways *to the transcendental reduction itself*. As I have mentioned, in Husserl's last work he investigates two non-Cartesian ways into phenomenology; but neither attains its goal until the transcendental reduction and its epoché have been reached (*Crisis*, §§55; 71). Without the purifying 'disconnection' of all natural, worldly beliefs, the transcendental perspective cannot be attained at all. For the transcendental perspective, you will recall, is that which sees the constituting role of consciousness with respect to every type of worldly object, ourselves included. Examining how consciousness effects such constitution is now to be our sole concern as philosophers. Any concern with the reality of the things that are constituted would be a sheer *metabasis,* an incoherent reversion to a different, and essentially non-philosophical, sort of concern. Even if Husserl had abandoned the 'Cartesian way' – something for which, in fact, there is very little evidence – this would not amount to any 'departure from Cartesianism' of the kind imagined by Landgrebe and mentioned in the Introduction. There is no radical change in what Husserl took transcendental phenomenology to be: only a growing appreciation of the depths and complexities that it involves. Nor is a concern for apodictic knowledge what is distinctive of the Cartesian way, and therefore perhaps optional. For that is reaffirmed in the *Crisis* both generally and in the context of each of the non-Cartesian ways (e.g., 192, 263, 275 [188, 259, 340]). What *is* characteristic of the Cartesian way is an *initial* focusing on the philosophical need for apodictic knowledge, and a consequent critique of all 'positive' knowledge, as a *reason* for practising the transcendental reduction and becoming a phenomenologist. The Cartesian way is therefore the 'epistemological' way to phenomenology. And to this there certainly are alternatives – as Husserl demonstrates in the *Crisis*. In this late work, one route to phenomenology proceeds through psychology, and one through reflection on the 'life-world' (about which more later). Such 'ways', however, offer *alternatives* to the Cartesian way, they are not a *replacement* for it. If this were not so, it would be deeply puzzling why, after having sketched out alternative ways into phenomenology and pointed out possible shortcomings in the Cartesian way in the early 1920s, Husserl should have followed that very way in the *Cartesian Meditations* itself. Moreover, both of these alternative routes to phenomenology are indicated in this text: the psychological way at the end of §35, and the way through the life-world in §59. I believe that Husserl's critical observations on the Cartesian way are best understood as expressing worries over how that way might be *misunderstood*. The worry is over 'presentation'. In the *Crisis*, for example, he says that 'a great shortcoming' of the Cartesian way is that 'while it leads to the transcendental ego in one leap, as it were, it brings this ego into view as apparently empty of content, since there can be no preparatory explication; so one is at a loss, at first, to know what has been gained by it' (158 [155]). For what all the non-Cartesian ways into phenomenology have in common (so that they may, in fact, be seen as but variations on the *one* alternative to the Cartesian way) is that, rather than starting with a worry over the possibility of knowledge as such, they engage in a reflection on the apparent accomplishments of knowledge in some specific area – such as psychology, or everyday experience. Led by the idea of absolutely grounded knowledge, Husserl believes that such a reflection will lead to the 'transcendental insight', and hence to the transcendental reduction. Such a route therefore involves recognition of a pregiven field of purported knowledge, which we can explore 'constitutionally'. By contrast, the worry is that, by being led on solely by a concern for apodicticity, the Cartesian way gets us interested only in the possibility of there being some apodictically secured entity. There is then a problem of knowing what to do philosophically with this fact. It is surely significant, however, that this issue simply does not arise as problematic in our present text, even though it follows the Cartesian way as single-mindedly as any. It is, indeed, explicitly raised at the beginning of the Second Meditation – 'what can I do with the transcendental ego philosophically?' (66) – but is immediately answered: the transcendental reduction presents us not with some blankly existent self, but with 'an infinite realm of being of a new kind, as the sphere of a new kind of experience: transcendental experience'. For after having secured the transcendental ego, what Husserl does in the following meditations is to take the most significant and basic kinds of object with which we know we are acquainted as 'transcendental clues', as presenting us with specific tasks for constitutional research (see, for example, §21). In contrast, it is Descartes's own procedure which 'remained barren because Descartes neglected . . . to direct his attention to the fact that the ego can explicate himself *ad infinitum* and systematically, by means of transcendental experience' (69–70). To be sure, if the 'Cartesian way' had consisted solely in a search for some apodictic truth, such a subsequent field of research would not have presented itself naturally to us as a task. The indefinite deferring of an apodictic 'critique' of transcendental knowledge would also be deeply problematic. But we have seen that this first meditation contains much more than such a search. In particular, and quite centrally, it contains the 'transcendental insight'. We begin with an apodictic critique of natural experience, and of course find it wanting. What is important, now, is the *way* in which it is found wanting. It is so in virtue of the 'Cartesian thought'. This thought then motivates the 'transcendental insight', which in turn motivates the transcendental reduction as the only way of capitalizing on the insight. This status accrues to the reduction because within it we concern ourselves solely with what is required of consciousness if there are to be objects out of consideration of any sort 'for us'. This reduction requires the epoché, because only by leaving all questions concerning the reality of objects out of consideration can we focus entirely on this *being for consciousness*. Without the epoché we are naïve: we take objects as ready-made 'things' that are simply *given* to us, and thus overlook the constituting role of consciousness. By detailed investigation into this role, into what precisely is required of consciousness for any type of object to be available to consciousness, we shall, since what an object is 'for us' simply corresponds to the particular formation of consciousness in which such an object is given, come to a fuller understanding of the nature of such objects – a fuller understanding of their 'sense', as Husserl will put it. Once the reduction has been effected, one has attained the standpoint of transcendental phenomenology, and there is no other way of attaining it. If, therefore, the reader has appreciated the philosophical importance, indeed necessity, of effecting such a reduction, the present introductory meditation of Husserl's has achieved its goal. The reader need have no worries that what follows in the subsequent meditations is a presentation of phenomenology that Husserl ever forsook (though, of course, he would always want to develop and modify it in detail). It is, however, precisely in what follows, in the detailed constitutional analyses, that transcendental phenomenology must prove its mettle. As Husserl himself says,

> The empty generality of the epoché does not of itself clarify anything; it is only the gate of entry through which one must pass in order to be able to discover the new world of pure subjectivity. The actual discovery is a matter of concrete, extremely subtle and differentiated work.
>
> (*Crisis*, 260 [257])

It is to this that we must now turn.

NOTES

1   Hence Husserl's perhaps initially puzzling remark in §7 that the lack of apodicticity attaching to the existence of a world is not a proof 'that, in spite of the continual experiencedness of the world, a non-being of the world is conceivable' (57).

2   Cairns's use of the term 'field' towards the end of p. 62 is misleading in this respect. The field of transcendental knowledge is precisely what has *not* been 'assured absolutely' at this point. Husserl's word is '*Erkenntnisboden*': the *basis*, not the *field*, of knowledge.

3 This is not, I should say, an uncontroversial claim. We shall consider the issue in some detail in Chapter 4.

4 I can, for example, easily imagine that the decimal expansion of π does not contain the sequence '731'. But if, on working it out, we discover that it *does* contain this sequence, we must conclude that it was never a genuine possibility that it should have lacked this sequence, since such mathematical truths are necessary. For the classic exposition of the issues involved here, see Kripke, 1980.

5 At the time of *Ideas I* 'phenomenological reduction' and 'transcendental reduction' are employed in materially equivalent ways. Only with the growing appreciation of the need to distinguish his philosophy proper from phenomenological psychology does Husserl come to use only the latter term in connection with the genuinely philosophical enterprise.

6 'Giving' is often translated as 'presentive'. Such intuitions are also often termed '*ursprünglich*' – usually rendered as 'originary' – in one of the senses that attach to this complex and central term in Husserl's philosophical vocabulary: see esp. *Int I*, 346ff.

7 The reader may wonder how this account is supposed to apply to the meaning of logical, abstract, and theoretical terms. We shall look into this matter in Chapter 3, but the short answer is that intuition is not necessarily *sensory* intuition.

8 As we shall see in the next chapter, Husserl's rejection of the view that at least our own subjective experiences are adequately given to us is based upon the essentially 'flowing', temporal nature of experience.

9 In fact, however, such an inference would be mistaken – as Husserl's own repeated insistence that the 'I think', at least, is apodictic itself indicates. The resolution to this apparent problem is that for Husserl the 'I think' relates to *transcendental* consciousness; and, as we shall see in the following chapter, this is not, strictly speaking, *in* time, but is 'super-temporal'.

10 The classic text here is Kern, 1964, §17. (His views are also available in English in Kern, 1977.) For what is in my view a more satisfactory account of the matter, see Drummond, 1975.

2

SECOND MEDITATION

§§12–22

We have, according to Husserl, discovered 'an infinite realm of being of a new kind' (66). This is the realm of 'transcendental experience', which is that of my 'pure' conscious life and all of its ingredients, together with all the 'pure' types of object that could possibly be given to – i.e., constituted in – it. This entire domain has, thanks to the epoché, been 'purified' of any positing of worldly realities, even the 'subjective' ones that psychology deals with. To describe this domain as a new *realm of being* will doubtless appear to many as something of a leap, perhaps even as an egregious mistake, given only the findings of the previous chapter. For surely we have as yet found only a new way of considering our conscious lives, or perhaps a new function that our lives fulfil. Surely no metaphysical or ontological conclusion, such as the term 'being' may seem to imply, is warranted at this stage? As I indicated in the previous chapter, I wish to defer consideration of any such issues until Chapter 4. For we can proceed, if it is allowed that Husserl has at least opened up a new type of enquiry: an enquiry into the constituting function of subjectivity, into how any kind of object is a necessary correlate to certain types of conscious state. This and this alone is to be our permanent field of enquiry as radical philosophers. The new science of phenomenology is to be one 'that is, so to speak, absolutely subjective, whose thematic object exists whether or not the world exists' (69). Here alone are we to find 'the deepest grounding of all sciences' (66). We are not, like Descartes, to concern ourselves with trying to infer the existence of things *outside* this realm of experience. Indeed, as I mentioned earlier, and as we shall see in more detail in Chapter 4, Husserl regards the very notion of such an 'outside' as nonsensical. We are to remain within this field and content ourselves as 'disinterested onlookers' (73), with faithfully describing and analysing what is there revealed to us. Transcendental phenomenology is to be 'the hermeneutic of conscious life' (*P&A*, 177). Since the conscious life in question is 'my own' for each radical philosopher, phenomenology is also nothing other than 'self-explication' (*CM*, 76, 97).

Despite the fact that in the previous meditation Husserl had placed much importance on the requirement of apodictic certainty in our philosophizing, and despite the fact that he claimed apodictic certainty of his own conscious existence – that of the *ego cogito, I think* – he begins this second meditation by repeating the claim, already noted in the previous chapter, that he is not as yet in a position to claim such certainty for this new *field* of transcendental experience: 'No matter how absolute this self-evidence of the existence of the ego may be for the ego itself, still it does not without further ado coincide with self-evidence for the existence of *the manifold data* of transcendental experience' (67, my emphasis). In the previous meditation he had pointed to the notorious fallibility of memory as warranting the suspicion that apodictic certainty may be restricted to the present moment of one's conscious life. In the present meditation he also implies that 'habitual properties' – by which he means mental dispositions and capacities, as well as character traits – may also fall outside the scope of such certainty. Indeed, a careful reading of the beginning of the present meditation will show that Husserl is not at this stage claiming apodictic certainty even for his present thoughts and experiences: 'The cogitationes given to me in the attitude of the transcendental reduction – given as *perceived*, recollected, and so forth – must not yet be declared absolutely indubitable with respect to their *present* or past existence' (67, my emphasis). And further down the same page he implies that we start with apodictic certainty *only* of the '*ego sum*', of 'the bare identity of the "I am" '. Securing the necessary *field* of transcendental subjectivity therefore emerges as problematic. Because of this, Husserl promises a critique ('criticism' in Cairns) of transcendental experience, by which he means an assessment of transcendental knowledge to see if it matches up to the benchmark of apodictic certainty. Without this, Husserl says in various places, we shall labour under 'transcendental naïveté' (e.g., *EP II*, 170).

Although in the present work Husserl gives no extended treatment of what might survive such an apodictic critique, he does give us some indications. He points out, for example, that although we may not have apodictic knowledge of the particular contents of the ego's transcendental life as it has unfolded through time, we can have such knowledge of the *structure* of the ego (67). You have, for example, apodictic knowledge that your transcendental life, whatever particular thoughts and experiences it contains, is *temporal* in nature: it 'flows'. Though *what* your past concretely has been is not a matter of absolute certainty, that you *have* a past is. And in a text dating from a few years before these meditations, Husserl claims that we have apodictic certainty concerning our recollections of at least the immediate past (*APS*, 374). But even if we were to grant this, it may not seem to offer us very much; certainly not an 'infinite realm' for research. Two points should be made in this connection. First, as we shall see in the following chapter, transcendental phenomenology was always intended to be *eidetic* phenomenology. Husserl is not, that is to say, primarily interested in concrete facts – even transcendentally purified ones – but in *essences*: in particular, in the necessary a priori structures and norms of any possible consciousness whatever. Even though the existence of the individual transcendentally meditating ego may be apodictically assured, this actual ego and its life are to serve a merely illustrative role in the search for *essential possibilities*. Here, in the Second Meditation, Husserl briefly indicates this fact:

There is also an a priori science which confines itself to the realm
of pure possibility (pure representableness, pure imaginableness),
and which instead of judging about the being of transcendental realities, judges about a priori possibilities, and thus at the same time
prescribes rules a priori for realities.

(66)

Even the sceptic will grant that there is a whole range of *possible*
pasts that I may have had. What Husserl is further interested in is,
for example, what relations must necessarily hold between any
such past and my actual present if that past is to be my actual past,
and the kind of temporal structure that any actually extended
conscious life must possess. Second, Husserl points out that transcendental phenomenology must proceed in two stages, the second
of which will carry out the apodictic critique of transcendental
experience. The first stage, without such a critique, is one 'that is
not yet philosophical in the full sense' (68). Here we explore transcendental experience 'with simple devotion to the self-evidence
inherent in the harmonious flow of such experience' (*ibid.*). This
reference to harmoniousness suggests that we are, at this first
stage, to content ourselves at the transcendental level with something analogous to the 'empirical indubitability' of the objects
of natural experience that we noted in the previous chapter. The
Cartesian Meditations as a whole operates at this first stage, in as
much as the promised critique is never carried out: 'Meanwhile we
understand questions about the range of . . . apodicticity . . . to be
set aside' (70). Although such questions do, perhaps, need finally to
be addressed, the first stage of phenomenology, with which we
shall content ourselves in these pages, is already of fundamental
importance. At one point Husserl distinguishes the transcendental
reduction from an 'apodictic reduction' – one which, within the
transcendental field, restricts attention to what is truly apodictic –
and says that 'before I practice apodictic critique, I must have a field
for that critique: in the present case, a realm of experience. And
this – that of transcendental self-experience – I first acquire thanks
to the method of the transcendental reduction' (*EP II*, 80). We shall
content ourselves with exploring this domain without undue

concern for the ultimate prize of apodicticity.[1] For, as we saw in the previous chapter, we already have a reason for being philosophically interested in such a field: namely, the priority that attaches to transcendental research over against any 'positive', and therefore 'naïve', enquiry. Because of this, we can proceed secure in the knowledge both that we are engaging in, if not 'first philosophy', at least one that is prior to any other discipline, and that our findings will, in virtue of the harmoniousness to be found in pure experience, have at least the certainty of any empirical enquiries. (For this sort of approach, see, for example, *APS*, 367–8.)

INTENTIONALITY

Although pure consciousness is to be our true field of enquiry, such enquiry would not be particularly interesting were not consciousness essentially possessed of a certain feature that will guide all our subsequent research. That feature is *intentionality*: consciousness is, essentially, a consciousness *of* things. The term 'intentionality' is a relatively late arrival in the vocabulary of analytical philosophers, and it has been used in a variety of senses. Some use it to stand for the ability of certain 'mental states' to be about, or to have reference to, certain items in the real 'external' world. The issue is standardly presented in the context of a transcendental realist perspective, the problem being that of how we can get 'outside' consciousness. A construal of intentionality in this way fails ultimately to have any meaning in relation to Husserl, however, since he is an idealist. But even leaving that issue to one side, this first issue is not in any case equivalent to intentionality as Husserl understands it, because intentionality characterizes not only our awareness of 'external' objects, but also our reflective awareness of our own mental states and processes (whether transcendentally purified or not). Moreover, such a construal of intentionality sees the issue as being how distinct existences, distinct *entities*, can be epistemologically or cognitively related. But this, from Husserl's point of view, conflates two issues: intentionality itself, as directedness to objects, and a distinct question concerning the *reality* of objects. Others in the analytical tradition have attempted to explicate intentionality by reference to the well-defined semantic notion of intensionality.[2] But not only does this give rise to uncertainties of its own – e.g., the context ⌜S veridically saw x⌝ is extensional, but visual perception is an intentional phenomenon; and many treat 'It is a law of nature that . . . 'as intensional, but it has nothing obviously to do with intentionality – if there is any interesting connection between the two notions at all, the direction of explanation will have to go from the originally intentional mental phenomena to the linguistic phenomena that are their expression. The closest one comes within the analytical tradition to Husserl's notion of intentionality is the claim that a mental state or event is intentional if and only if it has an object, but one that need not actually exist. Ponce de León searched for the Fountain of Youth, and a child can await Santa Claus, though there are no such entities. However, although this is indeed true of most intentional states, it is not universally true. For we have, according to Husserl, apodictic certainty concerning some objects – if only it be one's own self. Our consciousness of such objects would be a case of intentionality, and yet apodicticity wholly excludes possible non-existence. Moreover, even when the non-existence of an object is a possibility, this possibility itself fails to give us a *fundamental* explication of intentionality. Husserl, by contrast, gives an account of intentionality that accounts for and makes intelligible the possible non-existence of an intentional object when this is possible.

'The word intentionality', writes Husserl, 'signifies nothing else than this universal fundamental property of consciousness: to be consciousness *of* something' (72). To 'intend' an object simply means to have, or to be mentally directed to, an object in any way at all – in perception, thought, memory, imagination, anticipation; in desire, emotion, and so forth. It signifies the same as to 'mean' (*meinen*) an object. Hence the full expression of the Cartesian certainty is not '*cogito*', but '*cogito – cogitatum*' (74) – to be interpreted as 'I am conscious – of something'. Strictly speaking, this is *all* that Husserl means by 'intentionality'. In fact, it is easy to misconstrue even this apparently simple claim. For it is easy to assume that Husserl is trying to explain the intentional 'of' by appeal to an already understood, everyday notion of consciousness.

In fact, however, the order of elucidation is ultimately in the reverse direction: we are to understand what consciousness is in terms of the special 'of-ness' that relates us to objects. For as we shall see, Husserl freely speaks of activities and states of consciousness that are not at all 'conscious' in the usual sense. The notion of consciousness is not one that the phenomenologist is simply to take over from everyday thought. It is, rather, one that must be fashioned anew in the course of phenomenological explication. This is, indeed, true of phenomenology's 'conceptual apparatus' in general. Concepts and terms are to be defined anew, in an 'original' manner, in the context of a pure description of the subjective accomplishments that are 'seen' in transcendental reflection (e.g., 180). Phenomenological concepts thus emerge, and are refined, in the course of phenomenological investigation itself. Nevertheless, Husserl will begin by focusing on conscious states in an everyday sense, so as to unearth the relatedness to an object that is manifestly to be found in those states. The problem is fully to comprehend what is involved even in this apparently simple notion of being conscious of something. When this has been done, such intentional relatedness to objects, which alone is definitive of consciousness, can perhaps be extended beyond the domain of what would ordinarily be regarded as states of consciousness.[3] The first step in comprehending what is involved in even this everyday notion of being conscious of something is recognizing the role of *synthesis* in our mental lives: 'Elucidation of the peculiarity we call synthesis first makes fruitful the exhibition of the cogito, of intentional experiences, as consciousness-of, and so first makes fruitful Franz Brentano's significant discovery that intentionality is the fundamental characteristic of mental phenomena' (79). In order properly to appreciate Husserl's understanding of intentionality, and hence of consciousness, we need to see why 'synthesis' is necessarily involved in it.

One thing that the phenomenological reduction involves is a turning of attention away from things in the world and towards our subjective experiences. When we do this, according to Husserl, about the first thing that leaps to the eye is the *multiplicity* of subjective processes that corresponds to the awareness of even the simplest object. You can't get much simpler, experientially, than perceiving a material object. In perception a material object seems simply to be there, 'bodily', before you. But

> reflective experience teaches us that there is no progressively per-
> ceived thing, nor any element perceived as a determination within it,
> that does not appear, during perception, in multiplicities of different
> appearances, even though it is given and grasped as continuously one
> and the same thing. But in normal ongoing perception, only this unity,
> only the thing itself, stands in the comprehending gaze while the func-
> tioning processes of lived experience remain extra-thematic,
> ungrasped, and latent. *Perception is not some empty 'having' of per-
> ceived things, but rather a flowing lived experience of subjective
> appearances synthetically uniting themselves in a consciousness of
> the self-same entity existing in this way or that.*
>
> (*EB*, 238)

This passage comes from the beginning of the first draft of Husserl's first attempt since *Ideas I* to introduce his philosophy to the public: his *Encyclopaedia Britannica* article 'Phenomenology'. At that time, at least, he clearly thought that this is the first thing one needs to know about phenomenology. In our own text he gives a concrete example of the sort of thing he has in mind:

> If I take, for example, the perceiving of this die as the theme for my
> description, I see in pure reflection that *this* die is given continuously
> as an objective unity in a multi-form and changeable multiplicity of
> manners of appearing, which belong determinately to it. These, in
> their temporal flow, are not an incoherent sequence of subjective
> processes. Rather they flow away in the unity of a synthesis, such that in
> them we are conscious of one and the same thing as appearing. The one
> identical die appears, now in near appearances, now in far appearances.
>
> (77–8)

Synthesis is this relation between different conscious states in virtue of which, despite the difference, an *identical* object stands before consciousness. In virtue of such synthesis, even after the

bracketing of the world and the turn to pure subjective experience
we still find a duality of object and of subjective processes in which
an object is given – a duality that involves a *unity* on the side of the
object as contrasted with a flowing *multiplicity* on the side of the
subjective processes. This seems initially to have come as a revelation to Husserl. In the 'Five Lectures' of 1907, one of the first-fruits
of Husserl's adoption of the transcendental perspective, we find the
following passage:

> If we look closer and notice how in the mental process, say, of [perceiving]
> a sound, even after the phenomenological reduction, appearance and
> that which appears stand in contrast, and this in the midst of pure given-
> ness, hence in the midst of true immanence, *then we are taken aback*.
> (*IP*, 11, my emphasis)

It is because of this (and returning to the *Cartesian Meditations*)
that 'inquiry into consciousness concerns two sides' (77), which he
terms the 'noetic' (concerning what is subjective in so far as it
involves a directedness to objects) and the 'noematic' (concerning
the object) (74). Only where we have such a duality do we have
intentionality. Intentionality is the name for a certain 'achievement' or 'accomplishment': that of the consciousness of identity
from within the 'Heraclitean flux' (86) of flowing subjective life.
Any object is a 'pole of identity' (83) within such a flux. Because of
this, it is always possible, in principle, to 'return' to an object, to
intend it once again, as one and the same, in a new mental act.
Where this is not possible, talk of an 'object' is inapplicable (e.g.,
FTL, 140–1, 251; *APS*, 326–7).

So the first step towards understanding Husserl's notion of
intentionality is the recognition that objects do not stand in a one-
to-one relation to the subjective states or processes that intend
these objects. This is, indeed, the precise meaning of 'constitution'
in Husserl. He introduces this notion in the Five Lectures as follows: ' "Constitution" means that things given immanently are
not, as it first appeared, in consciousness as things are in a box, but
rather that they present themselves in something like "appearances" . . . , appearances that in a certain sense create objects for the

ego in their changing and highly peculiar structure' (*IP* 71). So, to speak of consciousness 'constituting objects' is simply to advert to this way in which an object comes about as a pole of identity within the flowing multiplicities of conscious processes, solely as a result of these processes.

Husserl has, therefore, uncovered a sense of 'transcendence' that is to be found *within* the sphere of pure consciousness. After the epoché we yet find that consciousness carries a relatedness to an object *within itself* (71), such an object being 'immanent in the flowing consciousness, descriptively in it' (80). In order to clarify this notion of transcendence-in-immanence Husserl introduces the technical term *'reell'*, usually rendered by Cairns as 'really inherent' or 'really intrinsic'. Something is really inherent in consciousness if it is literally a *constituent* of the flow of consciousness, if it is something that we *live through* – like a perceptual experience, a process of thinking, an emotion, a sensation, and anything that is a constituent part of such mental phenomena. Something is, by contrast, transcendent if it is not thus a really inherent part of consciousness. So even wholly unreal objects, such as hallucinated objects, are transcendent, for they too are not literal constituents of consciousness, but rather poles of identity in relation to the multiple flow of the subjective processes that are genuine constituents of consciousness. As Husserl says at the very end of the First Meditation, no doubt to stave off the charge of subjective idealism,

> Just as the reduced Ego is not a piece of the world, so, conversely, neither the world nor any worldly object is a piece of my Ego, to be found really inherent in my conscious life as a really inherent part of it, as a complex of data of sensation or a complex of acts. This 'transcendence' is part of the intrinsic sense of anything worldly.
>
> (65)

This is asserted after the transcendental reduction has been effected, so that the world and its objects here in question are mere 'phenomena'.

In relation to the perception of material objects – which Husserl commonly takes as an exemplary form of awareness – the object of consciousness is clearly transcendent to the flow of experience, since there is always more to it than 'properly' appears in such experience. This book that you see before you, for example, has a rear side that is not currently appearing to you. You could turn it over, of course, and directly experience its cover; but when you do so, you necessarily lose the original appearance of these two pages. This is true of even the simplest and smallest of perceptible bodies. If, switching to another sense, you could entirely encompass a small object in your hand, you would achieve a tactile appearance of the entirety of the object's surface; but even here there are the inner parts of the object which necessarily cannot be felt at the same time. Even when we turn to a two-dimensional phenomenon such as a shadow, which has no hidden or occluded parts at all, we still find a transcendence of the object to any really inherent components in the experience that intends it. For even a shadow presents a different appearance when seen aslant from that which it presents when seen full on; and if I walk up to it, it will come to occupy a greater expanse of my visual field than it did before. When I thus alter my viewpoint on the shadow, the sensory components of my experience change, but the object, even when taken precisely as it appears to me, does not: it does not even *appear* to change shape, or size. What changes, and what is *taken* as changing, is but my perceptual relation to the object – my 'perspective' on it. It is similar even in the case of a quality of an object such as a colour. For as the phenomenon of 'colour constancy' shows, qualitatively different sensory states may be involved in the presentation of what appears as the *same* object-colour, albeit under different lighting conditions. Husserl speaks in this connection of physical objects and features of such objects being *adumbrated* by the really inherent sensory features of perceptual experience (*Ideas I*, 74, 202–3; *LI* VI, §14b). It is important to realize that such facts do not rely on any natural beliefs concerning the reality of objects in the world. The point is not that we just 'know' that bodies have rear sides and inner parts and so forth. The point is, rather, that such objects *appear as* having such a nature, whether they really do so or not: that we unreflectingly *take* them in this way, and that so taking them is definitive of the *kind* of object and experience in question. This fact remains after the epoché, since it concerns the sheer 'descriptive character' of certain of our experiences. Even if you convince yourself that you are now visually hallucinating, this book will continue to appear as a three-dimensional material object with hidden aspects. This is definitive of an object's having, as Husserl puts it, the 'sense' *material body*.

The fact that perception of a material object involves a reference to aspects of it that are not sensorily registered in that very experience should remind us of a topic that we have already (in the previous chapter) seen Husserl deal with: the emptiness of a 'meaning intention' compared with its 'fulfilment' by perceptual contact with the very object that was emptily meant. What Husserl discerns is that an 'empty intending' is to be found even in perceptual experience of an object's bodily presence: 'Each individual percept is a mixture of fulfilled and unfulfilled intentions' (*LI* VI, 690 [714]). When you look at this book, it appears as a material object hiding a part of itself from your gaze. It can appear like this only because the subjective 'accomplishment' of perception involves a reference to the hidden side – something that is absent from merely experiencing a sensation, which does not even seem to have any hidden aspects.[4] That there is such a reference in your perception of this book would become clear if you picked the 'book' up and discovered that it was really but two sheets of paper: for you would be *surprised*. The 'reference' to the hidden aspects here takes the form of an *anticipation*. Conversely, if things are really as they seem, then, when you turn over the book, your perception of the cover *fulfils* and *confirms* the originally 'empty' reference to it. If you are already familiar with this book, you will have a fairly determinate expectation of what you will see when you turn it over. If, by contrast, you espy a wholly unfamiliar object, this will not be the case. Nevertheless, if the thing looks like a material body of some sort at all, you will necessarily have *some* expectation concerning its hidden side: at the very least that it has got one. *Intentionality resides precisely in the presence of empty, unfilled components in experience*:

Intentional analysis is guided by the fundamental recognition that, as a consciousness, every *cogito* is indeed (in the broadest sense) a

meaning of its meant, but that, at any moment, this something meant
is more (what is meant is more) than what is meant at that moment
explicitly. In our example, each phase of perception was a mere side of
the object, as what was perceptually meant. This *meaning-beyond-itself*,
which lies in any consciousness, must be considered an essential
moment of it.

(84)

Indeed, Husserl tends to think of 'intentional acts' primarily in terms
of empty intending, often contrasting such acts with 'fulfilling acts'
(e.g., *LI* V, §13). Nevertheless, even the latter are truly intentional
despite the 'fullness' of sensory presentation – but only because
they too harbour within themselves empty intentions that involve
a 'meaning-beyond'. Intentionality essentially involves absence.

Husserl frequently employs two related terms to express our
intentional directedness beyond what is strictly registered in
sensory appearance: 'apperception' and 'appresentation'. When
you look at some material object, you only 'properly' see a limited
aspect of it; indeed, with an opaque object, a limited aspect of its
surface. Only this is 'exhibited', as Husserl puts it, in your sensory
experience. And yet you take yourself to be perceiving a coherent,
three-dimensional body with hidden sides because of the empty
intentions directed to those hidden aspects. Husserl expresses this
by saying that you *apperceive* the thing as a coherent body. So you
apperceive something when you perceive it *as* a thing of a certain
sort, and when so taking it involves appreciating something about
the thing that goes beyond what is properly registered, or 'exhibited', in the sensory state involved in the perception. Apperception
is a 'perceiving-in-addition-to' ('ad-perception'). Since, as we have
just seen, Husserl holds that *all* perception involves such a 'meaning beyond' what is properly given – an apperceptive 'surplus', as
he calls it on one occasion (*LI* V, 399 [567]) – he holds that all
perception is apperception. He then says that the aspects of an
object that are 'properly' seen *appresent* the other, essentially
implicated, but only emptily intended aspects of the thing.

Before moving on, we should perhaps dwell a little on Husserl's
claim that consciousness is essentially characterized by intention-

ality – that *every* state of consciousness is a consciousness of some object or other – since this is a claim that has been frequently contested. The first point to make in this connection is that Husserl does not deny that there are really inherent elements in consciousness that lack intentionality. As we shall see later in this chapter, Husserl recognizes 'sensory data' as going to make up any perceptual experience: elements which account for the sensuous immediacy that distinguishes such experience from mere thought or imagination. And Husserl regards such elements as intrinsically bereft of intentionality. Such sensory elements are, however, but elements in more complex acts – full-blown perceptions – which as a whole *are* intentional in character. It is only to such concrete, integral acts as a whole that Husserl attributes intentionality. There are, however, two sorts of concrete conscious states that have often been seen as lacking intentionality even as wholes. First, there are sensations. A pain, for example, is commonly thought not to be 'of' anything, but to be a sort of brute presence in consciousness. On the other hand, several philosophers have argued that even feeling a pain does indeed involve a directedness to an object. To have a pain in your foot, for example, is, on this view, to be *aware of your foot* in a certain way. And, at least as far as normal experience is concerned, Husserl agrees with this latter view. The possibility of so being aware of your foot when in pain has its preconditions, however. In particular, your body must already have been 'constituted' for you. For is not a very rudimentary form of consciousness conceivable in which pains occur prior to the emergence of any awareness by the subject of its own body? Perhaps the consciousness of a foetus in the womb, at some stage of its development, is an actual instance of such a possibility. If so, then sensations would not necessarily involve an intentional directedness to anything. In fact, for reasons we shall investigate later in this chapter, Husserl denies that even the awareness of such 'neat' sensations can be accounted for simply by the brute presence in consciousness of some non-intentional pain 'datum'. Even in relation to such sensations Husserl will draw a distinction between the object and our awareness of it.[5] So, even in relation to sensations, a brute, non-intentional 'raw feel' is, for Husserl, but an abstraction from a more comprehensive, integrated act.

The second type of integral state of consciousness that may be thought to cast doubt on Husserl's claim is *mood*. For cannot some moods – e.g., certain sorts of anxiety, general boredom, malaise, a feeling of uncanniness – wholly lack a specific intentional object? Indeed, they can, as Husserl fully realized; but this does not deprive them of intentional directedness. For, as we shall see in greater detail in Chapter 3, intentionality does not always involve a directedness to determinate objects. As far as moods in particular are concerned, as early as the *Logical Investigations* Husserl indicated that he regarded them as possibly involving an intentional relatedness to an *indeterminate* object (*LI* V, §15b). Such a lack of determinateness is not unique to moods. A different sort of case of indeterminate intentional reference is where we try, and fail, to remember the name of something. Here we are, as it were, not so much intentionally 'directed' to something, as intentionally groping. Husserl himself, in the passage just referred to, mentions 'obscure drives or pressures toward unrepresented goals' and 'an idea had before we give it verbal expression' as further examples of the phenomenon. So, to return to the case of moods, although we may not be able to put our finger on the object of our anxiety, this does not mean that anxiety is some blank, self-enclosed state. In a passage from later in his life, Husserl writes of a mood as 'a unity of feeling that lends a colour to all that appears' (M III 3 II 1, 29). The German word for mood – '*Stimmung*' – connotes for Husserl (as it did, more famously, for Heidegger) an *attunement* to one's environment. And in late manuscripts Husserl relates mood to the tenor of our life as a whole (e.g., A VI 34, 22). Something that so intimately concerns our 'situation' in life can hardly be regarded as devoid of intentionality. At the limit, therefore, a mood can be taken as being intentionally directed at the world, or reality, as a whole – a possibility that Heidegger would capitalize on.

THE CONCEPT OF HORIZON

In order to express the interplay of presence and absence at the heart of intentionality, Husserl introduces a term that has remained central to all later developments of phenomenology: 'horizon'. Husserl standardly makes a distinction between an object's *inner horizon* and its *outer horizon*. Its inner horizon comprises what we have recently been considering as 'absent' in a perception of an object: the further parts and aspects of the object itself that are not exhibited in a particular experience of the object, but are only 'emptily meant'. A thing's outer horizon, by contrast, comprises things that are not parts or aspects of that very thing at all, but which are yet implicated in any consciousness of it. It is one of Husserl's basic insights that the 'meaning-beyond-itself' that is constitutive of intentionality is a meaning not only beyond the sensorily registered parts of an object towards the whole, but beyond the thing itself as a whole. For every material object is essentially located in space. Every individual perception necessarily has the sense of being but a particular 'view' on one segment of the world. Every scene necessarily gives upon another, and that upon yet another, in an unbounded space that can be indefinitely explored with respect to the other objects that it may contain – other objects that it *must* be *capable* of containing. This reference beyond a given perceived thing to its spatial environment is essential to that object appearing as the *kind* of object that it is: namely, as a material body. This outer horizon, for any subject with any 'experience of the world' at all, will not be just an empty potentiality. For we all have an arena of familiarity, a zone in which we can 'find our way around'. Space reaches out into almost wholly indeterminate 'uncharted territory' only beyond this zone. We are not, however, constantly turned towards even the familiar objects of our 'home territory': they function mostly as *background* to the particular objects with which we are attentively concerned at any given moment. To express this idea of background, Husserl introduces a distinction between 'actual' and 'potential' (or 'inactual'), between 'explicit' and 'implicit' consciousness. Perception in the full sense of the word involves, for Husserl, an explicit 'seizing' of an object, a turning of attention on to something. He in fact reserves the terms *cogito* and *cogitatio* for acts (which may not be perceptual) in which, through attention, one is *explicitly* turned towards something. It is these that we naturally consider first in order to get a grip on the notion of intentionality as a 'consciousness of'. And yet any such 'cogitatio' that is a perception is always a seizing of something *from out of a background of objects that are 'co-given'*. Among such merely co-given objects, closest to hand are those that fall within our perceptual field and are sensorily registered, but which we are not attending to:

> In perceiving proper, as an attentive perceiving, I am turned toward the object, for instance, the sheet of paper; I seize upon it as this existent here and now. The seizing is a 'seizing out'; anything perceived has its experiential background. Around the sheet of paper lie books, pencils, an inkstand, etc., also 'perceived' in a certain manner, perceptually there, in the 'field of intuition'; but, during the advertence to the sheet of paper, they were without even a secondary advertence and seizing-upon . . . Every perception of a physical thing has, in this manner, a halo of *background intuitions* . . . , and that is also a '*conscious mental process*', or, more briefly, 'consciousness' – and, indeed, 'of' all that which in fact lies in the co-seen objective 'background'.
>
> (*Ideas I*, §35, translation modified)

Visually, at the present moment, only your awareness of this book, or perhaps these words, is a *cogitatio*, an 'explicit' consciousness in the mode of 'actuality'. Your awareness of the objects that lie towards the periphery of your visual field is not; it is an 'implicit' or 'non-actual' awareness. Husserl also calls it a 'potential' consciousness, since it sustains the possibility of your turning your attention to these objects, and 'seizing' them explicitly.[6] Apart from the possibly odd vocabulary, there is nothing of note in this. Husserl, however, extends these observations to encompass what lies *beyond* your field of vision. You have a consciousness of what lies beyond the edge of your visual field, indeed of what lies behind your back. Husserl is not crediting you with some 'sixth sense'; he is simply pointing out that you have an awareness that *something is there* – even if it be only a practically empty region. That you have an appreciation of the extension of space beyond the limits of your perceptual field goes towards constituting your explicit consciousness of what does lie within the perceptual field *as a consciousness of something in the world*, as a scene *arrayed in space*. This 'appreciation' is not a mere conceptual representation, mere 'knowledge' that there is a wider world. It is a *perceptual* fact, implicated, 'implicit', in any world-directed perception. Husserl here has the surely sound thought that a given perception would not be phenomenologically of a material object in a spatial scene at all if it did not sustain the possibility in principle of changing your viewpoint and coming to perceive objects in neighbouring regions – a possibility which we appreciate as motivated by perceptual consciousness itself. In a similar way, and returning to an object's inner horizon, your awareness of the rear sides of material objects is implicit or potential. Seeing an object harbours within it – within its 'sense', Husserl will say – the possibility of perceiving more of it. If you did not take there to be any 'more', the object would not be appearing to you, be 'apperceived' by you, *as* a material object at all. In both cases we have horizons, external and internal, which are 'predelineated potentialities' (82) – predelineated by the very 'sense' of any actual perception. As potentialities, they point forward to possible actualizations or fulfilments. Hence, we can 'ask any horizon what lies in it, we can explicate it and uncover the potentialities of conscious life at a particular time'. When we do this, 'precisely thereby we uncover the object-sense meant implicitly in the actual *cogito*' (*ibid.*). 'Object-sense' (*gegenständlicher Sinn*) is a technical term that Husserl often employs. Any object has a certain 'meaning' or 'sense'. The kind of object that it is entails various possibilities and impossibilities for consciousness in relation to it. A material object, for example, must be located in space along with possible neighbouring objects, and must allow itself to be perceived from various perspectives. Conversely, both of these are excluded from an object of a fundamentally different ontological type, such as an *after-image*. Such possibilities and impossibilities are part of the 'sense' of such objects. We know these things, and a priori, because objects, under the transcendental reduction, just are what they are *for us*: their nature is exhausted by our possible experience of them, experience in which the things are themselves *given*. Objects can have such different natures only because of the different kinds of processes of consciousness that intend them. By excavating the complex mental accomplishment to which a given type of object corresponds, unearthing the forms of intentionality that lie implicit in such an accomplishment, we shall concretely explicate the 'sense' of such an object.

The notion of horizon has a yet wider employment, however – something that may serve to allay a worry that some readers may have been harbouring about the preceding explication of Husserl's notion of intentionality. For if an empty intention is necessarily involved in any intentional act, what are we to say of our awareness of our own, current, conscious states? For Husserl certainly regards such reflective awareness as characterized by intentionality, since it is 'of' something; and yet elements in our own mental lives hardly have aspects that can be brought into view or changed in appearance as a result of different perspectives we might take on them. They are not, it would seem, 'adumbrated'. We do not even have to turn to reflection to make the point: bodily sensations hardly feature an 'absence' that can be only emptily intended. Sensations seem to *fill* consciousness. In fact, in his earlier writings Husserl contrasted 'transcendent' and 'immanent' objects on just this score: an object such as a material thing is transcendent precisely because it cannot wholly be encompassed in an originally giving experience, whereas experiences themselves are immanent precisely because they are so encompassed. We simply 'live through them', as Husserl puts it; completely. Experiences are given 'adequately', transcendent objects 'inadequately' through adumbrations (e.g., *Ideas I*, §§41–2). So another way of expressing the present worry is to say that, on the present construal of intentionality, it looks as if the idea of something being given adequately in an intentional act would be incoherent. In fact, although Husserl would continue to respect a distinction between immanent and transcendent objects, between those that are and those that are not themselves really inherent parts of the stream of consciousness, and to do so in terms of the possible presence of perspective and hiddenness, he came increasingly to see that adequacy, understood as a complete and total presence of an object to and in consciousness, was indeed impossible, even where awareness of our own conscious experiences is in question. Of particular note in this connection are later amendments that Husserl made to the passage in *Ideas I* just referred to. These later remarks qualify his attempt to contrast awareness of immanent subjective processes and of transcendent 'external' objects by reference to the lack of any adumbrations in the former. What he now says is that it is not that mental processes are not adumbrated at all; it is, rather, that they are not adumbrated 'one-sidedly'. There is no possibility here of diverse adumbrations *at a single time* (*Ideas I*, 81). In other words, there are adumbrations in relation to 'immanent' conscious processes, but they are *temporal* in character. For although every phase of such a process is a really inherent part of our subjective life, our *awareness* of any such process points beyond the present moment so as to include *past* phases of the process. Hence, Husserl can say in the last Meditation that *every perception* is such that 'it posits more as itself-there than it makes *actually* present at any time . . . provided only that we understand "presenting" in a broader sense' (151). Even subjective states and processes, since they too, according to Husserl, can be 'perceived', therefore have their horizon. In their case the horizon is time – a topic we shall be investigating shortly.

'SENSUALISM' AND THE SENSE-DATUM THEORY

We can perhaps appreciate Husserl's distinctive understanding of intentionality more fully by contrasting it with an opposed position that he is principally intent on rejecting. It is what he terms 'sensualism' (76). It is also commonly known as 'sensationalism', and it dominated philosophy and psychology during the period prior to Brentano's 'significant discovery'. According to this approach, when we reflect upon sense-experience we find, as what is immediately given to consciousness, various sensory 'data': colour-patches, sounds, various tactile qualities, and so on. These are supposed to be *both* 'really inherent' in the flow of consciousness *and* objects of awareness. As Hume says at one point,

> Every impression, external and internal, passions, affections, sensa-
> tions, pains and pleasures, are originally on the same footing; and . . .
> whatever other differences we may observe among them, they appear,
> all of them, in their true colours, as impressions or perceptions.
>
> (Hume 1739/40, p. 190)

Since it was commonly held that there is no distinction to be made
between, for example, a pain and our experience of it, it is here
being claimed that there is, at the fundamental level, across the
whole range of experiences, no distinction between an act of awareness and what the awareness is of. There is no noetic–noematic
duality of the sort that is at the heart of the doctrine of intentionality. The fundamental elements of conscious life are 'meaningless
sensations': meaningless because giving us, of themselves, no
notice of anything beyond themselves. They are brute data, lacking
intentionality. Therefore there is, on such a view, no place for that
in virtue of which diverse mental states can be equally directed to
one and the same object in differently adumbrated ways. There is
no essential role for empty intentions. Such 'sensualists' do, indeed,
recognize cognitive elements in consciousness in addition to sensations; but these 'ideas' are themselves taken to be but pale 'copies'
of sensations, and so they lack intentionality quite as much as the
mere sensations of which they are copies. Criticizing this position,
Husserl writes as follows:

> Consciousness is not a name for 'psychical complexes,' for 'contents'
> fused together, for 'bundles' or streams of 'sensations' which, without
> sense in themselves, also cannot lend any 'sense' to whatever mixture;
> it is rather through and through consciousness . . . Consciousness is
> therefore *toto coelo* different from what sensualism alone will see,
> from what in fact is irrational stuff without sense.
>
> (*Ideas I*, 176)

In Husserl's view, a being whose whole subjective life consisted of
nothing more than a succession of such sensations, if such is conceivable at all, ought not to be regarded as one possessing mentality
('*ein psychisches Wesen*', *LI* V, §9). No mere piling up of meaning-

less elements will take us out of what is meaningless. If something were wholly sensorily present to consciousness, it would not, in fact, really be present *to* consciousness at all: it would merely be present *in* 'consciousness', as a wholly meaningless 'piece' of subjectivity; and so what it was 'in' would hardly deserve the name 'consciousness' at all – at least not 'in the pregnant sense', as Husserl liked to put it, according to which consciousness is consciousness *of* something. It is precisely sense-giving 'empty-intentions' that are missing in the sensualist's account – those that are implicated in the synthesis that is involved in any state of consciousness whatever.

It is not, however, only this school of sensationalism that fails to appreciate the intentionality of consciousness. The sense-datum theory, though developed by the early Russell and Moore in conscious opposition to the sensationalist school, would be no better in Husserl's eyes. According to Moore, mental acts are 'acts of the mind or acts of *consciousness*: whenever we do any of them, we are conscious of something' (Moore 1953, p. 4). It is such acts as these, he held, that are the indisputably *mental* items in the world. In every case such an act is to be sharply distinguished from the object of which we are conscious in that act:

> The entity which is experienced may be of many different kinds . . . But, whatever be its nature, the entity which *is* experienced must in all cases be distinguished from the fact or event which consists in its being experienced; since by saying that it is experienced we mean that it has a relation of a certain kind to something else.
>
> (Moore 1922, p. 169)

Similarly, Russell writes that 'acquaintance is a dual relation between a subject and an object which need not have any community of nature. The subject is "mental", the object is not known to be mental except in introspection' (Russell 1913, p. 5). The term 'sense-datum' had been around since the closing decades of the nineteenth century, but these two writers appropriated it to stand for the object of any such act of awareness that is directed towards a sensory object. They both felt that the term 'sensation', as employed by the earlier sensationalists, expressed an incoherent conflation of act and object. However, despite this clear rejection of the sensationalist tradition, as far as concerns what Husserl sees as the essential issue here the sense-datum theorists and the sensualists are all in the same boat, since they all hold to a one-to-one correlation between objects and conscious acts. This is because, although the sense-datum theory does recognize 'acts of consciousness' as irreducibly different from objects (so that the one-to-one correlation is not that of sheer identity), these acts have no intrinsic character at all. They are purely 'diaphanous', serving simply to bring various objects to awareness. What this means is that every detectable feature in sensory experience is a feature of the *object* of that experience; and hence that every change in such experience is a change in the object of experience. The pure act awareness, being utterly featureless and everywhere the same, fulfils no role at all, except to open up the abstract possibility that what are objects of awareness may themselves exist without being *objects*, without standing in any relation to an act of awareness. There is still no complexity on the 'mental' side of things *vis-à-vis* objects of awareness.

This may seem unfair to the sense-datum theory. Such a theory, after all, hardly claims that sensation, or the sensing of sense-data, is all that is to be found in our mental lives. The bulk of the philosophy of mind is to be devoted to showing how more complex acts can be built up upon this basis. In particular, sense-datum theorists commonly recognize a distinction between 'sensation' and 'perception', and thus will have no difficulty in accepting Husserl's notion of an 'apperceptive surplus' that was mentioned earlier in this chapter. And if they do not follow the 'sensualists', as commonly they do not, in supposing that all cognitive elements in conscious life other than sensation are but pale copies of sensation, one may perhaps wonder if there is a significant difference between this school of thought and Husserl. More precisely, perhaps Husserl's disagreement with a possible sense-datum theory amounts to little more than a question of methodology: Where do you start from? This may seem to be reinforced by what Husserl says in the *Cartesian Meditations* when he claims that to start from anywhere other than 'the things themselves', from the testimony of the 'pure – and, so to speak, still dumb – psychological experience' (77) is a fundamental mistake. He goes on to make clear what he takes such primary data to be: 'The truly first utterance ... is the Cartesian utterance of the *ego cogito* – for example: "I perceive – this house" or "I remember – a certain commotion in the street".' In short, consciousness relates primarily to more or less 'rich', everyday objects, not sensations or sense-data. As he says more fully in the *Crisis*:

> The first thing we must do . . . is to take the conscious life, completely without prejudice, just as what it quite immediately gives itself, as itself, to be. Here, in immediate givenness, one finds anything but colour data, tone data, other 'sense' data or data of feeling, will, etc.; that is, one finds none of those things which appear in traditional psychology, taken for granted to be immediately given from the start. Instead one finds, as even Descartes did . . . , the *cogito*, *intentionality*.
> (236 [233])

Although the question of the reality of the world has been 'disconnected' from our philosophical enquiring, our experience's being as of such a world is in no way denied or altered. Indeed, a chief purpose of the epoché is to allow us disinterestedly to 'see' natural experience of the world in its true colours for the first time, undistorted by prejudice. And such experience does not, of course, give itself as having to do with sense-data or colour patches, but with the objects of everyday life. Indeed, this faithfulness to the lived character of everyday experience is principally what is popularly connoted by the term 'phenomenological'. It is perhaps commonly associated even more strongly with Husserl's erstwhile student, Heidegger, who nicely expresses the approach in the following passage:

> We never . . . originally and really perceive a throng of sensations, e.g., tones and noises, in the appearance of things . . . ; rather, we hear the storm whistling in the chimney, we hear the three-engine aeroplane, we hear the Mercedes in immediate distinction from the Volkswagen.

> Much closer to us than any sensations are the things themselves. We
> hear the door slam in the house, and never hear acoustic sensations
> or mere sounds.
>
> (Heidegger 1977, 364 [156], translation modified)

Such 'faithful description' may, however, be thought to be of
limited philosophical value. After all, it is not as if a sense-datum
theorist (or even a 'sensualist', for that matter) need *deny* such
statements. The real philosophical task is surely to analyse and
account for such everyday appearances. In fact, Husserl agrees with
this. 'The proper task of reflection', he writes, 'is not to repeat
the original process, but to consider it and explicate what can be
found in it' (72–3). Indeed, when one reads through the *Cartesian
Meditations*, one repeatedly finds Husserl offering us *analyses* of
various phenomena of consciousness: not only unfolding what is
intentionally 'implicit' in experience, but also unearthing elements
that are 'really contained' in consciousness, digging down into
the infrastructure of everyday experience. This is, indeed, one of
the most striking differences between Husserl and Heidegger. For
the latter operates purely descriptively and hermeneutically at the
level of fully constituted, meaningful, human life – explicating,
in Husserl's terminology, what it is to be a 'person'. Not until we
go beyond such description, however, and begin to analyse such
intentional achievements, tracing their preconditions down to the
pre-personal level of 'anonymously functioning subjectivity', are
we doing transcendental philosophy according to Husserl (see, e.g.,
Ideas II, Supplement XII, esp. Section II, §12). We shall return to
this disagreement between Husserl and Heidegger in the next
chapter; but the immediate point of importance for us is that the
supposedly radical disagreement between Husserl and the sense-
datum theorists may now be disappearing from view. The situation
only becomes worse, apparently, when we find Husserl writing
that 'in what cases, and in what different significations of the
phrase, data of sensation can . . . perhaps be tendered legitimately
as components [of intentional experiences]: that is . . . a special
result, to be produced by a work of uncovering and describing'
(77). Although he does not go into this matter in the *Cartesian*

Meditations, elsewhere Husserl does repeatedly treat sensory data as 'legitimate components' of sense-experience. Indeed, he (characteristically) introduces his own technical term to refer to them: 'hyletic data' or '*hylé*' (the Greek for matter, or stuff). When such sensory data are discussed in some detail in *Ideas I*, §85, Husserl makes three claims about them, two positive and one negative. First, they are positively characterized as 'sensation contents'. They include bodily sensations such as pain, and 'no doubt also the sensuous moments belonging to the sphere of "drives" ', but also, and most relevantly for us, those sensation contents that lend sensuous immediacy to sense-perception: 'color-data, touch-data and tone-data, and the like'. Second, they are, along with the *noetic* functions, said to be 'really inherent' in consciousness – in contrast to what is *noematic* or but intentionally present to consciousness. Third, and negatively, they are characterized as having '*nothing pertaining to intentionality*'. It is the noetic components of mental life that give it intentional directedness to objects. Sensuous data 'present themselves as stuffs for intentive formings, or sense-bestowings', the latter being the job of noetic processes. Such data are 'components in more inclusive concrete mental processes which are intentive as wholes; and more particularly we find those sensuous moments overlaid by a stratum which, as it were, "animates", which *bestows sense*'. So we may well wonder if Husserl's phenomenology is not, at least in part, but a mirror image of the constructions that a sense-datum theorist might offer – a question that presents itself with some urgency when we eventually find Husserl starting to talk about principles of 'association' (as in §39 of the *Meditations*) – part of the stock in trade of sensationalism in particular.

In fact, we are not dealing here with a simple matter of reverse presentation, despite some parallels that do emerge. For one thing, although Husserl himself frequently employed the terms 'sense-data' (*Sinnesdaten*) and 'hyletic data', these are not literally '*data*', they are not 'given' to consciousness (at least in normal, non-introspective experience). They are not, as they were for the sense-datum theorists, primary *objects of awareness*. For it is the *noetic* functions in our conscious life that determine what objects we are aware of; and such functions, even in simple sense-perception, direct us primarily to phenomenologically 'rich' objects such as houses, commotions in the street, and cars – at the very least, to material bodies arrayed in space. Second, and relatedly, a hyletic datum is but a *dependent aspect* of any conscious experience – one that we can focus on introspectively only by *abstracting* from a concrete phase of experience that equally and necessarily contains intentive functions. This implies, finally, that intentionality, for Husserl, albeit in different forms, goes 'all the way down' – even down to the level of 'sensations' or 'sense-data' themselves. As he writes in one manuscript, 'Every one of our hyletic data is already a "developmental product", and so has a hidden intentionality that points back to a synthesis' (F I 24, 41a). There is no possible experience that does not involve that 'meaning beyond' which is the hallmark of intentionality. By failing to begin with intentionality, the sensualists and the sense-datum theorists are incapable of ever truly recognizing it. Perhaps surprisingly, Husserl's increasingly sophisticated account of sensory data results from his investigations into the nature of our consciousness of time – a topic that surfaces on a number of occasions in the *Cartesian Meditations*.

TIME-CONSCIOUSNESS AND *HYLÉ*

One manifest aspect of all the (non-abstract) objects of which we can be aware is their temporal character. Events occur at times; processes unfold in time; and material objects persist for some time, however briefly. All have their positions in time, and are related to one another in terms of 'before', 'after' and 'at the same time as'. We are aware of them *as* having such a temporal character. Such a character, as pertaining to constituted objects, is itself, of course, an accomplishment of consciousness. So one thing the phenomenologist will have to do is give an account of the intentional performance in virtue of which objects possessing such a temporal character are available to consciousness. Furthermore, experience itself unfolds in time, and particular experiences are temporally related to one another. Indeed, as we are about to see, it is only *because* consciousness is itself temporal that temporal objects can be constituted for consciousness. Husserl regarded our consciousness of time, and in particular our consciousness of the temporal character of consciousness itself, as the most fundamental of all intentional accomplishments, since it underlies and alone renders possible every other feature of conscious life. Husserl also thought that this was the most difficult of all subjects for phenomenological clarification (*Time*, 276).

Let us suppose, to take Husserl's favourite example in this area, that I hear a melody. This, whether we take it as a real melody sounding in the objective world, or a 'bracketed' melody as pure phenomenon, is a temporal object: it takes time to unfold, during which time one note follows another. What is involved in my being aware of such an object with its temporal character? Well, one thing that is required is that my experience of it be extended in just the way that the musical object is: 'The consciousness of a time itself ⟨requires⟩ time; the consciousness of a duration, duration; and the consciousness of a succession, succession' (*Time*, 192). The flow of the melody through time must be matched by a flow of my experience, each now-point of my experience registering the currently sounding phase of the melody. But as Kant was perhaps the first to recognize, this by itself does not suffice to account for our awareness of the phenomenon. For if, as I am hearing a certain note in the middle of the melody, the previous note, which I have just heard, had altogether dropped out of my consciousness, so that now it is as if it had never been heard, I should not now be experiencing the present note as *following on* from a previous one, and so should have no overall awareness of the melody as something *extended* in time. What we need to recognize is that, as Husserl says, 'each perceptual phase has an intentional reference to an extended section of the temporal object' (*Time*, 239). There is a problem to be addressed here because, in short, a succession of experiences, in this case the experiences of each note of the melody, even in a single subject, does not obviously entail an experience of succession. Nor, indeed, does an enduring, unchanging experience obviously entail an experience of permanence – as when we hear a continuous, unchanging tone for a while. Here, too, at each point at which I am hearing the phase of the tone that is now sounding, the earlier stretches of the tone must somehow be 'retained in grasp', as Husserl puts it, if I am to be aware of the extended continuity of the tone. Furthermore, such a grasp on what my immediately past experience has afforded is necessary even for me to hear the melody or the tone *begin* sounding: starting to experience in a certain way does not obviously entail experiencing something of a certain sort starting. For in this case I need to have now, as the first note begins to sound, an awareness that just before now I was aware of silence. As a matter of fact, although they may not be immediately obvious, the above *are* cases of entailment for Husserl – but only because experiences themselves necessarily have a depth-structure that is itself far from obvious, and which needs to be unearthed by careful phenomenological analysis if we are to understand the phenomenon of time. And the first element we have encountered in this essential structure of consciousness is a holding-in-grasp. 'The past would be nothing for the consciousness belonging to the now if it were not represented in the now; and the now would not be now . . . if it did not stand before me *in that consciousness* as a *limit of a past being*. The past *must* be represented in this now as past' (*Time*, 280).

In addition to featuring the 'holding in grasp' of prior moments that we have just mentioned, consciousness must be *continuous*, at least while we are awake. Experiences are not strung together like beads on a thread, however closely packed. Its manifest phenomenological character is that of a 'flow'. This must, of course, be granted whenever we are aware of a continuously unfolding phenomenon, such as a continuous tone. An experience of something continuous requires a continuousness in consciousness. But even where the objects of our awareness are not continuous – as when we hear a series of discrete pips – our awareness of such a phenomenon must involve a strict continuity of consciousness. For such pips are presented to us as discrete only in virtue of each one being preceded and followed by a relevant silence. We have to be aware of this silence, this non-sounding, as such if we are to be aware of the discrete sounding of the pips. And the pips will be perceived as further apart or closer together in time depending on how long these silences are perceived to be. Perceiving a silence is not the absence of any awareness, but is itself an intentional achievement. There must be a continuous awareness of the silence and then a pip in order for the pip to be perceived as discrete.

Putting these two points together, we see that consciousness must involve a *continuous synthesis*. Whenever an experience (such as a perception) presents its object as *now*, such presentness makes sense only as emerging out of a lived, experienced past: 'The present is always born from the past' (*Time*, 106). The appearance of any present phase of the world is at the same time a slipping into the past of another, immediately preceding phase of the world. And this is equally true of the phases of your own experience, should you be turned reflectively towards it. This slippage is experienced as such, and is the basis of all talk about the 'flow' of time. Husserl gives the name 'retention' to the 'holding in grasp' that allows such slippage to be experienced. Retention is not memory, in the usual sense of recollection, which is a *regaining* of a past object as something over and done with, something that is achieved in discrete acts of recollecting that fix and focus on some past phenomenon. Retention is, rather, at least initially to be understood as our appreciation of a present *as it slips into the past*, continuously, thereby serving as the basis for our sense of a past in the first place. Retention is what makes recollection possible. It is not an act, but a *process*: a continuous 'intentional modification', as Husserl puts it, of an actual present as it falls into the past. In addition to such retention, every present moment of consciousness also possesses what Husserl calls 'protention', whereby we have a sense of the immanent future phase of our experience about to come to presence. This is not expectation in the usual sense, which is a discrete act and which presupposes it. It is, rather, a sheer, continuous openness to the new – even if it be but the newly unchanging. Because of protention, waking life is 'a living-towards, a living that goes from the now towards the new now' (*Time*, 106). What, specifically, is protended is determined by what we have immediately experienced: 'The style of the past is projected into the future' (*Bernau*, 38). Hence, Husserl can speak of protentions as offering us 'an analogy' of what has just been experienced, and as 'a shadow that is cast ahead' (*APS*, 288, 289). In addition to such backward- and forward-facing aspects, each conscious present features what Husserl calls a 'primal impression' or 'primal sensation'. It is, in fact, the moment of *hylé*. It is also the moment of *actuality*; of what is actually *new* and *now*: 'The now that is just sinking into the past is no longer the new but that which the new has pushed aside' (*Time*, 63). It is what others have been tempted to identify with the experiencing and experienced present in the strict sense. Although Husserl can on occasion refer to primal impression as being the 'now' in the strict sense (e.g., *Time*, 67), he is quite clear that 'primal sensation is something *abstract*' (*Time*, 326). In speaking of such a primal impression we are focusing on just one aspect of any actual, fully concrete moment in the stream of consciousness, for any such moment necessarily involves *all three* of the aspects just identified: primal impression, retention and protention. The reason for this is that primal impression, or *hylé*, like retention and protention, is itself a *process*. It is the continuous filling of consciousness, the constant incursion of the new. The retentional aspect of the present is, as it were, but the shadow of this impressional procession, a continuous intentional modification of that phase of the hyletic process that is 'pushed aside' by the new, actual phase. Indeed, this pushing aside, of which we have seen Husserl speak, just is this process of modification that the actualizing of *hylé* brings about. The modification that is in question here is of what is 'really inherent' in consciousness into what is but intentionally present. Suppose you have just now heard one of those discrete pips that I mentioned earlier. While you actually heard it, a certain hyletic datum was really contained in your stream of consciousness. As soon as the pip stops sounding, that datum ceases actually to exist. What is really contained in your consciousness in this new moment is (apart from new hyletic data and renewed protention) a *retention* of that pip, which contains the pip in but an 'irreal' (*irreell*), or intentional, manner, and hence as no longer *actual*, but past. The pip, in short, has been modified from being originally perceived to being retended in virtue of the relevant hyletic datum being modified from being 'really inherent' in consciousness to

being intentionally present to consciousness: 'As primal presentation has "really inherent" core data in it in so far as it contains
these data unmodified, so every primal retention has core data in it,
though not really inherently, in so far as it contains these data
modified' (*Bernau*, 212). The flowing, processive present is a process of what is *reell* 'passing over' into what is *irreell* (*Bernau*, 213).
The protentional side of things is also but another modificational
aspect of the welling up of new hyletic data, though in an inverse
sense: this time our empty directedness to the impending future
is continuously being filled by new, really inherent data. Hence
Husserl can say that 'primal presentation', the welling up of new
hyletic data, is itself the 'filling' of protention (*Bernau*, 7, 14).

As the stream of consciousness flows onward, the formerly present phases of experience do not retentively slip into an undifferentiated, general past. As we are in the middle of hearing a melody,
for example, our present sense of indeed hearing *a melody* – i.e., of
now hearing a *part* of a longer temporal object – requires that the
elapsed phases of the melody be retained in grasp in a certain *order*.
This is possible because, as a present phase of experience
retentively slips into the past, it does so with its own retentive
grasp on its own immediate past (together with *its* retended past).
This prior past, therefore, itself slips further away into the past
from the perspective of the current present. As the present streams
on, all these nested retentions undergo a continuous modification,
which constitutes a structured flowing away of experience, and the
objects therein constituted, into the past (see, for example, *Time*,
No. 50). This is part of what Husserl intends when, at the beginning of §18 of the *Cartesian Meditations*, he writes of 'an all-
ruling, passively flowing synthesis, in the form of the continuous
inner consciousness of time'. The further into the past, from the
living present, that we penetrate, the more we find obscurity and
indefiniteness, because such continuous retentional modification
proceeds up to a necessary limit:

> With this intentional modification there goes hand in hand a *gradual
> diminution of prominence*; and precisely this has its limit, at which
> the formerly prominent subsides into the *universal substratum* – the

so-called *'unconscious'*, which, far from being a phenomenological nothing, is itself a limit-mode of consciousness.

(*FTL*, 280)

As a phase of experience slips retentively into the past, it not only in this way gradually loses clarity, it also increasingly disengages from our attention (*Bernau*, 263). Although we must 'hold in grasp' the earlier phases of a melody we are listening to, we are not naturally *focused* on them as they slip into the past. That would involve an unnatural, reflective, phenomenological switch of attention. Rather, our attention is caught by what is newly being presented to us: 'In the living present that which makes an appearance as primal impression has, *ceteris paribus*, a stronger affective tendency than what is already retentional. Precisely for that reason, being affected is inclined uniformly to the future as far as the direction of its propagation is concerned. Intentionality is predominantly directed to the future' (*APS*, 156. See also *Time*, 118). Returning, however, to the 'substratum' of the 'unconscious', which contains the 'sedimentation of retentions', Husserl characterizes it as having the form of 'sleeping' consciousness (*FTL*, 255). Here we have a case of something I pointed out earlier in the chapter: the way in which intentionality comes to determine our understanding of 'consciousness', rather than conversely. This 'unconscious' substratum is yet a 'mode' of consciousness, because it must be characterized as harbouring intentionality. It is a *'reservoir of objects* that have been livingly established in the process of the living present. . . . [S]ense is still implicitly there' (*APS*, 177, my emphasis). This is shown by two capacities possessed by the contents of such a 'reservoir'. First, these 'sleeping' modes of consciousness can be awakened by recollection, reactivating that which, as unactivated, therefore already has its intentional reference.[7] For recollection involves a *double intentionality* (*Time*, 182–3). If, for example, I now recall a particularly striking bird I saw yesterday, my recollection is, of course, directed to the bird: that is its 'object'. But I am also recollectively related to my *seeing* the bird. I might, for example, recall the *clear presence* of the bird; but clarity was a feature of my *perception*. Indeed, I can recall the bird *only because* I awaken my past perception of it. My recollection *inherits* the perception's intentional object. That is why, if I am genuinely and accurately recalling the bird, it can only appear in my mind's eye in the perspective from which I saw it. Yesterday's perception, 'sunken' though it is, before any recollecting, in an obscure 'unconsciousness', yet retains its intentional directedness. Moreover, in such recollection, we have a certain synthesis: the present recollection is directed to *the same* object as the perception, and has the sense of so doing while we live through it. But synthesis, in general, is 'a mode of combination exclusively peculiar to consciousness' (77). Only consciousness can be synthesized with consciousness. It is not a mere matter of causal connection, since it essentially involves a sense of *identity*. Hence the 'unconscious' memory is a mode of consciousness. The same conclusion is indicated by the second capacity pertaining to the contents of the retentional reservoir. For what is thus dormant, or 'implicit', in consciousness can yet affect new experiences that are directed to new objects. Our past experience of the world 'colours' our later perceptions. We 'read' the world in the light of our past. More precisely, the empty intentions, which make up the 'apperceptive surplus' that is an ingredient in any perception, have their ground and origin in the reservoir of our past experience. This will be a major topic for us in the following chapter. For the moment it is enough to see that, since this reservoir is contributing empty *intentions* to new experiences, it must, as thus intentionally charged, be a mode of consciousness.

Because any present moment of consciousness necessarily has its *three* aspects of retention, protention and primal impression, any resuscitation of a past experience in the 'reservoir' through recollection, however short it may have been, will be the resuscitation of that which possesses all three aspects. Any such experience will be revivified *as* having a backward reference to an experiential past lying even further back in our past, and as having a forward, protentional reference: 'Every memory contains expectation-intentions whose fulfilment leads to the present' (*Time*, 52).[8] Recollection does not, however, recuperate such protentions precisely as they originally were, for now, in retrospect, they are *fulfilled* protentions: 'They are not only there in the process of catching what is coming; they have also *caught* it. They have been fulfilled, and we are conscious of this in the recollection' (*ibid.*). It is thanks to recollection that we have a sense of time itself as a *static* framework in which changeable events can be allocated a position once and for all: 'objective time', as Husserl commonly calls it. The 'now' is not itself a location in time, but rather a 'point of view' that gives us different 'perspectives' on our experiences, and the temporal aspects of objects constituted therein, as they flow away, with increasing 'distance', into the past. Husserl frequently calls these perspectives 'running-off modes' (e.g., *Time*, No. 53), but also, as we have already seen, and with an eye on the analogy with the appearing of physical objects through changing sensory data, 'adumbrations'. A temporal object such as an experience nevertheless has a fixed and unchangeable location in time due to its changing relation to the ever-changing present. A point in time, such as 5.15 a.m., 26 July AD 1756 is a *fixed* point in time, and whatever happened then is eternally fixed as happening then. This has sense for us because we can, in principle, repeatedly return, in recollection, to the *same* constituted period in the past and recognize it as the same, in relation to other segments of our lives: 'Temporal objectivity is produced in the subjective temporal flow, and it is essential to temporal objectivity that it be identifiable in recollections and as such be the subject of temporal predicates' (*Time*, 108).

Although I do not know that Husserl ever tried to (or could) justify it, he in fact believed that every experience is permanently laid down in the reservoir of the unconscious, with both of the above powers to affect future experience. *Nothing* is ever *wholly* lost to consciousness (e.g., *APS*, 266; *Bernau*, 46). Indeed, Husserl draws an even more striking conclusion from his analysis of inner time-consciousness. The present is essentially a flowing present; it is 'not something *toto coelo* different from the not-now but is continuously mediated with it' (*Time*, 40). Every present is necessarily 'the filling of a past' (*APS*, 378) – more precisely, of that immediately elapsed present which is now immediately past. But if every present is *essentially* a flow, the conclusion is . . . that consciousess's lived time is *infinite*: 'The I that lives onwards is immortal – *N.B.*, the pure transcendental I, not the empirical worldly I, who can very well die' (*ibid.*). Since a present without retention is also unthinkable, the pure life of consciousness is also infinite in the reverse direction, back into the past: the 'absolute *arising* of consciousness from unconsciousness is nonsensical' (B II 2, 4b). Hence, 'Transcendental life and the transcendental I cannot be born; only the human being in the world can be born. I, as transcendental I, was for ever' (*APS*, 379). And again: 'As coming to an end is thinkable only in the process [of conscious life], whereas the coming to an end of the process itself is not thinkable, so is a beginning thinkable only in the process, but not as the beginning of the process' (*APS*, 378). This does not mean that conscious life will continue for ever in its variegated, awake form, and that such has always been in train. It is far more likely, thinks Husserl, that large stretches will involve a 'sleeping' consciousness, where attention is aroused by nothing because sensory fields lack any kind of differentiation (B II 2, 6), 'a silent and empty life, a dreamless empty sleep' (*APS*, 380) – one which, however, is not just nothing, any more than is the reservoir of memory recently discussed. Because of this, any such sleeping consciousness can in principle be awakened. We shall be looking more closely at such 'metaphysical' aspects of Husserl's phenomenology at the end of Chapter 4.

So far we have looked at temporal objects and at our experiences in which such objects are constituted. There is, however, a whole further, deeper dimension to Husserl's account of temporality that we have yet to touch upon, at least explicitly. The reason for this additional level of enquiry is that our experiences themselves are temporal objects: 'It belongs to the essence of the perception of a temporal object that it is a temporal object itself. Under all circumstances it has a temporal dimension' (*Time*, 232). Since this subjective process itself endures, and has a temporal location in relation to other experiences, its *own* phases must be synthetically linked together, through continuously modified, nested retentions and protentions, if I am to be aware of it as enduring, and they must be related to protentions and retentions in other phases of my experience if they are to be regarded as having a position in time. It may be odd to speak of the perceiving of an object as itself an object.

However, it certainly can become an object – as in phenomeno-logical reflection. And as we shall see in the next chapter, Husserl holds that any object to which we attentively turn our regard (in the present case, reflectively) must *already* have been constituted in its unity and 'pre-given' to us. Hence its temporal unity needs accounting for even prior to actual recollection. What Husserl says in the *Cartesian Meditations à propos* our conscious life as a whole can, with the indicated omissions, be applied to any individual experience: 'Only because it already appears as a . . . unity can it also be "contemplated", in the pre-eminent manner characterising acts of paying attention and grasping, and be made the theme for a . . . cognition' (81). According to Husserl, even when we do not reflect, we at least *experience* or 'live through' (*erleben*) the experi-ences themselves, and we experience their temporal extendedness. For such an experience – a perceptual experience, for example – has, as we have seen, its 'really inherent' parts. There are, for example, the changing series of sensory data in virtue of which we are aware of changing features in the object of our perception, which 'adum-brate' those features. It is, in part, *in virtue of* our experiencing these sensations that we perceive the changing features or aspects of our object. The persistence of the perceived object therefore involves an experienced persistence of the perceiving of the object. After all, we are certainly aware of a perception itself terminating or changing in various ways, even when we are intent upon its object. In short, the temporality of experience itself must be accounted for. And for precisely the same reason that we encountered in relation to the objects of experience, this must be done by reference to the threefold structure of the present that allows awareness to extend beyond the present. But if, as we have established, objects are temporally constituted in experience in vir-tue of the latter's threefold structure, in what is the temporality of experiences themselves constituted? For they themselves, even though immanent in consciousness, have their temporal coherence and their positions in the flow of time on which we have varying perspectives from the ever-changing viewpoint of the present. A certain perceptual experience, say, is now experienced as currently unfolding; and later the *same* experience is remembered as, let us say, just preceding the onset of toothache. Husserl is therefore forced to dig yet deeper down into the domain of consciousness, and he finds a level even deeper than that of temporally extended and evanescent 'experiences': that of 'absolute consciousness', as he calls it (*Time*, Supplementary Text 54), or 'primal consciousness' (*Bernau*, 264). We now see that 'primal impression', 'retention' and 'protention' do not ultimately refer to really inherent features of experiences themselves, as temporal processes, but to really inherent features of absolute consciousness itself, in which all temporal processes are themselves constituted. In virtue of this, consciousness is *internally related to itself*. Husserl speaks in this connection of a 'lengthwise intentionality' (*Längsintentionalität*) as that which runs through absolute consciousness itself (*Time*, 80–1). It is specifically this that Husserl intends when he writes, in the *Cartesian Meditations*, of 'one aspect of the ego's marvellous being-for-himself: here, in the first place, the being of his conscious life in the form of reflexive intentional relatedness to itself' (81). Only because of this can discrete, unitary experiences, and the objects constituted therein, themselves be appreciated temporally. Husserl speaks in this connection of 'transverse intentionality' (*Querintentionalität*), which is directed to constituted, unitary, temporal *objects*: first of all our experiences, and thereby, to 'transcendent' objects (*Time*, 82).

But what of the 'absolute flow' itself? If it is a subject for phenomenological reflection, we can presumably become aware of *it* as temporal. As Husserl himself says, 'I surely do know of the flow of consciousness *as* a flow. I can look at it' (*Time*, 378). But if I am aware of the flow as itself unfolding in time, as having its phases and extents that I can look upon as unities temporally related to one another, shall we not have to recognize a yet still deeper level of consciousness in which the flow itself is constituted as temporal, and so on *ad infinitum*? Husserl raises this problem in the present meditation, when he speaks of 'a paradoxical fundamental property of conscious life, which seems thus to be infected with an infinite regress' (81). We cannot go into all the problems that this issue raises – such as the fact that, even if the regress is stopped, we would seem to be landed with a flow that *constitutes itself*, something that Husserl himself says seems shocking, indeed absurd, though he attempted to render the possibility plausible (e.g., *Time*, 378–80). In the context of Husserl's overall philosophy it is more important to see how he thinks the regress *can* be stopped. And this is ultimately because he refuses to regard the absolute flow as a process unfolding in time. Husserl insists that temporal predicates do not literally apply to it: it is, strictly, pre- or supra-temporal. Husserl can call the absolute flow a 'process'; but whereas it makes sense to suppose that any truly temporal process should unfold more quickly or slowly than it actually does, the absolute flow 'has the absurd character that it flows precisely as it flows and can flow neither "faster" nor "slower"' (*Time*, 370). Indeed, even calling it a 'flow', as Husserl repeatedly does, is metaphorical:

> The flow is something we speak of *in conformity with what is consti-tuted* . . . It is *absolute subjectivity* and has the absolute properties of something to be designated *metaphorically* as a 'flow': the absolute properties of a point of actuality, of the primal source-point 'now', etc. In the actuality-experience we have the primal source-point and a continuity of reverberation. For all this, we have no names.
>
> (*ibid.*)

This is what Husserl means by a phrase he came to use very frequently – the 'living present' (e.g., *Int III*, 348) – and he most commonly describes it as 'standing-streaming' (e.g., *Int III*, 590, 670). It is 'standing' because it does not move or process *through* time; it is 'streaming' because of the threefold hyletic-retentional-protentional 'process' that it involves – or, rather, that it *is*. It does not flow through time; it is, rather, that time flows through, or wells up, within, it – the absolute, living source-point of all consti-tution. It is this absolute flow that we, as transcendental subjects, finally are. In fact, as will become clear in the next chapter, such an absolute streaming is *more* basic than any 'I' or 'ego': it is, in itself, an 'I-less streaming' (*Int III*, 598), because in it a personal, centred self is constituted. It is this that is 'ultimately and truly absolute' (*Ideas I*, 163). In the beginning was (or better: is) the 'flow'.

The consciousness of time, of *immanent* temporality – not just the temporality of experiences, but ultimately the temporality of that absolute consciousness in which such experiences themselves are constituted – is fundamental for phenomenological research because it is presupposed by every other constitutive performance. This is what Husserl means when he says, in our present medita- tion, that 'the fundamental form of this universal synthesis, the form that makes all other syntheses of consciousness possible, is the all-embracing consciousness of internal time. The correlate of this consciousness is immanent temporality itself' (81). Every worldly thing that I perceive is perceived as having some duration, however short. Underlying any perception of objective change or stasis there is the consciousness of inner time as constantly elapsing, which is but the experience of our own conscious life continuously flowing. Temporal objects, whether immanent or transcendent, are themselves temporal only because they are constituted unities within a flow of absolute consciousness. For were there *no* such temporal synthesis at the level of lived experience, there would be no synthetically unified objects for us of any sort whatsoever.

This is of immediate relevance to us because of its bearing on the question of *hylé* – the sensory ingredient in consciousness. *Hylé* cannot be equivalent to *sensation* as traditionally conceived by the 'sensualists', or to sense-data. For these would be *constituted uni- ties* according to Husserl (e.g., *PP*, 486); whereas in their respective theories they are taken as ultimate constituents in, or relata of, conscious life. Hence, in a work from the 1920s, Husserl can criti- cize the 'sensualists' not, as he may have appeared to do earlier, on merely methodological grounds, but for 'constructing the life of consciousness out of data as, so to speak, finished objects' (*FTL*, 252). In contrast to this, Husserl asserts that 'even in the immanent "internality" of the ego, there are *no objects beforehand*' (*FTL*, 253). *Hylé* (and for this reason this mass term is more appropriate than the count-noun 'hyletic datum') is, however, *prior* to all con- stitution, being an ultimate constituent of conscious life. It is in no sense 'given' to us – not even in reflection, which also gives us but constituted unities. It is unearthed only by *analysis* of our conscious life, and is brought into the picture to do justice to the manifest sensory aspects of that life. Its recognition involves an *abstraction* from experience, in however simple a form we imagine experience to be, since any experience must at least already involve the syntheses of internal time-consciousness, and therefore constitution. Husserl will sometimes say – and other than pointing out its sensory character, this is perhaps all one can say about it – that *hylé* is what is 'alien' to the ego. By this Husserl does not mean that it is in any way ontologically independent of consciousness, since it is 'really inherent' in it: 'We do indeed say that a hyletic datum is alien to the I; but this alien thing has the peculiarity that it can belong to only a single individual subject . . . What is hyletic has this in common with every experience' (D 3, 11). By 'alien' to the ego Husserl means that *hylé* is distinct from and prior to any *activity*, of however low a grade, on the part of the ego. It is what, at least when differentiated, *affects* the ego in the primally impressional moment, drawing the ego's attention – a topic we shall be investigating in the next chapter.

Intentionality is essentially characterized as a 'meaning beyond'. What we have found in the analysis of temporality is such a 'meaning beyond' that is presupposed even by the experiencing of sensation, or what some would construe as the awareness of sense-data. For any such awareness involves retention and protention, which point beyond what is present, beyond 'primal sensation'. At this basic level we are, of course, a long way from intentional functions that direct us to the phenomenologically rich objects that occupy us in our everyday lives. How such richer intentionality is built up upon the necessary basis of internal time-consciousness is an issue that will bulk large in the next chapter.

INTENTIONAL ANALYSIS

Phenomenology as intentional, or constitutional, analysis proceeds in a number of directions. First, and most obviously, it involves *correlational* investigations concerning the noetic and noematic sides of consciousness. Any noema, any object just as it is intended, is to be investigated by analysing the complex mental performance in which the object is constituted. This will lead to the unearthing of the 'really inherent' components of conscious life (both noetic and hyletic). One aspect of such correlational analysis is what we might call 'foundational analysis'. For certain mental acts will be seen to exhibit a *stratified* complexity – one intentional layer being founded upon and presupposing another – which it will be our task to bring to the light of day. Correlated with this, there will be a stratified complexity in the object. We shall be investigating this topic in Chapter 3. Another aspect of such intentional analysis, as we have already seen, is what we may call 'horizonal analysis': unpacking the implicit, empty intentionalities that are present in any conscious act:

> We can ask any horizon what lies in it, we can explicate (unfold) it, and *uncover* the potentialities of conscious life at a particular time. Precisely thereby, however, we uncover the object-sense meant implicitly in the actual cogito ... This sense, the *cogitum qua cogitum* ... becomes *clarified* only through this exposition of the given horizon and the new horizons continually awakened.
>
> (82)

From first to last, Husserl's investigations are controlled by his adherence to the 'principle of all principles'. Phenomenological research must ultimately be guided by 'the things themselves'. Since these are self-given only in intuition, *it is to intuition itself that all analysis and clarification must be oriented.* All merely empty intentions point back, as intentional 'modifications', to intuitions in which things are given – and ultimately to originary intuitions in which they are 'self-given'. Hence, Husserl can speak of explicating an intentional performance 'in respect of its *rightful content – that is, its fulfilment content*' (123, my emphasis). This privileging of intuition is, in fact, reflected in the practice of horizonal analysis, since the latter is 'a matter of uncovering the intentionally implicit in the experience as a transcendental process, a matter of explicating systematically the predelineated horizons *by a conversion into possible fulfilling self-evidence*' (98, my emphasis). For what is actually involved in 'explicating', concretely realizing, the horizon – the inner horizon, let's say – of some type of physical object, short of actually circumnavigating it, is our *imagining*, as concretely as possible, what we should perceive of the object as we explore its formerly hidden sides and aspects. Now, although, as Husserl repeatedly says, imagination operates in the realm of the 'as if', it has a privilege over any mere empty thinking, because it presents its objects as they would appear when perceived. Imagination is an intuitive act, and as close as we can come to original experience of a thing without its actual presence. When we concretely imagine some material object, we must perforce imagine it in some particular orientation with respect to us. Even though we can, in such a 'fantasy-mode', quickly survey the entirety of a vast object – even the earth, or the solar system – this is but a speeded-up version of the kind of thing we could in principle perceive. Even though we may not explicitly imagine ourselves in the imagined situation, the fact that we are ineluctably 'as if there' is indicated by the oriented perspective from which we must imagine any object we can possibly imagine. In imagination, not only is some object as if it were there, some perception of ours, in which such an object would be given, is as if it were occurring. Therefore imagination gives us an 'as if' *reality* (94). Because of this, although I have so far contrasted empty intentions with the 'fullness' of perceptual experience, as Husserl himself often does, even imagination can serve something of a fulfilling – more precisely, an 'illustrating' or 'clarifying' – function. Although imagining an iguana, say, is far from actually seeing one, being able to imagine one puts you in a more 'authentic' or 'proper' cognitive position than someone who has merely heard of iguanas and knows that they are a certain kind of reptile. So horizonal explication presupposes the 'original right' of intuition, in so far as it involves the imaginative conversion of empty intentions into their intuitive illustrations:

> One and the same object can, a priori, be intended in very different modes of consciousness (certain essential types: perception, recollection, empty consciousness). Among them the 'experiencing' mode, the original mode of consciousness of the object in question, has a precedence; to it all others are related as intentional modifications. But *intentional* modification has, quite generally, the *intrinsic* property

of *pointing back* to something unmodified. The modified manner of givenness, when, so to speak, we interrogate it, tells us itself that it is a modification *of* that original. That makes it possible for the subject of consciousness . . . , starting from the particular non-original manner of givenness, to strive toward the original one, and perhaps to presentify it explicitly or to make the object-sense 'clear to himself'. The fulfilling clarification takes place in a synthetic transition in which the object of a non-original mode of consciousness is given as one and the same as the object of consciousness in the mode 'experience' (the mode 'it itself' translation), or else as one and the same object 'clarified' – that is to say, as it 'would' be itself given in a 'possible experience' . . . Every manner of intentional givenness, as a 'consciousness-of', can be *'statically' explicated* in this fashion.

(*FTL*, 276, translation modified)

Husserl's slogan 'To the things themselves' is not only a curb on fanciful speculation. It is, more importantly, an indication of a theory of meaningfulness. Any 'empty', merely symbolic thinking has the content that it does only in virtue of its inherent relation to a possible experience in which the relevant object is itself given 'in person'. Were it not for this relation to experience, such thought really would be *empty* – i.e., devoid of determinate content. When you think of an iguana, in virtue of what does this thought of yours have a determinate content? How does it relate to a specific sort of thing? Husserl's contention is that such a thought, being initially 'empty', is properly related to what it is supposed to be about – iguanas – only if it is internally related to your ability in principle to encounter the reptile in your experience and knowledgeably proclaim 'This is the thing itself' – an ability that naturally (though not necessarily) goes together with an ability to imagine the thing in question. 'An empty representation in general', writes Husserl, 'is only a potentiality for what is present as actuality in the corresponding intuition' (*APS*, 244). Now, it is not, of course, that if you lack such a recognitional ability with respect to iguanas, you cannot in any sense be said to be able to think of them. And much has been made of the supposed importance of this last fact, especially in the United States, in recent years. (Works by Hilary Putnam and Tyler

Burge, such as those cited in the bibliography, have been particularly influential in this regard.) On such an approach, people can be said genuinely to think of iguanas – iguanas themselves enter into the 'content' of his thoughts – even if they cannot recognize an iguana, and so cannot convert their empty intendings into fulfilling, or even clarifying, intuitiveness. Perhaps that is true; but it touches Husserl's account not at all. He can happily recognize such cases; but he would point out that they are cases of *inauthentic* thinking. Such people's thought having a reference specifically to iguanas depends, for example, upon the recognitional ability of others in their linguistic community. For if *nobody* knows an iguana when he or she sees one, all our thought and talk about them would be referentially indeterminate, if not downright bogus. As Husserl puts it at one point, 'Precisely because each self-giving consciousness gives its object as the thing itself, it can establish a right, correctness, for a different consciousness (for an intending of something unclearly, or quite confusedly, or for an intending . . . that in some other way is not self-giving)' (*FTL*, 142, translation modified). All the cases that are amenable to the Putnam–Burge style of psychological attribution involve some sort of unclarity and imperfection in the subject's thinking. But it is just this kind of thinking that *we cannot ultimately be content with*. It is precisely in opposition to contentment with such inauthenticity – which leads to the petrifaction of thought, and ultimately of the human spirit – that Husserl's return 'to the things themselves' was undertaken.

Husserl goes yet further in his privileging of 'experience'; for he asserts that *it is only in intuitions that objects are constituted*: 'Perception is the originally giving consciousness of individuals. The object is constituted . . . with respect to its sense and mode of being in the primal mode, in originality' (*APS*, 243; compare *Time*, 41). By contrast, he says of empty representations that 'in the proper sense no object-sense is constituted in them' (*APS*, 72). All empty intentions feed off prior intuitions in which the relevant objects have been 'primally instituted'. Therefore phenomenology must include *genetic analysis* in addition to the above 'static' investigation. The earlier aspects of intentional analysis are so closely related that they are generally all in play in any extended discussion of Husserl's. However, although necessarily implicated in phenomenological research, it was only gradually that Husserl came to see the necessity of genetic analysis. We shall consider it explicitly in the next chapter.

The pretension of transcendental phenomenology is to lay down the essential constituting conditions for all possible types of object. The task is to

> make understandable . . . how, within the immanency of conscious life and in thus and so determined modes of consciousness belonging to this incessant flux, anything like fixed and abiding object-unities can become intended and, in particular, how this marvellous work of *constituting* identical objects is done in the case of each category of objects.
>
> (85)

Achieving this will allow the phenomenologist to lay down, a priori, a universal ontology that will serve as the basis for all possible science (see, e.g., §59). We are now in a position to appreciate more adequately the grounds for such a pretension. It arises from the unique clarity and intelligibility that attaches to constitutional analysis. For although philosophy has commonly sought a priori knowledge, such knowledge itself can be 'naïve' – and will be when it is a matter merely of analysing concepts, at a distance from genuine intuition. Indeed, naïveté will only be left entirely behind when a priori knowledge is demonstrated as having 'originated from ultimate transcendental-phenomenological sources' (181). In constitutional analysis we exhibit objects as *ideal structures of consciousness itself*; and we make something fully intelligible to ourselves when, but only when, we exhibit it as a 'formation' of consciousness. This kind of understanding, Husserl says in the Fourth Meditation, is 'the highest imaginable form of rationality' (118). By contrast, 'No objective science, no matter how exact, explains or ever can explain anything in a serious sense. To deduce is not to explain . . . The only true way to explain is to make transcendentally understandable' (*Crisis*, 193 [189]). In the following chapter, we shall penetrate deeper into the infinite tasks of such transcendental self-explication and clarification.

NOTES

1 By the time of the *Cartesian Meditations* Husserl had already come to associate the 'apodictic reduction' with a restriction to what can be found within the 'concrete present' (e.g., *EP II*, 465–7), within what Husserl increasingly came to call the 'living present' – a subject we shall broach in the section on time later in this chapter.

2 A linguistic context is intensional if the substitution of one extensionally equivalent expression for another in that context is not guaranteed to preserve the truth-value (i.e., the truth or falsity) of the original sentence. Referring expressions are extensionally equivalent if they refer to the same thing; predicates if they are true of just the same things; and sentences if they have the same truth-value.

3 Indeed, as we shall see later, there is even an intentionality that is not directed to fully constituted *objects*. This, too, is a later refinement of the notion.

4 Such a sensation may have *unattended* aspects: you may not notice that a sensation has grown slightly more intense, for example, or that there is a slight throb to it. But these are not *hidden*, wholly unrepresented by what is really inherent in the stream of consciousness.

5 Husserl had not always recognized such a distinction: not in the early *Logical Investigations*, for example. The need to make such a distinction was borne in upon him as a result of his in-depth analyses of our consciousness of *time*, as we are soon to see.

6 Centrality in the visual field and attention commonly go together; but not necessarily. Were you to direct your attention, without shifting your gaze, and unnaturally, to what lies in the periphery of your visual field, this would be a 'cogitatio', and you would then have but implicit awareness of this book.

7 Recollection is not restricted to objects that have fallen out of our clear retentive grasp. We can recollect things which are still in the process of 'flowing away' in relative clearness (e.g., *Time*, 367). The essential difference is that recollection is a discrete act that attentively re-presents a past stretch of experience and the object constituted therein, as a unity, whereas retention involves a *continuous* hold on a phase of consciousness and object as it passively flows away.

8 This is also true of retentions, which hold in grasp the protentional aspects of earlier phases of our experience. (On this, see especially *Bernau*, 2–49.)

3

(MOST OF THE) FOURTH MEDITATION

§§30–39

Because the short Third Meditation paves the way to important metaphysical conclusions that are explicitly drawn only in the last two sections of the Fourth, I propose to treat them together in a single chapter. Because, furthermore, those conclusions are intimately related to the topic of the fifth and final meditation, whereas the bulk of the intervening Fourth Meditation continues to display the variegated character of phenomenological research that we are in the course of exploring, I shall deal with the Third and Fourth Meditations in substantially the reverse order. Another reason for this procedure is that the metaphysical position towards which the Third Meditation will attempt to move us is out-and-out idealism – a position with which very few today will have any sympathy at all. The order of presentation that I am about to adopt has the virtue of underlining just how much of Husserlian phenomenology can be discussed, and perhaps accepted, without even broaching the idealism to which, in Husserl's own firm opinion, it inexorably led. The

Fourth Meditation, aside from its final two sections, introduces us to three new facets of transcendental phenomenology: genesis, passive synthesis, and the eidetic reduction. Before these themes are introduced, however, Husserl turns his attention more squarely to the transcendental ego itself, which is the accomplisher of the intentional performances we have so far been investigating.

EGO, PERSON, MONAD

In our radical philosophical turn from naïve dedication to the world towards an exploration of pure consciousness, the first thing that has attracted our attention has been intentionality: the way in which, through synthesis, the flux of experience gets polarized into unities of sense, in virtue of which we are conscious of identifiable and reidentifiable objects. So what has principally attracted our attention on the subjective side of things has been the flowing, changing character of the experiences that we live through, in contrast to the relative stability of objects. Husserl now points out that a second kind of polarization occurs in the unfolding of transcendental life – one that effects an abiding stability on the subjective side of things. For even on the subjective side, reflection discovers not just the 'Heraclitean flux' of lived experiences, but also an *ego* – an 'I', a 'self' – who is the *subject*, and the identical, abiding subject, of these experiences. In the *Cartesian Meditations* Husserl simply asserts that we have apodictic certainty of the full Cartesian *ego cogito*: I am guaranteed that it is *I* who am 'thinking'. He thus simply ignores the suggestion, famously made by Lichtenberg, that Descartes had gone too far in claiming absolute certainty for the 'I think': all he was really entitled to, so the suggestion goes, is the claim that 'thought' (i.e., conscious experience) is occurring. Although Husserl does, as we have seen, promise a 'critique' of transcendental experience, such a critique would concern the range of what is apodictic *beyond* the 'I think', whose own apodicticity is never questioned. In fact, the Lichtenberg's objection is not worth taking seriously. The only beings who can make anything of the present meditations are those who are capable of reflecting on their own conscious lives; such reflection itself is as apodictic as any other conscious act; and reflection without a subject makes no sense whatever. Rather more surprising, however, is Husserl's ignoring the suggestion that the self may be nothing but – if not a mere Humean 'bundle' of experiences externally related to one another (for this would contradict the essentially flowing nature of experience that we investigated in the previous chapter), then – the flowing experiences themselves. For he certainly does think that the self is more than this. This is all the more surprising because Husserl himself was formerly of that opinion. In the *Logical Investigations* we find a discussion that echoes the famous passage in the *Treatise* where Hume claims that

> for my part, when I enter most intimately into what I call *myself*, I always stumble on some particular perception or other, of heat or cold, light or shade, love or hatred, pain or pleasure. I never can catch *myself* at any time without a perception, and never can observe any thing but the perception.
>
> (Hume 1739/40, 252)

Of a 'self' as a subject supposedly different from the experiences we actually live through, Husserl himself stated, 'I must frankly confess ... that I am quite unable to find this ego, this primitive, necessary centre of relations' (*LI* V, §8). However, in a notorious footnote that he added to the second edition of that work, which came out at about the same time as *Ideas I*, he claims that 'I have since managed to find it'! It is the existence of such a 'substantial' self that Husserl assumes in our present work.

What Husserl particularly focused on in his middle period as evidence for such an ego was *attention*. We can shift our attention from one part of a sensory scene to another (and without moving any sense organs); we can attend to one aspect of a given object and then to another; we can attend to the thoughts or imaginations passing through our minds rather than to what is sensibly appearing to us, and so forth. Husserl commonly speaks of such phenomena in terms of a 'ray' of attention emanating from the ego, illuminating one rather than another set of objects, all of which are given to us – though not, and not possibly, with the same degree of prominence. The mental processes that do not engage this ray of attention are, as we have seen, termed 'inactual' or 'potential'. They make up the ever-present background to our 'cogitationes', these being the mental processes in which the ray is directed – in which, therefore, the ego is *involved*, or in which it 'principally lives' (e.g., *Ideas I*, §§37, 45). In other words, the ego is unearthed in relation to mental *activity*. Astonishingly, it was not until the beginning of the nineteenth century that philosophy came fully to recognize the irreducibility of activity – not only 'mental', but also kinaesthetic for that matter – to any set of impressions, or perceptions, or sensations. The period occupied by Hume and Lichtenberg is notable for the failure to see this. When figures such as Fichte and Maine de Biran began to acknowledge this fact, we have the dawning of a new era in philosophy – one still insufficiently widely appreciated. The scope of this appeal to activity should not be underestimated, since *every* 'cogitatio' involves some form of activity, according to Husserl.

Even if this is accepted, however, we have still not gone as far as Husserl wishes us to go. For the self that is in question in the *Cartesian Meditations* is not the human subject, nor even the subject of psychology – what Husserl calls the 'soul' – but the *transcendental ego*. Even Sartre, who acknowledged the constituting function of consciousness, thought that this was going too far, and asked, 'Is not this psychic and psycho-physical me enough?' (Sartre 1992, 18–19 [36]). Heidegger, too, parted company from Husserl over this point: something that is evinced most clearly, perhaps, in his initially collaborative exchanges with Husserl in connection with the latter's *Encyclopaedia Britannica* article. To stop with Sartre and Heidegger, however, would, in Husserl's eyes, be entirely to miss the transcendental perspective which alone is truly philosophical. For the psycho-physical ego is itself a worldly, and hence constituted, object. Husserl agrees with Heidegger that a 'person' necessarily has a world (at least as phenomenon) in which it is caught up, and by which it is motivated. But that we appear to ourselves as embodied, mundane individuals is an intentional accomplishment that needs accounting for by constitutional analysis. Here, as everywhere, we must enquire behind the phenomenon and unearth those subjective processes which alone allow such a phenomenon to arise. Behind every *constituted* we must find a *constituting* (and hence transcendental) ego. We should not, on the other hand, construe Husserl's transcendental ego along the lines of the intellectualism so roundly criticized by Merleau-Ponty. The transcendental ego is not the calm, wholly rational orderer of its own life; and its mundanization is in no sense whatever analogous to a Neo-Platonic 'fall', but the necessary form of consciousness's self-realization, as we shall see later. In fact, when we penetrate to the very depths of constitutional analysis, we shall find processes of what Husserl calls 'passive synthesis', and these are not 'ego-acts', not effected by a specifically active ego. Such processes are involved in the constitution of the transcendental ego itself. Nevertheless, ego-acts are necessarily involved in the constitution of a world: it hardly makes sense that a world should exist for a subject who never noticed anything! And so we cannot rest content with any merely worldly self. Even if there is 'pre-egoic' constitution, it is 'pre-' the transcendental ego; and whatever is 'pre-' the transcendental ego is itself transcendental – i.e., is 'prior' to the world as phenomenon.

The purpose of the present meditation, however, is not to prove that there is a transcendental ego, but to show that it is not merely some empty 'pole' of identity on the subjective side of things, 'any more than any object is such' (100). Although Husserl initially associated the transcendental ego with activity, he now speaks of it as 'active *and affected*' (100, emphasis mine). Indeed, he now introduces his explicit treatment of the ego with a consideration of something that may at first sight seem far removed from activity: namely, habitualities. The ego is not only 'a pole of his acts' but also 'a substrate of habitualities' (103), such habitualities being characterizing 'properties' of the ego. They are, more specifically, mental dispositions and capacities. In fact, however, although habitualities are clearly not themselves activities of any sort, they all, as we shall soon see, originate in activity on the part of the ego.

Husserl introduces the topic of habitualities by referring to the effect that *decisions* have on us. When I make a decision I am changed in a certain way. This is not a merely formal or logical

change, amounting to no more than the fact that I am now someone who has so decided, whereas before I was not. For this will be
true even if I have revoked my decision. Husserl is interested in the
change that is wrought in me when I make a decision and *stand by
it*. This orients or disposes me in a certain fashion; and should I
revoke the decision, I should be yet differently disposed. Although
such habitualities are clearly subjective – they are properties of *me*,
even to the highest degree of transcendental purity – they cannot
be viewed as 'a continuous filling of subjective time with experiences' (101). I possess them when my mind is wholly directed
elsewhere, and in the deepest sleep. They, too, have an abiding
identity through the flux of subjective experience – one which
points, therefore, to the abiding identity of that of which they are
determining properties: the self. They are properties of the transcendental ego because they have intentional implications. For one
thing, they colour our conscious experiences – something we shall
be exploring shortly. But they also, like all potentialities, have possible realizations. In the case of decision, for example, we have
possible 'returns' to the content of the decision in which I recognize
and reaffirm a position *as mine*. Given the focus of the *Cartesian
Meditations* so far, Husserl not unsurprisingly begins with cognitive decisions – that is to say, judgements. If, for example, you have
decided that some UFOs have really been extra-terrestrial space-
craft, you are now someone who is *of* that opinion, as we say; and
this fact carries weight in your cognitive life. Although not
unshakeable, it will influence what other propositions you are willing to accept, and what inferences you deem acceptable. But such
decisions are, of course, not limited to the merely cognitive domain.
For your habitualities encompass your intentions and your values.
Indeed, habitualities in general go to determine what we call a
'personality' or a 'character' – the 'abiding style' with which one
lives one's life (101). They are essential to what Husserl terms
a 'person'.[1] Another term which Husserl introduces to denote
the self is 'monad'. By this he means the transcendental ego taken
'in full concreteness' (102): taken, that is, together not only with
its habitualities (the 'person'), but with its entire, actual intentional life and the objects therein constituted. (The Leibnizian

connotations of this last term are not to be underestimated, as we shall see in the next chapter.)

What Husserl now principally focuses on is the way in which our habitualities are correlated with the character of the world – the world 'for us', of course. When we institute the transcendental reduction, we do not, as some critics have suggested, reduce ourselves to some worldless, disembodied subjectivity. Nothing, *qua* phenomenon, changes when we effect the reduction. In particular, the world remains on hand for us, albeit within 'brackets'. Indeed, it is one of the principal tasks of phenomenology to interrogate the phenomenon *world* as such, to unearth the formerly anonymous intentional states and activities that allow a world to appear to us, and thereby to understand more fully the complex, structured sense that the world, *qua* phenomenon, has. When we so reflect, we immediately recognize that the world is not a mere totality of objects, or entities: it has, and necessarily, a certain *structure* – one which is specifiable, in part, in terms of *familiarity*. The following is an extract from one of Husserl's most extended discussions of such a world-structure:

> Along with the ones now actually perceived, other actual objects are there for me as determinate, as more or less well known, without themselves being perceived or, indeed, present in any other mode of intuition. I can let my attention wander away from the writing table which has just now been seen and noticed, out through the unseen parts of the room which are behind my back, to the veranda, into the garden, to the children in the arbour, etc., to all the objects I directly 'know of' as being there and here in the surroundings of which I am immediately co-conscious . . . But not even with the domain of this intuitionally clear or obscure, distinct or indistinct *co-present* – which makes up a constant halo around the field of actual perception – is the world exhausted which is 'on hand' for me in the manner peculiar to consciousness at every waking moment. On the contrary, in the fixed order of its being, it reaches into the unlimited . . . My indeterminate surroundings are infinite, the misty and never fully determinable horizon is necessarily there.

> (*Ideas I*, 49)

Such a structured world necessarily arises for me thanks to two facts. The first is that the perceptual world is *spatial* in character, every object in it having an internal and external horizon. The latter, in particular, means that every scene necessarily gives on to another – even if it be but an empty waste – that can in principle be attained and explored. Although the walls of my study in a sense currently restrict my awareness of the surrounding world, they are but temporary screens between me and the whole surrounding world, which is constantly *there* for me – indeed, in a sense, *perceptually* there, since implicated in the very character of my awareness as perceptual. That I take there to be such a world is not a result of perception being augmented by a fringe of images. Such images may well occur to me, but they may not. And even when they do occur, what they serve to do is merely to fill out in a more or less determinate way the details of the wider layout of the world which, as world, as the implicated horizon of my present and of any possible perception, is *already there*. The second fact is that every cognitive achievement of mine becomes an 'acquisition', on the basis of which the parts of the world that are not actually being perceived by me have an abiding character. As Husserl says in the present meditation,

> My activity of positing and explicating being establishes a habituality of my Ego, by virtue of which the object, as having its manifold determinations, is mine abidingly. Such abiding acquisitions make up my surrounding world, so far as I am acquainted with it at the time, with its horizons of objects with which I am unacquainted – that is, objects yet to be acquired but already anticipated with this formal object-structure.
>
> (102)

As I explore the world, I come across objects and zones that are, in the everyday sense, unfamiliar. But the *radically* unfamiliar, that which would be discontinuous with my former experience, is inconceivable. However weird, any object must at least conform to the basic structures of perceivability that have governed my actual experience – for example, being perceptually 'adumbrated', with an inner and an outer horizon, the latter leading back, in principle, to my zone of familiarity. Unfamiliarity is 'a mode of familiarity' (*EJ*, 34 [37]), to which it points back, and from which it derives its sense. Husserl commonly sums all this up by saying that the world has a certain *style*.

Husserl can refer to the world as 'the firmest and most universal of all our habitualities' (*EJ*, 424 [350]). Because the sense of a world is horizonally implicit in every perception, and because what kind of world exists for us is a function of our habitualities and our ongoing experience, Husserl can say that 'the problem of explicating this monadic ego phenomenologically (the problem of his constitution for himself) must include *all constitutional problems without exception*. Consequently the phenomenology of this self-constitution coincides with phenomenology as a whole' (102–3). Because of the noetic–noematic parallelism, the phenomenon of the world (for me) can be read off from a complete analysis of my subjectivity. But inversely, and because of the same parallelism, I can be read off from my world. As Husserl says in a late text: 'To interpret [*auslegen*] the world ontologically is to interpret humanity therein, in its complete and concrete structure' (*Int III*, 617).

STATIC AND GENETIC PHENOMENOLOGY

Husserl has described habitualities as 'acquisitions'. They presuppose, therefore, an 'establishment' or 'institution' (*Stiftung*) in the past. We encountered this notion briefly in the Introduction, but it is now time to give it its full recognition as a central concept of phenomenology. In virtue of such a reference back in time, habitualities are but a special case of a feature of transcendental life the importance of which Husserl came increasingly to appreciate, and which increasingly influenced his phenomenological method. That feature is (transcendental) *genesis*, and the method it gives rise to is termed 'genetic phenomenology'. The kind of enquiry that has so far been primarily indicated in these pages, and with which it is natural for the 'beginning philosopher' to start, is termed 'static phenomenology'. When we turn from our involvement with the world to a pure reflection upon our own experiencing self, we do not find an inchoate mass of experiences, but a coherent intentional experiencing of a world. Such a putative world, and the various kinds of objects within it, are *already* constituted for us. Hence we can take the latter as 'transcendental clues' for intentional analysis, which involves explicating the senses of the experiences in which such objects are intended by us. As we have seen, the interest and the challenge here reside in bringing to light the intentional performances that are *implicit* in such experiences, and implicitly determining for what is prescribed by their 'object-senses'. Static phenomenology is *noetic–noematic horizonal analysis*. Such a procedure does not, however, exhaust our phenomenological interest. For in addition to asking what various kinds of experiences contain, or amount to, there is a question about the *preconditions* for having such experiences and their objects. Here we ask, not what lies *in* such experiences, but what historically lies *before* them. At the moment, for example, sitting in my study, I look around and see many books. 'Implicit' in my perceptual experience are empty 'anticipatory and attendant meanings' that point to the unperceived pages and print that I take them to contain. It is such implicit intentionality that makes it the case that these things appear to me *as books*. This would not, however, have been true of me if I had looked around this very same room at the age of two. At that age I had no idea what books were. At that age I should have seen things that were but *unfamiliar things* of various shapes and colours. My present experience is what it is because of my past experience. The horizons that objects have are, as here, indicated by the habitualities, the cognitive 'possessions', that the experiencing subject has acquired. In *all* intentional acts there lie implicit, empty intendings. But why, in any given case, just *these* implicit intendings and not others? This, too, calls for phenomenological investigation: not 'horizonal', but, as it were, 'archaeological'. The genesis that is the subject of such an investigation will, as we have just seen, be a genesis *of the self* – of the kind of self that is capable of the intentional accomplishments in question.

It is hardly surprising that phenomenology should have such a genetic dimension, since, as Husserl has indicated at several points in these Meditations, the most fundamental form of conscious life is temporality, and the fundamental level of constitution is the constitution of time itself. We are always, and necessarily, in the process of becoming, and all objects are fashioned in the flow of consciousness. As Husserl claims in the heading to §37, time is 'the universal form of all egological genesis'. Now, what is of particular note in connection with genetic phenomenology is the role of retention. We have already seen the way in which retention is essential to the existence of the living present. What is of equal importance, and crucial in the present context, is the way in which retention harbours implications for possible future experience. One such implication is, of course, possible recollection. But there is another:

> Every manner of original givenness has a *double genetic after-effect*. Firstly, its after-effect in the form of possible recollective reproductions, *via* retentions that attach themselves to it quite immediately by a process of original genesis; and secondly, its 'apperceptional' after-effect, which is such that anything (no matter how it is already constituted) that is present in a similar new situation will be apperceived in a similar manner.
>
> (*FTL*, 279)

Husserl gives an example of the sort of thing he has in mind in the Fifth Meditation: 'The child who already sees physical things understands for the first time, say, the purpose of scissors; and from now on he sees scissors, as such, at a glance – but naturally not in an explicit reproducing, comparing, drawing an inference' (141). This 'understanding for the first time' is a case of *Urstiftung*: the primal instituting of a sense which henceforth is available for informing our intentional lives. As Husserl says elsewhere, 'With each new kind of object (genetically speaking) constituted for the first time, a new type of object is permanently prescribed, in terms of which other objects similar to it will be apprehended in advance' (*EJ*, 35 [38], translation modified). All apperceptions point back to such an initial establishment of a sense.[2] For otherwise it would be arbitrary which empty intentions were engaged in perception on any particular occasion. We should not then be able to attain transcendental clarity in this area.

Note that it is only an 'original givenness' in a first-hand experience of an object that can play this primally instituting role. This is because all other modes of intentional directedness are mere presentifications, which, as we saw towards the end of the previous chapter, have the character of *intentional modifications* of 'original' consciousness, intrinsically pointing back to the latter. When we recollect something, for example, we recall how on some previous occasion the thing perceptually appeared to us; and when we imagine something, we imagine how something would appear to us in some possible perceptual experience of it – representing it 'as if' we were perceiving it. That is why the objects of such intuitive presentifications are always represented as spatially oriented to us in some way, just as are perceptual objects. And if intuitive presentifications are thus secondary to 'first-hand' experience, empty ones are even more evidently so, since they require, as we saw in the previous chapter, a reference to intuition to clarify their sense. Since such a 'pointing back' by presentifications to original presentations is part of the very sense of the former, it can be recognized by 'static' analysis. What Husserl came increasingly to see was that such pointing implicates a genetic, temporal dimension:

> The *original form* of consciousness, *experience* in the broadest sense . . . , has not only a static but *also a genetic priority* to its intentional variants. *Genetically too the original manner of givenness is* – in a certain fashion – *the primitive one* . . . No mode of non-original consciousness of objects belonging to a fundamental sort is essentially possible, unless there has previously occurred, in the synthetic unity of immanent temporality, the corresponding mode of original consciousness of the Same – as, *genetically*, the *'primally instaturive'* mode of consciousness, back to which every mode of non-original consciousness points genetically (as well as statically).
>
> (*FTL*, 278)

It is not, of course, that we cannot experience an object non-originally unless we have previously experienced it originally. As Husserl himself points out, 'In a completely empty anticipation, for example, something can be indicated for us that we have never seen' (*FTL*, 278). But, as mentioned earlier, unfamiliarity is but a modality of familiarity. And so the fundamental *type* of any object that we may dream up will of necessity be familiar to us. As Husserl says in the *Cartesian Meditations*, 'What we call unknown has, nevertheless, a known structural form: the form *object* and, more particularly, the form *spatial thing, cultural object, tool,* and so forth' (113).

It is important to note that Husserl's genetic enquiries are intended to be genuinely transcendental in nature. We are not at this point to fall back into some merely empirical psychological enquiry. Although the claims Husserl makes in this connection have the status of 'laws of causality in a maximally broad sense – laws for an If and Then' (109), they have a higher 'dignity' than any nexus of natural causality discovered by empirical investigation – causality 'in the narrow sense', as Husserl calls it. According to Husserl, not only the psychologist, but even the physicist, has no insight into why the basic laws of nature that he or she accepts are as they are. This is why such 'laws' can be subsequently revised – even, like Newton's, after generations of acceptance. Nor do we have any understanding of the causality that we see at work in our everyday experience of the natural world. We see that the world has a certain causal 'style' to it. Colliding bodies, for example, of different shapes and sizes and masses have characteristic modes of behaviour, which we rely on. Indeed, that the world has some such reliable style is transcendentally necessary for there to be a world for us at all, since recognition of a world corresponds in large part to the habitualities we have acquired through our experience, and such habitualities are precisely forms of reliance. A *wholly* undependable *world* makes no phenomenological sense. But, again, we have no insight into why the world has this causal style rather than some other. At least we have, and can have, no such insight by focusing on the natural world itself. By contrast, what Husserl is concerned with in his genetic enquiries are *essential compossibilities* that are determinable a priori. Certain forms of experience and comportment necessarily exclude others, and necessity can attach to the *order* in which they make an appearance in a conscious life.

Husserl believes that we can attain transcendental clarity even with respect to such genetic issues.

One might, however, question whether we really are capable of having such insight into the rules of transcendental genesis. One might wonder, indeed, if it is even empirically impossible that, say, a young child should do theoretical physics, or that I should take these things around me in my study to be books without ever having seen or heard of a book before. For these may seem to be among the kinds of thing that Husserl thinks he can rule out *in principle*. In fact, they are not, precisely as they stand, the sort of thing that Husserl is interested in. 'Young child', for example, is a term applying to a human being, a constituted object within the world, whereas Husserl is concerned with genetic necessities within the sphere of transcendental consciousness. Similarly, reference to my familiarity with books should not be taken as a comment on my *psychological* life; for this, too, is bound up with the positing of a real world. Nevertheless, such issues do point to questions that can be raised at the transcendental level. For it is not, of course, that there are, in any individual case, *two* streams of consciousness – a worldly, psychological one, and a pure, transcendental one. It is the *same* flowing life, which from the absolute perspective is understood as transcendental consciousness, that 'mundanizes' itself as a human being in the world (e.g., *Epilogue*, 145–7; *PP*, 342–4). We constitute *ourselves* as human by virtue of our transcendentally constitutive, intentional performances. In other words, there is something about our intentional lives that accounts for our experiencing ourselves as embodied subjects in a world. So there is a story to tell about the horizons of sense that are involved in having such an object of awareness as *my body*. And there is a further constitutional story to be told of how we in some way 'locate' our experiences in such a body as 'psychological' processes. Still, given that we do, it follows that to each empirically identified psychological state or process there will correspond states and processes in the stream of pure transcendental life. If there are genetic necessities in the latter, there are corresponding ones in the former.[3] So it looks as if Husserl is committed at least to saying that if I, as a transcendental ego, now constitute my surrounding world as one containing books, then I must, at some earlier stage of my transcendental life, have lived through an active 'institution' in which the sense 'book' was originally constituted for me. Or, if a book is not a sufficiently 'basic' type of object, such a claim must be upheld in respect of the type 'physical thing', or 'spatial thing'.

There are two principal grounds on which one might have doubts about such a position. The first is that certain apperceptive possessions may be *innate*. For although no one is going seriously to suggest that we might come into the world equipped with an innate idea of what a book is, the suggestion that we have at least some innate 'acquisitions' surely cannot be ruled out of court without discussion. Such a suggestion gains plausibility the more basic we make the intentional performances in question. And as we have seen, it is precisely the more basic types of apperceptions that Husserl believes have to be primally instituted. He certainly thinks that the sense *material body* is one that has to be originally constituted at some time in our lives:

> The fact that we objectivate physical things, and even see them at a glance ... refers us back, in the course of our intentional genetic analysis, to the fact that the *type*, experience of a physical thing, had its rise in an earlier, primally institutive genesis, and that the category, physical thing, was thereby instituted for us with its initial sense.
>
> (*FTL*, 278)

Or, as he puts it more simply in the *Cartesian Meditations*, a child has to 'learn to see physical things' (112; see also 110). Elsewhere, after mentioning the constitution of inner time, he goes on to speak of the '*genetically higher* levels, the levels of what is transcendent, ... the constitution of nature' (*Int II*, 38, my emphasis; compare *ibid.*, 115). And in a passage that relates the complexity of an intentional performance to a genetic complexity, he writes as follows:

> In our experience, in every one of our perceptions of physical things, there lies a horizon of possible experience, and thereby they refer to a genesis of this experience which must have its building up of levels

> where lower apperceptions develop, lower ways of experiencing with restricted horizons. Then new unities of experience, experience of a higher level as a result of higher horizons etc., due to new experiential connections.
>
> (*Int II*, 115)

In Chapter 1 we saw Husserl claiming that he was an empiricist in the true sense of the word. In that context he was speaking in connection with his understanding of self-evidence. We now see that he is also some sort of empiricist in connection with genetic issues. Indeed, he can self-consciously echo Hume's talk of 'impressions' and 'ideas' in expressing his own position on these matters: 'Every qualitatively unmodified presentification points back to memories that must be prior, every "idea" to an earlier impression, at least as concerns the constructive elements and the form of connection' (*Int I*, 349).

On the other hand, Husserl was quite insistent that phenomenological enquiry forces us to recognize innate factors in consciousness. 'Every transcendental I', he can write, 'has its innate endowment' (A VII 17, 46a). Sometimes what is claimed to be innate is a certain *structure*. In the manuscript from which I have just quoted, for example, what is in question is the basic structure of temporality. He can, however, speak of innateness in connection with more specific issues. He states, for example, that a newly emerging monad will possess individual characteristics that have been inherited from its parents (e.g., C 17 V ⟨1⟩, 84). Moreover, as we shall see later in the present chapter, Husserl credits us with various innate *instincts*, and he refers to them as 'an intentionality that belongs to the original, essential structure of psychic being' (C 8 II, 16a). Indeed, he claims that a 'primal child' (*Urkind*) is 'instinctively oriented toward the world' (E III 3, 5a). Such instinctive intentionality, as we shall see shortly, has a role to play in the fundamental constitution of the world. Husserl speaks, for example, of a 'pre-I' emerging into the world with an 'innate habituality' and with an *inherited empty horizon* that will become the horizon of the actual world upon the acquisition of experience (*Int III*, 605). Where Husserl draws the line in relation to innateness, however, is with innate 'empty representations' (*leere Vorstellungen*). He writes that 'it is the basic failing of bad nativism that ... it presupposes inborn "representations" ... One is not yet a phenomenologist if one brings in "empty representations" ' (*Int II*, 335). At one point, Husserl asks, 'The first act: What is its "basis"?' And he answers as follows:

> The I already has the 'world horizon' – the primally incipient horizon, in which the human world horizon is implicitly born ... The primal horizon, the *inheritance*, is in its primal sense an empty horizon. The first *hylé*, the first affecting thing, becomes the first thing grasped ... The I before this awakening, the pre-I that is not yet living, has yet already a world in its own way ... : its inactual world 'in' which it is unliving, and for which it is not awake. It is affected, it acquires *hylé* as the first filling – the first share in the world of the awake.
>
> (*Int III*, 604)

Husserl here speaks of an innate orientation towards the world in terms of an 'empty horizon'. And he elsewhere contrasts such an empty horizon, which may be possessed innately, with an empty 'representational horizon' (*Vortstellungshorizont*), which cannot (*Int II*, 334). When you or I see a physical body, we immediately take it to be such – i.e., to be a coherent, three-dimensional body occluding part of itself from our view – despite the fact that what is 'exhibited' to sight is but one side of the body. We immediately *presume* that there is more to the object than is exhibited to the 'naked eye'. This presumption, which has a more or less determinate content, and which goes towards making up the internal horizon of such an object, is precisely the sort of 'empty representation' that Husserl denies to be possibly innate. In contrast to the passage quoted earlier, where Husserl alludes to Hume and says that unmodified presentifications point back to prior memories, he can speak of ' "inheritance" without memory, and yet a kind of "fulfilment" by awakenings, etc.' (K III 11, 4a). The reason why such an 'inheritance', or innate endowment, can, unlike empty representations, exist without prior memories is indicated by the word 'awakenings'. For what Husserl has in mind here as innate possessions are but *instincts*, albeit structured ones. The 'human world horizon' that develops in the newly awake monad is the 'fulfilling explication of the universal instinct-horizon' (E III 9, 3a). So, although we may well be predisposed to pass to ever higher apperceptive levels on the occasion of suitable experiences, these experiences themselves are genetically necessary antecedents for any actually possessed apperceptive endowment. Determinate content enters only with such experience. Otherwise, we should be landed with innate 'empty representations'. Husserl insists, however, that such determinate content, requiring a primal institution in actual experience, includes even such 'formal' elements as materiality. On one occasion, Husserl counters the suggestion that the ability to perceive physical objects as such might be innate by saying that 'the behaviour of those who have been blind from birth and have been operated on of course counts against it, for they must learn to see with effort' (*Int II*, 333). Not only is this dubious in itself (as I have argued elsewhere: Smith 2000); more significantly, it is far from having the sort of a priori status one would have expected. Indeed, to this reader's mind at least, many of Husserl's genetic pronouncements seem somewhat doctrinaire.

A second ground for querying Husserl's conviction that genetic claims can be established a priori, and one that may come even more readily to the modern mind, is the thought that a neurosurgeon could in principle rearrange a person's cortex so as to induce almost any experience and capacity, irrespective of that subject's past experiential history. To take an extreme case, one that was implausible in the context of the previous objection from innateness: could not such a surgeon tamper with the brain of someone who has never come across a book in his or her life in such a way that this person is now capable of perceiving something as a book, and does so now? Husserl's response to any such suggestion is unambiguous: he denies that intentional acts, even at the 'natural' level of psychology, can be causally determined or explained by physical processes. The occurrence of sensations, yes; but not intentional acts. Husserl even denied that any causal relations at all, in the strict sense, obtain between worldly items and intentional acts. He did not deny, of course, that we can affect what someone is thinking about or perceiving. Shouting 'Fire!' in a crowded cinema is known to have a dramatic effect. From the outside this may look like sheer causal determination. Indeed, if we use the term 'causality' in a wide enough sense, it *is* causality; but that is only because one species of such generic causality, of the mere 'if . . . then', is what Husserl calls 'motivation', which is found only within consciousness, and which essentially involves intentional relations. Once you have caused a sensation to occur in a person's stream of consciousness, this may well lead to a certain intentional act that otherwise would not have happened. But the relation of sensation to intentional act is motivational. This is of relevance in the present connection, because one of Husserl's basic reasons for adopting this position concerns the very issue of genesis we are now dealing with. For in an argument that is almost the inverse of Davidson's well-known argument for 'anomalous monism', Husserl claims that the mental realm, at least above the level of mere sensation, is governed by norms of intelligibility and sensefulness that have lawful genetic implications. Such norms are a priori, and govern mental life with absolute necessity. If our whole mental life were but a causal product of our brain activity, if the stream of consciousness could be arbitrarily deflected and rearranged by fiddling with the brain, there would be no such necessities. So such interference is not possible, even in principle. (See *Ideas II*, §63; compare Davidson, 1980).

ACTIVE AND PASSIVE SYNTHESIS

We have, so far, touched upon only one aspect of genetic phenomenology. We have seen that any apperception of an object that is not itself original points back to some prior apperception of the same basic type of object. But there is still a question of how those originating apperceptions themselves arise in consciousness. For there would be a regress *in infinitum* if all apperceptions pointed back to prior apperceptions. It is at this point that a distinction Husserl makes between *passive* and *active synthesis,* and therefore between passive and active genesis, plays an important role. Since Husserl commonly associates the pure ego with activity, it should come as no surprise that he explicates the distinction between passivity and activity in terms of whether the ego is 'involved' or not. Or rather, since, in a complex, typically human consciousness, there are many intentional levels featuring different degrees of activity and passivity, the distinction is explicated in terms of the *degree* to which the ego is involved. At the highest level of active synthesis we have *inventions*, where someone, typically after painstaking effort and reflection, contrives something new. In any such operation the subject will be dealing with objects that are *pre-given* in relation to the novel invention. Invention isn't creation *ex nihilo*. The novelty consists in a new structuring – i.e., synthesizing – of elements already known. The inventor of the wheel, for example, would and must have been familiar with a spatial world, loads that need to be moved, circular objects, and so forth. And this is true of active synthesis universally: it is an operation that presupposes objects that are *passively pre-given* in relation to the active achievement. It is not just technological inventions that have their place in this highest sphere of active genesis. All 'intellectual' and 'spiritual' accomplishments have their place here. For example, in a very late paper known as 'The Origin of Geometry', Husserl gives a fascinating account of the genetic preconditions of our present-day familiarity with geometry (*Crisis*, Appendix 3 [6]). At a lower level of activity we find the fashioning of non-individual objects and categorial formations. We shall be looking into this matter more fully in the next section; but the kind of thing Husserl has in mind is the fact that we not only perceive objects, but can actively articulate them, and relate them to one another. For instance, I can not only see, say, a green vase, but consider the vase as 'subject' and its greenness as 'property', and thereby fashion a new categorially articulated object: the state of affairs that consists in the vase's being green. Or, as a result of counting, I can now perceive some objects as a group of six. Indeed, any perceiving *that* some state of affairs obtains involves an active synthesis that goes beyond simple sense-perception. In order to see that the cat is on the mat, for example, it is not sufficient that I see the cat on the mat. The object that corresponds to the judgement here is the cat's *being* on the mat, one that requires that we articulate the perceived scene into different objects and relate them one to another.

In relation to both of the above levels of active synthesis, it is straightforward perception of individual objects that passively pre-gives the objects to be synthesized:

> Anything built by activity necessarily presupposes, as the lowest level, a pre-giving passivity; and when we trace anything built actively, we run into constitution by passive genesis. The ready-made object that confronts us in life as an existent mere physical thing . . . is given, with the originality of the *it itself*, in the synthesis of passive experience.
>
> (112)

Since this level precedes even the formulating of logically articulated judgements – 'every judging presupposes that an object is on hand, that it is already given to us, and is that about which the statement is made' (*EJ*, 4–5 [14]) – Husserl calls it the level of *pre-predicative experience*: 'Those judgments which are primary in themselves are . . . judgments of experience. They are preceded by the self-evident givenness of individual objects of experience, i.e., their pre-predicative givenness' (*EJ*, 21 [27]). Even the simple perception of a physical object, however, is not an entirely passive affair, since perception – at least perception 'in the pregnant sense' – means *attentive* perception; and attending to something is an activity of the ego. So even here there must be pre-given objects. These objects form the *background* to any object that is attentively perceived. As our gaze wanders across a scene, and we notice now this object, now that one, the very experience of noticing itself intimates that what is now noticed was formerly *there to be noticed*: it was passively pre-given to the active exercise of attention. Husserl speaks in this connection of an object *affecting* the ego:

> 'To affect' means to stand out from the environment that is always co-present, to attract interest to itself, possibly interest in cognition. The environment is co-present as a *domain of what is pre-given*, of a *passive* pre-givenness, i.e., of what is always already there without any attention of a grasping regard, without any awakening of interest.
>
> (*EJ*, 24 [30], translation modified)

Objects' power to affect us answers to a *perceptual interest* that governs our waking lives. This is a basic cognitive drive, one aspect of which is the fact that simple noticing tends naturally to develop into more considered contemplation of the object – one that possibly, indeed often, leads to fully articulated judgement concerning it and its relations to other objects. When we 'succumb' to the attractive power of an object, the first response is a 'turning toward' the object attentively, and this is the most primitive form of ego-activity. Although Husserl can refer to it as 'receptivity', he also states that 'receptivity must be regarded as the lowest level of activity' (*EJ*, 83 [79]). Nevertheless, although such ego-activity is present in any properly attentive perceiving of an object, the syntheses that unfold in the course of perceptual exploration are wholly passive. When, for example, I explore the inner horizon of an object by bringing into view its formerly hidden rear side, although I am active both in attending to what I see and in moving myself so as to attain differing perspectives on the object, the synthetic 'coverings' of previously empty intentions by the new sensory intuitions that then occur do so without any contribution from me. In *Ideas II* Husserl called this sort of synthesis 'aesthetic' or 'sensuous', and wrote, 'The *categorial* synthesis is, as a synthesis, a spontaneous act, whereas the *sensuous synthesis, on the contrary, is not*. The synthetic connection is itself, in the first case, a spontaneous doing and performing, a veritable activity; in the second case it is not' (*Ideas II*, 19). However, although such an aesthetic synthesis is passive, it is not blind – not a matter of a mere succession of data. It is, rather, guided beforehand by that 'apperceptive surplus' which is ingredient in any perception, and which contains the empty intentions that constitute the object's horizon. This apperceptive capacity is *presupposed* by any such perception, and so there is yet more of a genetic story to tell. The typical familiarity of the world is not only, as static phenomenology teaches, a complex intentional achievement, but also, as we have now come to expect, a complex genetic result. This extends down even to basic type 'physical object':

> In *early infancy*, then, the pre-giving field of perception does not as yet contain anything that, in a mere look, might be explicated as a physical

thing . . . We can, the meditating ego can, penetrate into the intentional constituents of experiential phenomena themselves . . . and find
intentional references leading back to a *history*, and so make these
phenomena knowable as formations subsequent to other, essentially
antecedent formations.

(112–13)

There are several lower layers to the perception of any physical
object, and we cannot enter upon a proper discussion of this aspect
of Husserl's philosophy here. But briefly, the picture is as follows.[4]
A physical object is immediately apprehended as an intersensory
thing. Even if I am just looking at a typical material object, it looks
like something that can be touched. The visually perceived object,
in other words, has an inner horizon that can be explored tactually.
Such an apperception points back to a primally instituting experience in which a mere 'sight-thing' was synthetically experienced as
touchable. This is because a consciousness is conceivable in which
visually perceived things bear no relation to tactile experience. As
Husserl puts the matter in one passage, 'In a certain manner we can
systematically dismantle our completed experience (perception, the
original experiential apperception); if we exclude certain experiences from the genesis, and so assume that certain groups of
experiences would never have existed, we can reflect on how perception must have been fashioned with respect to its horizons' (*Int
II*, 115). A complex relation between the two senses is necessary if
such intersensory objects are to be constituted for the subject.
Moreover, even purely visual 'phantoms', as Husserl calls them,
have their preconditions. For they are perceived as located at various positions in space; and this itself involves a complex relation
between visual experience and the *kinaestheses* (the experiential
expression of our ability to move our bodies). As I move my eyes
from side to side, my visual data undergo lateral displacement; and
as I walk up to an object, it comes to occupy a greater expanse of my
visual field. A consciousness is thinkable in which such visual-
kinaesthetic dependencies did not hold. We can, at the limit, conceive of a consciousness in which *no* visual change was consequent
upon *any* kinaesthesis. For such a subject visual objects would not

even be apperceived as in space – for this means, for Husserl, being in principle reachable by some movement on the part of the subject: 'Space itself, the form of the physical world, is nothing other than the system of the places into which I can transfer myself' (*Int II*, 507).[5]

What we find at each of the above levels are two things. First, that an awareness of a type of object is possible *only if* certain features of consciousness are constituted: e.g., you cannot see physical objects as such without seeing them as coloured and shaped. And second, that these latter features *are* possible for a consciousness *without* certain other features that are essential to the previous objects: e.g., one might, visually, have perceived *only* coloured shapes (because kinaesthesis is absent, or not integrated with visual experience). Since it is synthesis alone that can give rise to objects on a given level from the possibly unintegrated objects of a lower level (material objects from sight-things and touch-things), and since we are entirely below the level of properly *active* synthesis, Husserl sees this entire domain of synthesis and genesis as governed by *association* – 'a fundamental concept belonging to phenomenology' (113–14). Indeed, at one point Husserl can say that 'all unities of experience are unities due to association' (*Int II*, 348). The term 'association' makes us think of the kind of 'sensualistic', empirical psychology that dominated the eighteenth and nineteenth centuries; but Husserl's conception of the matter could not be more different from this. Not surprisingly, he regards it as a field in which one can make progress a priori: he calls it 'a realm of the *innate* a priori, without which, therefore, an ego as such is unthinkable' (114). This is because it 'is a matter of intentionality' (113). The associationistic psychologists thought of association as involving some sort of mental causality – one typically patterned expressly on physical causality. But simply pointing out that one sort of phenomenon pops into the mind whenever another of a certain sort is present, as a matter of brute causal law, makes nothing at all intelligible; nor would a reduction of such brute uniformities to the laws of neurology, if that were possible. What Husserl is interested in is not 'laws of succession' for mental processes, but the meaningful appurtenance of one thing to another in experience.

Items in experience, thanks to empty intentive moments, bear *intentional, directed* relations to one another. And what we find in the building up of an ego is increasingly complex sedimentations of *sense*, which the phenomenologist is called upon both to analyse and to trace in their development. Without the development of a phenomenological language, centred on intentionality, such a task cannot even so much as be properly conceived, let alone carried out.

We have not, however, finished our 'descent' into the foundations of intentional life. For even the data of the separate sense modalities, which is where we have arrived, are not without their preconditions. The most elementary sort of visual field imaginable has an extension and the possibility of containing various elements; but it also constitutes a unity as against a realm of auditory or tactile data. Moreover, single elements in such a visual field themselves have a unity. Both of these phenomena involve associative synthesis involving 'homogeneity' and 'heterogeneity'. Husserl discusses the way in which a red element against a white background will attain a phenomenal unity because of contrast; and several reds spots against the same background will appear similar because of homogeneity:

> What in a purely static description appears to be likeness or similarity must therefore be considered in itself as being already the product of one or the other kind of syntheses of coincidence, which we denote by the traditional term *association* . . . It is the phenomenon of associative genesis which dominates this sphere of passive pregivenness established on the basis of syntheses of internal time-consciousness.
>
> (*EJ*, 77 [74])

The mention of this last level of synthesis, that whereby time itself is constituted thanks to the impressional, retentional and protentional aspects of the living present discussed in the previous chapter, brings us to the absolute basement in our descent through the stratified, founding levels of conscious life. Here we are entirely at the level of 'sub-personal', 'associative' causality (*APS*, 386).

Although Husserl can regard as passive all the syntheses pertaining to perceptual consciousness that we have recently run through – in contrast to the active shapings of objects that we find on the 'predicative' and 'spiritual' levels – he will sometimes reserve this characterization for the last three sorts of synthesis: of homogeneity, heterogeneity, and temporality. Here Husserl recognizes a *total* passivity unconnected with any activity of the ego in even the weakest sense: 'The objects of receptivity are pregiven in an original passivity ... Their apprehension is a lower level activity, the mere act of receiving the sense *already preconstituted in passivity*' (*EJ*, 299–300 [250–1], my emphasis). This narrower circumscription of the term 'passive synthesis' has, I think, the following rationale. It does not seem to make any sense to suppose that disparate visual and tactile data, for instance, should originally attain a synthetic unification in an intersensory object *without the subject's attention being directed to the new object*. The 'primal establishment', whereby a sheer visual appearance acquires an 'apperceptive surplus' of tactile significance, is surely one that needs to be *noticed* by the subject. It is for this reason that I said earlier in this chapter that all habitualities originate in some activity of the ego. This is because all such are acquired as a result of some primal instituting, and this requires that the ego at least attend to, be 'turned to', the newly constituted object. On the other hand, we do not have to attend to a red spot against a white background in order for that spot to be constituted as a unity, since its sheer heterogeneity suffices for that, and for its having the power to attract attention. And although, because of the impressional moment, attention tends to be operative in the 'living present', the flow of consciousness itself would continue even if it weren't.[6] Hence, in the final meditation Husserl glosses 'pure passivity' as the forming of data 'regardless ... of whether they are noticed or unnoticed' (142). At this level of pure passivity, there is not even anything pre-given to be synthesized. And yet, since synthesis takes place, there must be something to be synthesized. As we know from Chapter 2, this is *hylé*, the sensory 'matter' or 'stuff' of experience. Husserl sometimes regards it, as we shall see in Chapter 4, as the one irreducibly contingent and inexplicable aspect of reality.

EIDETIC PHENOMENOLOGY AND THE NATURE OF THOUGHT

In §34, in the middle of his discussion of genetic considerations, Husserl finally makes explicit something that he has been tacitly assuming all through these *Meditations*, and that has already been hinted at in some of his remarks to date: namely, that transcendental phenomenology is to be an *eidetic* discipline. It is, in other words, to be a study of *essences*, rather than of individuals or of concrete facts. Although the meditating philosopher perforce takes himself and his concrete life of pure consciousness as his initial theme, the sheer individuality of that life, and the purely contingent features that such a life will possess, are not our real concern. The final goal is, rather, a comprehension of transcendental consciousness as such, in all its possible forms. When Husserl discusses the nature of visual perception, for example, he clearly does not mean us to take him to be describing features of conscious life that may simply be peculiarities of Husserl's own ego. We are supposed to recognize them as true for all of us. As Husserl himself says, 'For good reasons, in the course of our descriptions such expressions as "essential necessity" and "essentially" forced themselves upon us – phrases in which a definite concept of the a priori, first clarified and delimited by phenomenology, receives expression' (103). Ultimately, the solitary meditating philosopher is to serve merely as an illustrative example of findings that are to hold of any transcendental ego whatsoever. Husserl commonly speaks in this connection of an 'eidetic reduction'. We have already come across the notion of reduction, of course, and we know what it means: a limitation of interest, 'a sort of methodical blind', as Husserl puts it on one occasion (*Int II*, 263). In the case of the eidetic reduction, we ignore any concern we have with factualities, and turn our attention only to essences and essential truths. Our true concern is with 'pure possibility' (107). Indeed, Husserl goes so far as to characterize the not-explicitly-eidetic presentation of phenomenology we have been investigating so far as 'empirical' (105). Not, of course, that the enquiry so far has been empirical in the usual sense of this word: after the epoché our enquiry has been into pure, transcendental consciousness. This has, however, been a concrete, individual consciousness: your own. Only when the move to the eidetic is made – a move that Husserl says was made by phenomenology (i.e., by himself) 'from the beginning' – can phenomenology establish itself as 'first philosophy', as true 'philosophical science' (106).

Essences are, in fact, but one type of 'ideal' object – a general class about which it is high time something was said. For although much of what Husserl says may so far have appeared plausible where perceptual experiences of physical phenomena are in question, the reader may well have felt that it is distinctly implausible where *thought* is concerned. Husserl has claimed, for example, that any 'empty' intentional act points to a possible intuitive fulfilment in which the emptily meant object would be presented in itself. He has also claimed that any empty act refers us genetically to some such intuition as primally instituting, at least as far as basic types of object are concerned. But is this at all plausible in relation to, say, our ability to think of the present economic climate, or Euclidean geometry? How, indeed, does the notion of 'the things themselves' get a purchase in relation to the domain of thought – at least when it ranges beyond merely thinking about particular objects? The answer to such questions is that Husserl draws a distinction between empty and intuitive acts *within the domain of thought itself*. Being fulfilling is not the prerogative of acts of sense-perception. It is, indeed, for this very reason that Husserl has all along employed the term 'intuition', rather than 'perception', in expressing his basic epistemological claims. We have already noted that in *Ideas I* Husserl claims to be a true empiricist because he demands that all thought and theory be made answerable to 'experience'. What, however, commonly goes under the name of empiricism is mistaken, according to him, in identifying the self-givenness of objects, on which all cognition is indeed grounded, with experience 'in a narrow sense' that involves the *sensory* self-givenness of individual things. Hence Husserl's use of the term 'intuition' to stand for the entire range of acts in which something is given – a range that extends beyond what is sensory, or 'perceptible' in the ordinary sense. Whereas 'experiential intuition' gives us only 'realia' – i.e., spatio-temporal objects – there are other sorts of intuition that give us wholly different types of object, all of which are 'ideal'. Although Husserl doubts that the expression 'bodily present' is appropriate in relation to the intuition of such objects, he is insistent that they are as truly 'self-given' in their respective intuitions as are individual physical objects in sense-perception. Let us begin our necessarily brief survey of this so-far neglected area by considering what Husserl calls 'categorial intuition'.

Suppose you see a piece of white paper. The perception itself 'gives' you the paper, and it gives you its whiteness. It does not, however, give you the state of affairs which consists in the paper's *being* white. 'Being is nothing perceptible', as Husserl puts it (*LI* VI, §43). Or suppose that you see one such piece of paper and another. Perception itself will give you each, but it will not give you the 'and' – any more than will a painting: 'I can paint *A* and I can paint *B*, and I can paint them both on the same canvas: I cannot, however, paint the *both*, nor paint the *A and* the *B*' (*ibid.*, §51). In order for predicational states of affairs and collectives to come to our attention, we must go beyond the passive syntheses involved in perception and *articulate* the sensuously given objects. Such articulation goes beyond even perceptually dwelling on one aspect or another of an object, even when the aspect is what Husserl calls a 'non-independent moment' of the object (such as shape or colour, which cannot exist apart from the object whose colour it is) rather than a literal *part* (what Husserl calls a 'piece') of the object. I may, for instance, be perceptually intent upon the colour of a piece of paper. But though a mere 'moment' of the object, its colour is a 'real' (i.e., concrete) aspect of the thing, genuinely given in perception. By contrast, 'Being is nothing *in* the object, no part of it, no moment tenanting it, no quality or intensity of it . . . But being is also nothing attaching *to* an object: as it is no real ["*real*"] internal feature, so also it is no real external feature' (*ibid.*, §43). Similar remarks also apply to the conjunctive 'and', of course. The articulations that are in question here are more 'formal' in nature than anything that mere perceptual investigation could unearth. In the first of the above two examples, I have to articulate the thing before me into a subject and a property so as to be able explicitly to relate the one to the other in a subject–predicate judgement. And in the second, I have to count the objects and regard them as elements in a group. Such 'forms' can, nevertheless, be *intuited*. Indeed, after having claimed that being is imperceptible, Husserl immediately goes on to say that this is true only if 'a very narrow concept of perception' is in play. He is convinced that intuition is a genuinely unitary kind, comprising both sensuous and categorial types, because of the *fulfilling* role that both can play in relation to what, by contrast, must be seen as empty forms of consciousness. For just as a sensory perception can fulfil some empty anticipation, so an empty supposition can be fulfilled by literally seeing *that* things are thus and so. Since, although they are ideal, categorial forms are the ideal forms *of* sensuously perceivable objects, categorial intuition must be founded on intuition of the relevant objects. I must have the white paper intuitionally before my mind – at least in imagination – if I am genuinely to intuit the paper's being white, rather than merely emptily to think or believe this. Most of the time when we are thinking, we do not bother to do this, of course. But, then, most of our thinking is 'inauthentic' or 'improper'. It is, indeed, largely because of this that there is, in Husserl's eyes, such a great need for phenomenology to bring us back to 'the things themselves' – which we can now see to be a call to return not just to the 'bodily' presence of individual objects in sense-perception, but also to the self-given states of affairs and other objects of higher order that are given to non-sensuous intuition in all authentic thought.

This concern for a distinction between authentic and inauthentic thinking dates back to Husserl's very earliest essays in the philosophy of arithmetic. In his first book, for example, he distinguished between numbers that can and those that cannot be intuited. We can simply *see*, given the intellectual wherewithal, that two things are before us; or that five are. Husserl thought we could manage this up to about a dozen. But what of seventy-four? This is, in a sense, a different kind of number from the rest. It refers to the cardinality of a collective which we cannot intuit as such. So what sort of meaning can attach to such a large number? What kind of thinking goes on when we do arithmetic at this level? 'The concept 50 is given to us by the formation 49 + 1', writes Husserl. 'But what is 49? 48 + 1. What is 48? 47 + 1, etc. Every answer means pushing the question back a further step, and only when we have arrived in the domain of the proper number-concepts can we rest content' (*PA*, 229). It is not that Husserl wants, absurdly, to cast doubt on arithmetic when it advances significantly beyond the fingers of our two hands; but he does want to understand it. And simply recognizing that we can 'do' arithmetic at this level, and agree on results, is not to achieve such understanding. Husserl's suggestion is that higher numbers can be thought of only by mastering a certain numerical symbolism that relates them to intuitively graspable arithmetical objects. The system we are familiar with deals with groups of ten, so that seventy-four is represented as seven groups of ten plus four, each element here being intuitively graspable. And in a non-mathematical context, Husserl speaks of our usual hearing and reading of words as lacking 'an accompanying articulation of actual thinking, of thinking produced from the Ego, member by member, in synthetic activity. Rather, this course of thinking proper is *only indicated* (by the passively flowing synthesis of the sensuous verbal sounds) as a course of thinking *to be* performed' (*FTL*, 50). Again, the suggestion is not that this is anything but practically inevitable. But if we are interested in the clarification of sense – which, as self-responsible philosophers, we must be – then a cashing-out of such inauthentic cognitive activity by recourse to categorial intuition must be sought. And if no path leads to such intuition, our thinking is ultimately empty and futile.

Returning to our topic of the eidetic character of phenomenology, Husserl claims that we can also intuit *universal* objects. In particular, we can, according to Husserl, 'see' essences, and such seeing will make eidetic transcendental phenomenology possible. In his early treatment of these matters in the *Logical Investigations*, Husserl introduces the issue of universality by speaking of 'another set of categorial acts' (*LI* VI, §52). In fact, however, the intuition of universals is quite distinct from categorial intuition. The latter, if we focus just on states of affairs, rather than collectives and disjunctives, relates to the form of a state of affairs that corresponds to the logical form of a judgement. We can, Husserl says, present different forms of judgements in the following sort of way: '*A* is *P*', 'An *S* is *P*', 'Some *S* is *P*', 'All *S* are *P*', etc. Categorial form and categorial intuition relate only to the *unschematized* aspects of such statements. The schematized parts – '*S*' and '*P*' – represent what Husserl calls 'stuff' rather than 'form' (*ibid.*, §42). A particular predicative stuff might well be universal in character, however – as, for example, 'red' in 'All pillar boxes are red.' Husserl claims that we can intuit the universal *red*; but since this involves 'stuff', it cannot be categorial intuition that is in question here. In fact, after having spoken of 'another set of categorial acts', Husserl makes a distinction: 'We distinguish between *sensuous abstraction*, which yields *sensuous concepts* . . . and *purely categorial abstraction*, which yields *purely categorial concepts*' (*ibid.*, §60). Indeed, not only does universalizing abstraction not need to be categorial in nature, the categorial intuition of a state of affairs need not involve universal predicates. For in a judgement of the form '*S* is *P*', the '*P*' may stand for a 'real moment' of the individual *S* – the particular redness of this pillar box now in front of me, for example (which at most can be exactly like another pillar box's redness, but never identical to it). As Husserl says in a later text,

> We must, therefore, distinguish the first series of judgments, in which there is predicated of each substrate *its own individual moment* – S' is *p'*, S'' is *p''*, etc. – and, in contrast to this, the judgments in which *the same p*, as *everywhere the same*, is predicated as the *universal*, as the identically one in all, that which emerges in *p'*, *p''*, and so on . . . [In the latter] we no longer determine S' by *p'* as its individual moment but by *p as identically the same in* S, S', and so on . . . The judgment S is *p'* in which *p'* designates the *individual moment* in the individual object S is completely different from the judgment S is *p* in which *p* designates the *universal*, the *eidos*.
>
> (*EJ*, 389–90 [324–5]).[7]

So, at the eidetic level, we are dealing with a new type of intuition and a new type of higher-order object. Husserl often explains the possibility of seeing essences by reference to 'free variation'. We start with some intuitively given individual, either in actual perception or in imagination, and we 'modify' it, 'turning it into an arbitrary example which, at the same time, receives the character of a guiding "model," a point of departure for the production of an infinitely open multiplicity of variants' (*EJ*, §87). This should come as little surprise to the reader, for the eidetic character of phenomenology precisely means a concern with necessary truths concerning *pure possibilities*, rather than with merely 'empirical', contingent fact. Free imaginative variation is supposed to be the way we get a handle on such possibilities and their necessary a priori structures. As he says in the *Cartesian Meditations*, 'We, so to speak, shift the actual perception into the realm of non-actualities, the realm of the as-if, which supplies us with pure possibilities' (104). Now, the model that we start with is always a certain *kind* of thing. In the process of free variation we imaginatively produce for ourselves different objects that are yet copies of the model in so far as they are examples of the *same kind* of thing. In this process a certain 'invariant' emerges as

> the *necessary general* form, without which an object such as this thing, as an example of its kind, would not be thinkable at all. While what differentiates the variants remains indifferent to us, this form stands out in the practice of voluntary variation, and as an absolutely identical content, an invariable *what*, according to which all the variants coincide: an invariable *essence*
>
> > (*EJ*, §87, from which subsequent unattributed quotation in this section are also taken).

If, for example, I take as my model a certain musical note, I can imaginatively vary its pitch, its loudness, and its timbre. I cannot, however, vary it in such a way that it loses any of these attributes altogether. Any imagined object that lacked pitch or volume or timbre would not be a variant of the model *as a note*: 'The essence proves to be that without which an object of a particular kind cannot be thought, i.e., without which the object cannot be intuitively imagined as such.' In virtue of the necessary similarity that all the variants have to one another, they 'attain an overlapping coincidence . . . and enter, in a purely passive way, into a synthetic unity'. In this way the *eidos* is 'passively pre-constituted'; and the intuition of the *eidos* emerges with the '*active intuitive apprehension* of what is thus pre-constituted'.

The general sort of procedure envisaged here should not be at all unfamiliar to those acquainted with twentieth-century analytical philosophy, which for much of its history was dominated by an appeal to 'what I can imagine' as a test for possibility. A notable feature of Husserl's version of the procedure, however, is his stress on concretely, intuitively imagining the 'variants'. Empty 'theoretical' thinking about possibilities is answerable, for Husserl, to intuition of 'the things themselves'. Indeed, it is only because the variants are intuitionally brought to presence that Husserl can speak of an *intuition* of essences at all. For the idea is that as a result of the imaginative variation the 'necessary general form' *itself* becomes intuited as a higher-order object; and the 'clarity' with which such an essence comes to consciousness depends on the clarity with which the imaginings are effected. As we saw in Chapter 2, Husserl regards imagination as able to serve the important function of 'clarification' in relation to merely empty thinking, since it presents, albeit in the mode of 'as if', a perceptual experience of an object as self-given – one which would constitute 'confirming fulfilment' of the empty intention. In the present connection, imagination can make possibilities self-evident.

No doubt many at the present time are likely to be unimpressed by the pretension of such an exercise in imagination to be 'the way in which all intuitive essential necessities and essential laws and every genuine intuitive a priori are won' (*PP*, 72). One general theoretical worry we might have about the procedure is how we ourselves are supposed to ensure that we have indeed exhausted all the possibilities when we run through imaginative variants of our 'model'. For such a running through of images is what is supposed to give us the *infinite extension* of the possibilities that answer to the essence in question. Husserl certainly recognized that we cannot imaginatively flick through an infinite series of images in order to detect an invariant universal. He supposed, rather, that the implied infinity is grounded on the *freedom* with which we execute a finite series of variations, and on the character of 'exemplary arbitrariness' that thereby attaches to each image produced. Suppose that, in order to intuit the essence of a note, I imagine one of the sort produced by the open top string of a violin. Starting from this model I either arbitrarily imagine, say, a deep note on the bassoon, and then a high note on the clarinet, or I am led to imagine such by 'the aimless favour of association and the whims of passive imagination' (still from *EJ*, §87). In either case I recognize that the differences in the imagined objects are irrelevant to whether it is a note that I am intuiting: 'What differentiates the variants remains indifferent to us.' And in both cases I recognize the arbitrariness of the examples. Moreover, if I stop the imaginative exercise after a couple of examples, this too is arbitrary, for I *could* in principle have produced yet more:

> This remarkable and truly important consciousness of 'and so on, at my pleasure' belongs essentially to every multiplicity of variations. Only in this way is given what we call an 'infinitely open' multiplicity; obviously, it is the same whether we proceed according to a long process, . . . or whether we break off prematurely.

The single *eidos* comes to intuition as a '*unity in the conflict*'. For each variant is incompatible with each other: a tone cannot be *both* high and low, loud and soft, at one and the same time. It is precisely what thus conflicts among the variants that is 'indifferent' to us. However, 'things cannot enter into conflict which have nothing in common'; and this common basis for arbitrary conflict is the *eidos*, which comes to intuition in the intuitively varied conflicting series. We are dealing here with 'a unique consciousness with a unique content, whose correlate signifies concrete unity founded in conflict, in incompatibility. This remarkable hybrid unity is at the bottom of essential seeing.'

It is important to understand that such imaginative variation is not supposed by Husserl to be the way in which we acquire universal concepts. That we already possess such concepts is clearly presupposed by the account – in particular, by the way in which the initial model 'gives direction' to our production of images. General concepts as such arise, rather, when judgements relating to different objects that possess like features enter into a 'synthesis of the coincidence of likeness' (*EJ*, 388 [323]). I may, for example, notice the redness of a certain pillar box and explicitly, predicatively, ascribe its colour-moment to the pillar box as logical subject. I may then notice a similar, perhaps exactly similar, redness in some tomato, and predicate accordingly. The similarity of the two moments then founds the possibility not just of judging that the two subjects – pillar box and tomato – are similar, but that they are (qualitatively) *identical*. Imaginative variation has played no role here. And such variation is not required even when we go further and explicitly focus on such an identity as a universal object. Imaginative variation, with its essential moment of arbitrariness, is, rather, employed by Husserl to attain *pure* essences, unconnected with any factualities whatsoever – even the positing of a real world. In the work from which I have been quoting, *Experience and Judgement*, the discussion of imaginative variation occurs after a chapter which discusses 'empirical generalities'; and the later chapter is entitled 'The Acquisition of *Pure* Generalities by the Method of Essential Seeing' (my emphasis). Eidetic variation, in short, is intended *to lead us to the epoché*. In the present section of the *Meditations* Husserl speaks of 'abstaining from acceptance' of a thing's being (104), which certainly should remind us of earlier turns of phrase employed in connection with the transcendental reduction. And in other presentations of the eidetic move Husserl goes out of his way to echo the language we are familiar with in connection with the epoché. In one such, for example, he speaks of dropping the 'fact' of the world, though in a way that allows our conviction in its reality to remain unaffected (*PP*, 71). Elsewhere he speaks of putting our implicit positing of the world 'out of play' (*EJ*, 424 [351]). This amounts to saying that eidetic research requires the kind of total epoché that is involved in the transcendental reduction. Indeed, Husserl explicitly refers to 'the method of free variation and the consequent exclusion of all positing of real being' (*EJ*, 426 [352], translation modified). Only in this way will the essences with which we deal be 'pure', in the sense of not being tied to any actual matter of fact. The essences and essential possibilities in question should apply to any possible world and any possible form the consciousness may take.

This is the reason why, in the earlier discussion of the epoché in Chapter 1, I said that it and the transcendental reduction were 'intimately related', but not mutually entailing. For although, in the context of the First Meditation, a restriction to transcendental consciousness emerged as the point of effecting the epoché, we are now in a position to see that there are *two* directions that our theoretical interest can take when the fact of the world is bracketed: *either* a turn to the transcendental, *or* the present turn to the eidetic. The motives for the two moves are, however, distinct. The move to the transcendental is motivated by the need to overcome naïveté – a naïveté which is exposed, according to Husserl, by the unfolding of modern philosophy since Descartes, and which is fully recognized in the 'transcendental insight'. The move to the eidetic, by contrast, is motivated by nothing other than the demands of the idea of science itself. Here, as everywhere, 'the science of pure possibilities precedes the science of actualities and alone makes it possible as a science' (106).

FOUNDING

At a number of points in the exposition so far I have had recourse to use of the term 'found'. It was said, for example, that an act of categorial intuition is founded on an act of judgement. Since Husserl's concept of founding is not only one of his most important and widely employed phenomenological concepts, but also the cause of a historically important controversy, it deserves a section to itself. The notion of founding is relevant to us in so far as it concerns the necessity of one type of mental act being founded on another. Husserl does not, however, restrict talk of founding to mental acts. The term is first introduced by him in connection with a more general discussion of wholes and parts (*LI* III). As we have seen, Husserl distinguishes two sorts of parts: 'moments' and 'pieces' (or abstract and concrete 'contents'). The latter, but not the former, are separable from the whole of which they are parts. The leg of a table, for example, is a 'piece' of it, since it can be separated from the table; but the table's colour and shape are 'moments' of the table, since they cannot be so separated. Husserl employs the notion of founding in connection with this difference: 'If, by a law of essence, an *A* cannot exist as such except in a more comprehensive unity which ties it to an *M*, we say that an *A as such requires founding by an M'* (*LI* III, §14, translation modified). Founding, then, is a matter of *essential inseparability*. This leaves it open that two parts of a whole should be mutually founding, and Husserl explicitly recognizes such cases.

Even when we limit our attention to the domain of mental acts, the notion of founding is employed in various ways. Husserl says, for example, that an extended perception of something is founded on the constituent phases of the perception; and that the drawing of a conclusion is founded on the entertaining of premises (*Int I*, 348–9). What has generated most interest in Husserl's account, however, is his treatment of cases where one level of a complex act is founded on a lower, *concurrent* level. An example that Husserl often gives of such a case is that of valuing something. Such an act, or attitude, presupposes that an object is presented to or presentified by you in some fashion. We are still, here, in the territory of parts and wholes, for Husserl stresses that various 'act characters' so interweave as to produce a *unitary* intentional act. I do not see an object and then, as a separate act, value it. The valuing is so interwoven with the presentation that a single complex act results. In relation to the previously mentioned act, the valuing was a mere moment of it, since no valuing can take place in the absence of some act that intentionally directs you to the object itself; and the valuing itself does not give you this object. What the act of valuing gives you, rather, is a certain 'characteristic' of an object. We are already familiar with Husserl's concept of noetic–noematic parallelism. So far, we have seen this only in the context of 'cognitive' acts. Husserl applies it, however, to all higher-level 'act characters'. Because of this parallelism, a unitary object corresponds to the unitary presentational-valuing act: a *valuable object*. Although unitary, this is a complex noematic object, possessing internal stratification that mirrors the dependencies within the act that intends it. The valuableness of the object is founded on the physical object itself, just as the act of valuing is founded on, say, a perception that gives us the object itself. Although, in order for such a complex object to appear to me, I must engage in an act of valuing, it is not this act itself that I value: I value *the object*. And when I see a beautiful object, I find beauty *in the object*, not in me. Once again, there certainly is something in me that is relevant to the appearance of beauty – an aesthetic feeling or response of some sort. But it is not *this* that I find beautiful. Just as the noetic acts that are correlated with the noematic objects of 'straightforward experience' are not, except to a self-conscious reflective awareness, themselves objects, but, by virtue of their complex syntheses, constitute objects for consciousness, so an aesthetic act correlates with something noematic: it presents an object with an aspect of beauty (or its opposite). Husserl certainly admitted that there is a question to explore concerning the objectivity of values. But the 'things themselves', given in first-hand experience, cannot be gainsaid; and what such experience gives us as the things that are beautiful or valuable are various worldly objects, not states of our own 'minds'. We do not, however, initially relate to value or beauty as objects, but as characteristics that objects have. Valuational and aesthetic acts are not of themselves *objectivating*. We can, however, engage in a yet higher-order act which does 'objectivate' such characteristics, and then we do have value or beauty itself as an object – as when, for instance, I judge that the beauty of X is greater than the beauty of Y. Even here, however, it is not the aesthetic response itself that gives me this object *qua* object, but the higher-level objectivating act that is founded on the aesthetic act. So valuational and aesthetic acts are doubly non-objectivating. They neither give us the object that is valuable or beautiful, nor do they give us value or beauty as objects. (On the above, see *Ideas I*, §§95, 101–2, 108, 114; and *Ideas II*, §4.)

In relation to such acts there are, and can be, no cases of mutual founding. A valuing, for example, is founded on some objectivating act, *but not conversely*. This means, therefore, that objectivating acts can occur in the absence of any valuing, and indeed, in the absence of any other act-character whatever. The rule that holds here is 'one-sided separability: the lowest levels would be possible for consciousness if the higher levels were absent' (*Int I*, 354). Husserl's most general claim in this area is that what he calls 'straightforward experience' is founding for all other types of act that are directed to the fully constituted world. These latter fall into two categories. Within one category fall the sorts of acts we have been recently considering – 'attitudinal acts', we might call them, which include, along with aesthetic and evaluative acts, all emotional responses, as well as acts that involve recognition of objects as *artefacts*, or as possessing *social* and *spiritual* properties. To take something to be a lever, for example, requires a certain amount of practical engagement with objects in the world, a familiarity with how we can manipulate them. Conversely, however, we can have a great familiarity with worldly objects without the idea of a lever ever dawning upon us. At the root of all such hierarchies of founded acts there lies the simple experience of what Husserl likes to call 'the mere thing of nature'. In relation to such a founding level of 'straightforward experience', the higher-level acts involve an *enrichment of sense* of the very object that is experientially given to us as a whole. The other category of higher-order acts concerns the 'objects of understanding' with which we were concerned in the previous section: the logically articulated acts that give us states of affairs and collections, and the acts that give us universalities. Although 'straightforward experience' ultimately underlies these too, it is also required that we direct different 'rays' of attention to different things, or to different aspects of something. In order to judge that S is p, in order explicitly to predicate the one of the other, I need to have directed attention both to S as substrate and to p as moment; and the result is not an enrichment of sense of one or other of the initial objects, but an intuition of a wholly different kind of 'ideal' object. It is, however, the former class of higher-order acts that involve simple 'enrichment' that is our concern here. For Heidegger influentially criticized the philosophical tradition for having presupposed a 'spectator' account of our fundamental involvement with the world – a criticism to which, it is commonly held, Husserl himself falls victim in virtue of this specific employment of his notion of founding. According to such a 'traditional' view, our relation to the world is founded on a 'fixed staring at something that is purely present at hand' (Heidegger 1927, 61). In contrast to this, it is suggested, we should see ourselves as vitally 'engaged' with the world in multifarious, primarily practical, ways. The theoretical, 'cognitive' attitude, that which would give us *bare things* which would be simply *present*, is but one possible attitude for us – one, furthermore, that is not fundamental. Indeed, it presupposes a 'deficiency' in our fundamental comportment to the world. Many see in the position advocated by Heidegger the main shift in the history of continental philosophy in the twentieth century: from transcendental to *existential* phenomenology.

In fact, over and over again Husserl himself stresses that the theoretical attitude, that which leads to natural science, is an *unnatural* one – one that involves a disengagement from life and an abstraction from the richness of the 'life-world' which is our natural home:

> In ordinary life we have nothing whatever to do with nature-objects. What we take as things are pictures, statues, gardens, houses, tables, clothes, tools, etc. These are all value-objects of various kinds, use-objects, practical objects. They are not objects which can be found in natural science.
>
> (*Ideas II*, 27)

He can even say that 'the thematic direction of thought the natural scientist follows is a theoretical path away from the actuality of life' (*ibid.*, 374). Heidegger's criticism of the philosophical tradition was not, however, that it supposed that we are *nothing but* spectators of the world – which would be an absurd suggestion. What he objected to was the account that was traditionally given of the non-cognitive dimensions to human life – in particular, seeing them as *founded* upon straightforward cognition. Speaking of values, for example, Heidegger says that, traditionally, they 'would have their sole ultimate ontological source in our previously laying down the actuality of Things as the fundamental stratum' (Heidegger 1927, 99). One thing that existential phenomenology has insisted upon is that evaluative, emotional and practical aspects of human life make a *fundamental* contribution to the constitution of the world, and do not arise subsequently to simple cognition as some kind of 'colouring' lent to mere things. Emotion, for example, has its own, non-dependent intentionality. Heidegger says of '*Stimmung*' – commonly translated as 'mood', but connoting an *attunement* to things – that it is ontologically primordial and prior to cognition (Heidegger 1927, 136). And 'cognition', by contrast, is a *founded* mode of comportment (*ibid.*, §13).

There are, to be sure, many passages in Husserl that seem to embody the traditional picture. Indeed, elements of the picture certainly do correspond to things Husserl believed. He can write, for example, as follows: 'The subject has objects over against itself; it is a "representing" subject, and that is the foundation for its "comportment" toward the objects' (*Ideas II*, 278). And again:

> To begin with, the world is, in its *core*, a world appearing to the senses and characterized as 'on hand,' a world given in straightforward, empirical intuitions and perhaps grasped actively. The Ego then finds itself related to this empirical world in new acts, e.g., in acts of valuing or in acts of pleasure and displeasure. In these acts, the object is brought to consciousness as valuable, as pleasant, beautiful, etc.
>
> (*Ideas II*, 186; compare *EJ*, 54 [54])

In fact, however, when we penetrate more deeply into Husserl's writings, the standard interpretation of his thought does not stand up to scrutiny. Recall that, in relation to concurrent intentional acts, to say that one level is founding with respect to another is to say two things: that the latter is impossible without the former, and that the former *is* possible without the latter. But is it really possible that we should have 'pure', merely theoretical experience untainted by any 'affective' or practical element whatever? One move that Heidegger himself makes to render such a supposition unattractive is to claim that the sort of case that may come to mind as an example of a neutral registering of the passing show is itself but a modality of affectivity or 'attunement'. For example, we find certain things attractive, and others repellent. Here, clearly, some 'affect' is involved. But, claims Heidegger, finding things run-of-the-mill and unremarkable is itself a form of the very same kind of attunement – rather as something's being unremarkably at room temperature is yet being on the hot–cold spectrum. Now, in order to assess such a claim in its full generality, we should need to examine all of the different varieties of our comportment towards the world; for in some cases the claim may be plausible, and in others not. Rather than running through a case-by-case investigation, however, and so as to get to the nub of the issue, let us ask if Husserl thinks that it is ever possible to be in entirely 'pure' cognitive states, untainted by any features that are not purely 'presentive' or 'objectifying'. And to this question the answer is a clear No. To see that this is so, it suffices to examine Husserl's treatment of a topic of which mention was briefly made earlier in this chapter, when we examined Husserl's attitude to 'nativism': namely, *instincts*. Since, in addition to answering the preceding 'Heideggerian' critique, this topic is of quite fundamental importance in Husserl's (later) thought; since investigating this issue will finally put to rest the suspicion of an infinite regress that attaches to Husserl's claim about all apperceptions pointing back to primal experiential institutions; and since the nature of instincts is intimately related to the nature of *reason*, which will be one of our principal concerns in the next chapter, I believe the topic deserves a section to itself – one that will conclude this chapter.

TRANSCENDENTAL INSTINCTS AND 'DRIVE-INTENTIONALITY'

Throughout all conscious life, right down to its most basic substructure, Husserl discerns the play of *drives* and *instincts*. 'In the "beginning"', he writes, there is 'instinctive striving' (C 13 I, 6a). Indeed, 'All life is a continuous striving' (A VI 26, 42a). More particularly, instincts and drives inform and condition all of our *intentional* life, so that Husserl can come to speak of 'drive-intentionality' (*Triebintentionalität*) and 'instinct-intentionality' (*Instinktintentionalität*) (e.g., A VII 13, 20; C 8 II, 1). He speaks of 'transcendental instinct' as 'the universal tendency that in a sense runs through the whole of the intentionality of the ego' (C 13 I,

13b), and can even claim that 'the system of intentionality is a system of associatively interwoven drives' (A VII 13, 24a). He discerns in the original play of such instincts and drives a distinctive form of intentionality – a 'primal' or 'proto-intentionality' – that precedes and makes possible the familiar intentional directedness to objects in the world. Hence, he can refer to the innate system of instinctive drives as 'the primal predisposition of the I that all constitution presupposes' (E III 9, 4a). There is a genetic priority here, because we find in instincts an intentional directedness to something that is not yet constituted as an 'object': 'Striving is instinctive, and instinctively – and so, at first, covertly – "directed" at what are "later" first disclosed as constituted worldly unities' (A VI 34, 34b). In order to understand how Husserl can see instincts both as preceding and as making possible fully object-directed consciousness, we need to take note of a distinction he draws between *fulfilment* and *disclosure*. Fulfilment, which we have already encountered repeatedly in these pages, refers to the 'covering' of an empty intention by the object's presence in intuition. It presupposes that the empty intention is already intentionally directed to the object in question. When we are but instinctively directed to something, however, we do not yet 'know' what the goal of our inclination is. The instinct, and its 'target', are as yet 'undisclosed' or 'latent'. It is only when the instinctive drive is *satisfied* that the goal of the instinct is 'disclosed', thereby becoming 'manifest' – a process that is analogous to that of fulfilment proper (C 13 I, 6). Husserl on one occasion illustrates the kind of process he has in mind by reference to a baby at the breast, speaking of a 'direction towards drinking' being awakened in the baby by the smell of the mother's breast and by the sensation of its own lips moving. He then goes on to suggest that 'perhaps the smell alone awakens something further . . . that as yet has no "conscious" goal'. Only when drinking occurs, and the drive is satisfied, is that drive 'disclosed' as indeed having been directed to drinking (C 16, IV, 36b). It is thanks to such instincts that the monad at its most basic level can be seen as already intentionally directed.

In order to see how innate instincts can make possible an

eventual consciousness of a world, we need to focus on the 'birth' of a monad – which, as we now know, is the moment when the monad is first affected by *hylé*. Such affection is one aspect of a reciprocal process. For that which, on the side of the hyletic data, is called 'affecting' the I, from the side of the I is called 'tending, striving' (B III 9, 70). There is, therefore, an 'interest in sensory data and sense-fields before the objectivation of sensory data' (C 13 I, 11b). There is also, however, an instinct towards objectivation (C 13 I, 10–11), which underlies and drives forward our development towards a properly constituting conscious life. Of particular importance in this developmental story is the instinctive association of sensory data with kinaesthesia. Husserl calls the movements that changes in sensory data instinctively call forth 'involuntary', 'primal' kinaestheses (D 12 V, 11; C 11 IV, 10), and he speaks of them as involving a 'passive willing' (*Willenspassivität*) (M III 3 III 1 II, 103). It is only because of such movement, of course, that innate drives can be satisfied, and hence 'disclosed', at all. What is critical, here, is the *interplay* between changes in sensory data and kinaesthetic movement; and this, too, is instinctive (e.g., C 16 IV, 16; E III 9, 23). So three things are central for the possible emergence of a consciousness of objects: affecting *hylé*, the instinctive, affective turning of the attention, and instinctively motivated kinaesthesis: 'What is first in the constitution of the world in primordiality is the constitution of "nature" from . . . the threefold primal material: sensory core, sensory feeling, sensory kinaesthesis. To this corresponds "primal instinct" ' (B III 9, 67a).

With the 'disclosure' of instinctive drives through satisfaction we have not yet reached the constitution of objects. We are, as Husserl often puts it, at the level, not of being, but of 'pre-being' (*Vorsein*) (e.g., A VI 34, 34), just as we are dealing, not with an 'I', but with a 'pre-I' that is in the process of developing into an I through the constitution of a world of objects. However, because of the threefold innate endowment just mentioned, the nascent monad is not only 'directed', but directed (implicitly) to *the world*. For this endowment makes up the implicit, empty, 'primal horizon' of which we have already heard Husserl speak, and of which the eventually conscious world-horizon is but the 'explication': 'The instinctive intentionality of monads belongs to their worldly being and life. Their fulfilment is world-directed' (C 8 II, 16a). For with this threefold 'primal material' in place, the subject is in a position to start *exploring* what it is sensorily confronted with. Thanks to the fact that the sorts of passive, associative syntheses that we investigated earlier in this chapter are also in play, the subject is in a position to recognize and reidentify things that affect it – though at first strictly in relation to its striving to satisfy its innate instinctive drives: 'In the play of instincts: recognition, identification, differentiation – before something "objective" is constituted out of appearances. Recognition of a datum as the content of an enjoyment while one is satisfied' (C 13 I, 10b). The move from 'pre-being' to being, to the constitution of objects proper, is made possible precisely by such identifications: 'Instinctive affection [by *hylé*] leads to a turning toward and a grasping that is not yet the constitution of an entity. An entity is a possession that we have earned, that to which I already always have access as something that remains there for me' (A VI 34, 35a). Whereas the first, preobjective unities were 'interest-formations' (*Interessengebilde*) (C 13 I, 6), the first genuine objects are 'habitual accessible unities' (A VI 34, 36). The instinctive drive towards objectification is ultimately the drive for satisfaction that is derived from stable experiential unities. Instincts and drives do not individually well up in us, and are not extinguished when they are individually satisfied. The continuous striving of the ego means that such drives and instincts are *continuously* operative in our mental lives: 'All satisfaction is transitional satisfaction' (A VI 26, 42a). Hence, 'the instinctive pleasure in seeing is a process of instinctive intentions and fulfilments, and the fulfilments always leave something still open: the instinct-horizon extends further' (A VI 34, 36a). That our sensory fields are, given our instincts, invitingly accessible and indefinitely explorable in this way means that experiential structures can arise for the ego – structures that involve the first elements of founding. At one point Husserl speaks of 'the I . . . striving forward from fulfilment to new fulfilment: each fulfilment relative, each with a horizon of unfulfilled emptiness. Construction of *the genesis of foundings* in the developing I' (C 13 1, 10a, my emphasis). What, in

particular, guides the subject in its exploration of experiential unities is the instinctive search for what is *better*: 'Each higher level
begins with the attempt to realise . . . what is better' (A VI 34, 36b).
And what is 'better', at this level, means, of course, what better
satisfies the innate drives of the ego – that which *pleases* it. In
relation to sight, Husserl says that 'optically, that which pleases
most is always the optimum' (A VI 34, 34b). And, more generally,
he can write that to a subject's changing sensory fields there
belongs 'the constant general "satisfaction or dislike in sense-
perception", a general "interest" in one thing going along with
another [*Mitgezogen-sein*], which, thanks to the accompanying
kinaestheses, is instinctively directed to the constitution of what
is optimal, to the constitution of experiences of physical things, to
cognition of physical things' (B III 9, 67).

Husserl sees in this instinctive development of monads into conscious constituters of a world a 'universal teleology' (e.g., C 13 I,
13). Consciousness is innately and essentially directed in its striving life towards increasingly complex, stable unities in experiences.
Since, as we shall see in Chapter 4, this is ultimately the function of
reason, Husserl sees the development of consciousness as a grand
unfolding, or working out, of reason in the world. At the most
fundamental level it is at work in the primal instincts that drive
monadic striving. But such striving is guided by *pleasure*: 'Life is
a striving in multifarious forms and tenors of intention and fulfilment. In fulfilment, pleasure in the widest sense; in lack of fulfilment, a further tending toward pleasure as a striving that simply
craves' (A VI 26, 42b). That the living, awake monad constitutes a
world implies that innately implanted in that monad is an *interest* –
indeed a *pleasure* – *in being*, and in the stable unities of experience
that an experiential appreciation of being implies. For Husserl,
pleasure itself is teleologically directed. For Husserl, pleasure is the
handmaiden of reason.

We are now, finally, in a position to put to rest the worry that
Husserl's philosophy may embody an infinite regress of apperceptions presupposing apperceptions. Any apperception is directed to
an already constituted object, or one whose constitution is now
being 'instituted' for the first time in an original experience. But

such an experience will itself be world-directed, and hence presuppose 'prior memories'. Preceding all of this, however, and making it possible, are 'innate instincts as an intentionality that belongs to the original and essential structure of mental being' (C 8 II, 16a). It is their 'disclosure' that makes possible all apperception. The regress is stopped by the following claim, which I have already quoted, but which we are now in a position fully to understand: consciousness has an ' "inheritance" without memory, and yet a kind of "fulfilment" by awakenings' (K III 11, 4a).

We are also in a position to see that the 'Heideggerian' criticism of Husserl's philosophy is wholly without merit. It is not merely that Husserl says, repeatedly, that we have some sort of 'affective' relation to every object that we do or can encounter in the world – for this does not address the Heideggerian worry that every such instance may involve the traditional idea of some sort of 'colouring' being (always) added to an integral founding act of pure objectification, which latter constitutes our original relation to the world. No: for Husserl affection, drives, instincts go 'all the way down'. As he says at one point, 'Mere data of sensation, and, at a higher level, sensory objects such as physical things, that are there for the subject but are "value-free", are abstractions. Nothing can be given that does not move the feelings' (A VI 26, 42a). Or, as he also says, 'The I is a feeling I in relation to every content' (C 16 V, 68a). The important point is that this is asserted in relation to *every* content, including pre-objective content at the level prior to any 'cognition' or the possibility of a brute 'staring' at a world. Affective, striving engagement is not only involved in, but is *presupposed by*, every constitution of and relation to objects. It is 'the irrational that makes rationality possible' (E III 9, 4b).

If this is the case, however, what are we to make of the many passages where Husserl seems explicitly to embrace the traditional, 'pre-Heideggerian' position? Well, there certainly is a development in Husserl's thinking on this matter: he did not begin fully to appreciate the quite fundamental contribution of the 'affective' dimension of subjectivity to the constitution of the world until the early 1920s. On the other hand, there are passages even in the late works that may seem to express the more 'traditional' view (e.g., A

VI 34, 37, from 1931). Perhaps he did not attain a settled view on the matter. But the following, more interesting interpretation seems to me possible: that when Husserl says, for example, that a certain act of valuing is founded on, say, a perception of a certain object, what he means is that valuing *that object itself* is so founded. When we are related feelingly to a determinate object, that object must have been constituted for us as such; and it is indeed objectifying acts that produce such 'finished' objects. The determinate relation of all affective comportment *to objects* is therefore the work of such objectification. This does not imply that some valuing, or some other 'non-cognitive' response or drive, may not already be at work in constituting that object. It is just that these 'affective' and instinctive factors cannot yet be determinately directed to *that* object. For the latter needs to be fully constituted *as an object* for this to be possible. Indeed, as we have just seen, it is Husserl's view that such factors are always at work in the initial constitution of objects. For Husserl *agrees* with Heidegger that cognition is a founded mode of comportment. Although, when discussing founding, Husserl often focuses on those act-characters that lend an enrichment of sense to objects beyond what any objectifying act can offer, he also can employ the term 'founding' in relation to the complex substructure of perception itself, which we investigated earlier in this chapter in the section on active and passive synthesis. At the end of the Third Meditation, for example, Husserl speaks of a 'founding by levels' all the way down to the constitution of inner time-consciousness. In fact it is Heidegger who is a somewhat 'one-dimensional' philosopher in this connection, operating entirely on the level of fully constituted, personal life. With Heidegger, philosophy becomes mere hermeneutics. Husserl, by contrast, sees the importance for ultimate clarity in penetrating below the level of personal life, so as to investigate the complex layers of constituting, anonymous life that are presupposed by any account of our actual personal life. In one passage Husserl contrasts a mere 'spiritual-psychological "phenomenology"' with true transcendental phenomenology, and states that the former is but a positive science (*Ideas II*, 369–70). It is not a positive *natural* science, of course; but it is a mere positive science in the domain of the 'human sciences'. By implication and anticipation, Heidegger therefore emerges, in Husserl's eyes, as engaging in positive science, and not genuine philosophy – which, as we now know, in order to be genuine must be transcendental and 'archaeological'. Be that as it may, the most important issue in all of this from Heidegger's point of view is that any account of consciousness (or *Dasein*) that sees cognition as founding for all other forms of comportment towards the world will have prejudged the 'question of being' in favour of presentness-at-hand – the brute presence of a mere 'thing' as it would be registered in a 'pure cognition'. What Heidegger above all fears is that such a flat presence will be attributed to the being of subjects themselves. And he criticizes Husserl for not having adequately considered the peculiar form of being that attaches to *Dasein* (or 'personal monads' in Husserlian terminology), and for simply assuming that such being would indeed be that of such sheer presentness. As we are now in a position to see, however, it was precisely as a result of Husserl's depth-analyses of consciousness which penetrated below the level of everyday awareness and comportment that he discerns a wholly unique kind of being pertaining to consciousness. For Husserl says that it is 'drive-intentionality' that pushes forward one present into the next in that flowing life which a conscious monad enjoys (*Int III*, 595). At its root, conscious life is the absolute flow which temporalizes itself in a constant striving. The being of consciousness for Husserl, like the being of *Dasein* for Heidegger, is ultimately future-directed, striving temporality.

NOTES

1 As the discussion in §32 of the *Cartesian Meditations* indicates, 'person' is something of a term of art for Husserl, since he can on occasion call even non-human animals 'persons' in virtue of possessing habitualities. For an extensive discussion of this concept, and how it differs from both the pure ego and the 'soul' of the psychologists, see *Ideas II*, Section Three, and the various supplementary texts thereto.

2 The infinite regress that this claim may seem to involve will be addressed later in this chapter.

3 There is, to be sure, a distinction to be drawn between absolute, subjective time and the objective, constituted time of the world. They do not, and cannot, however, involve a different *ordering* of corresponding events.

4 For Husserl's most extensive treatments, see *TS*, *Time*, *Ideas II*, Sect. 1, and *EJ*, Part 1.

5 In fact, Husserl regarded the issue of the constitution of space as a huge and complex topic for phenomenological research, returning to it time and time again. It also has important implications for his account of intersubjectivity, as we shall see in Chapter 5.

6 Husserl seems to be committed to this position because of two claims he repeatedly makes. First, as we saw in the previous chapter, temporal synthesis is continuous (indeed eternal) within each monad. Second, as we shall see in the next chapter, Husserl thinks that monads are, for most of their existence, 'asleep' or 'involuted'; and he characterizes this state as one in which the ego is *affected by nothing*. Temporal synthesis must therefore be able to proceed without affection.

7 It should be said, however, that there is no neat separation of predicative articulation from abstractive generalization for Husserl. This is because predicative judgement relies on the offices of language, the predicates of which already have a universal significance: see *EJ*, §47.

4

THIRD MEDITATION AND PART
OF THE FOURTH

§§23–29, 40–41

The Third Meditation is by far the shortest of the five, occupying a
scant eight pages in the German edition. Moreover, some of the
ground covered in it amounts to but a development of material
already dealt with earlier in the work. Nevertheless, its importance
is out of all proportion to its size, since it is here that Husserl takes
the one major step towards showing that transcendental phenomenology leads us inexorably to idealism. However, although the
groundwork is laid here, Husserl does not explicitly draw this
conclusion until the last two sections of the Fourth Meditation:
'Phenomenology is *eo ipso* transcendental idealism' (118). I shall,
therefore, discuss these two sections as well as the Third Meditation in the present chapter, the overriding task of which, therefore,
is to evaluate the case that Husserl makes out for idealism.
The explicit topic of the Third Meditation itself, however, that
which I see as the cornerstone of his case for idealism, is that of
reality (*Wirklichkeit*).[1]

REALITY AND REASON

The topic of reality may initially appear a surprising one to emerge in the course of transcendental reflection, since the latter is made possible precisely by disconnecting any concern with the reality of objects – indeed, with that of the world as a whole. So it is important for us, before looking at what Husserl has specifically to say, to understand how this issue can even so much as arise after the transcendental reduction. The justification for Husserl's conviction that it can – that the topic of reality is, indeed, 'an all-embracing theme for phenomenology' (91) – is the 'transcendental insight' discussed in Chapter 1: the claim that anything that has any sense for us is something that is constituted in consciousness as having such a sense. For 'reality' is a notion that has a meaning for us. Something is real if and only if it matches up to what reality *means* to us – i.e., to a certain *sense* that is harboured within consciousness. So it is not only 'object-sense' that is constituted in consciousness – i.e., a kind of object – but also 'existential sense' – what it is for a given type of object to *exist* or to be *real*: both 'its "what" and its "it exists and really is"', as Husserl puts it (123). The latter, too, must be traced back to some feature of conscious life, since it, too, is 'a sense in or arising from my intentional life, from its constitutive syntheses' (*ibid*.). Moreover, and as we have already seen, every sense that we could possibly possess points to certain privileged forms of consciousness in which what is 'meant' is *originally given* to us. Just as any thought about a material object must be traced back to perceptual experience in which such objects are given originally, so our thoughts about the *reality or unreality* of such objects, if such notions ultimately have any genuine sense for us, must similarly be traced back to experiences in which these too are appreciated originally.

Our first question must therefore be: to which kind of experience, precisely, does the sense of 'being' or 'reality' correspond? The answer, as we have just seen, is going to refer us to 'originary intuition' or 'self-evidence' – something we encountered in Chapter 1, but which only now, in connection with reality, 'becomes our phenomenological theme' (92). It is not surprising that our sense of reality, in particular, should be related to originary intuition, since such intuition amounts to the actual 'seeing' – or, correlatively, to the 'self-givenness' – of objects. Indeed, at one point Husserl says that what is given in such an intuition 'is *the reality of what was emptily intended*' (*Int II*, 383). However, although it is unsurprising that self-evident intuition is to play a crucial role here, there may seem to be a certain vacillation in Husserl's writings over exactly what sort of self-evident experience is in question. For in several places – as in the last quotation – he writes as if what is in question is any simple 'seeing' and the certainty that necessarily goes with this. In *Ideas I*, for example, the predicate 'real' is claimed to be the noematic correlate of the sense-certainty that is ingredient in any straightforward perception (*Ideas I*, §103). Elsewhere he writes that 'the givings of things themselves are acts producing self-evident legitimacy or rightness; they are creative *primal institutions of* rightness, of truth as correctness' (*FTL*, 142). In the *Cartesian Meditations*, however, reality is said to be the noematic correlate, not of any self-evident act, but of self-evident *confirmation*. The predicates 'being' and 'non-being', we are told, 'are not given without further ado as phenomenological data when . . . the meant objects as meant are given'; they are, rather, 'intentionalities of a higher level' (92). Our sense of reality, of anything being real, therefore has its source in a certain sort of *synthesis*. As we know, in order to have synthesis, a single object must emerge as what is identically intended in the synthetically unified acts: synthesis essentially embodies a sense of identity. A 'self-evident confirming synthesis' requires, in addition, that one of the acts – a prior one – be 'empty' with respect to the object in question (either as a whole, or with respect to some part or aspect of it), and that one self-evidently present the object itself in the relevant respect. If, for example, I have a hunch that someone is standing behind me, and I turn and see that there is indeed someone there, this is a 'self-evident confirmation': the 'theme' is the same, and there has been a conversion from empty intending to 'bodily presence'. Again, if I inspect the rear side of some material object before me, this too is a self-evident confirmation, since once again the same thing (in this case a mere part of an object) is first intended emptily or presumptively, and is then given with intuitional immediacy. In such experiences of confirmation, in the transition from empty to fulfilled intentions, we *experience* something as *real*. As Husserl says in our present Meditation, 'A synthesis of self-evident confirmation . . . presents rightful or true reality itself' (95). Conversely, a course of experience in which a single thing is our abiding theme can lead to *disconfirmation*. I turn round, but there is nobody there; I move round the object, and see but the back of a shell, not the further parts of the massy body that I had expected. In such negations of initially empty intentions we have experience of the *unreality* of an object in one of the possible modes that this can take. Such conflict, leading to the 'cancellation' of an object, is for Husserl the one ultimate experiential origin of any sense that 'illusion' or 'mere appearance' can have of us: 'Mere appearance means that the course of harmonious experience is other than was prescribed for us by the preceding motivation and experience' (*Int III*, 49). Unreality has its origin for us in disappointment.

As the second of the above examples – the one involving the investigation of the rear side of an object – illustrates, disconfirmation can occur even in relation to perception, where the object in question was initially given 'in person' and with self-evidence. For although self-evidence gives us the thing itself, it does not do so apodictically. And this is because of what it leaves open – because of the merely emptily intended aspects of the object that are actually required if that object is really to be what it appears to be. Self-evidence can therefore conflict with self-evidence. Or, more precisely, what is now self-evident can conflict with what was formerly self-evident (and is still known to have been). In such cases where a perceived physical object is 'cancelled' because of the later course of experience, Husserl speaks of the original perceptual object 'exploding' (e.g., *Ideas I*, §138). Conversely, therefore, when such things do *not* happen, the unfolding course of perception has the character of confirmation. If I see a real vase, and go round and examine its rear side, I am not confirming any details of its originally facing side, of course; I lose that from view. But I *am* confirming that the originally perceived side was indeed a side *of a vase*, or at least of a coherent, three-dimensional material object.

Presumption about unperceived aspects of a material object are ingredient, as we have seen, in perception of the parts of the object that are seen: such a horizon is what gives them the character of *parts* of a *material body*. So when these presumptions are fulfilled in what Husserl calls a 'concordant course of experience', one in harmony with the initial presumptions, this reflects back, in a confirming manner, on the original phase of perception.

What this indicates is that a distinction between the account of reality that is perhaps expressed in *Ideas I* and elsewhere (according to which reality is the correlate of any 'originally giving' perception as such) and that which is to be found in the *Cartesian Meditations* (which sees reality as the noematic correlate of a certain sort of 'higher-order' intentionality) is somewhat artificial, since perceiving something is not a momentary act. Husserl frequently emphasizes the *interest* that is in play within perceptual consciousness as such. Perception 'in the pregnant sense' is, for Husserl, an attentive turning towards an object. And as we saw in Chapter 3, this turning-towards is possible only on the basis of our being passively *affected* and *attracted*. Such an attraction naturally incites an interest in the object, which is expressed in attentive consideration:

> The inception of an act of turning-toward, of paying attention to what exists, puts into play an activity with a tendency, a striving. It is a striving toward realization ... We can say that with this tendency is awakened an *interest* in the object of perception as existent ... [I]n this firm orientation on the object, in the continuity of the experience of the object, there is an intention that goes beyond the given and its momentary mode of givenness and tends toward a progressive *plus ultra*.
>
> (*EJ*, 87 [82])

And as he says a little later in the same work, 'Concrete perception is achieved in the working-out of its progressive striving, its tendency to attain new modes of givenness of the same object' (*EJ*, 93 [87]). So the distinction between perception and confirmation is somewhat artificial because *every phase* of a perception constitutes, in the usual case, a confirmation of the earlier phases. The artificiality of the distinction is made even clearer when we bear in mind that the examples I have so far used to illustrate Husserl's notion of confirmation within a continuing perception, and which have all concerned the inner horizon of an object, do not exhaust the possibilities of such confirmation. *Anything* in *any* horizon prescribed by the 'object-sense' of an experience will be capable of confirmation (or its opposite). This is because a horizon is a set of potentialities essentially prefigured by (experience of) a given type of object, and any such potentiality can be realizingly explored: '*Every actuality involves its potentialities,* which are not empty possibilities, but rather possibilities intentionally predelineated in respect of content . . . and, in addition, having the character of being realizable by the Ego' (81–2). Now, one important set of potentialities in relation to sense-perception are the 'kinaestheses' – and these do not all involve my marching up to an object to inspect it, or circumnavigating it. For it is part of the 'sense' of seeing a material object, rather than, say, a mere after-image, that if I move my head to one side, the object will be exhibited in a different part of my visual field:

> Only when, giving my kinestheses free play, I experience concurrent exhibitings as belonging to it, is the consciousness sustained of the one thing in actual presence, exhibiting itself in manifold fashion as itself. But if I ask myself what is implied in the fact that the thing-exhibitings belong to the altering kinestheses, I recognize that a hidden intentional 'if–then' relation is at work here: the exhibitings must occur in a certain systematic order; it is in this way that they are indicated in advance, in expectation, in the course of a harmonious perception . . . This is, then, the intentional background of every straightforward ontic certainty of a presented thing.
>
> (*Crisis*, 164 [161–2])

So the merest movement of the head while viewing an object, accompanied by the usual exhibition of the object in a correspondingly different part of the visual field, constitutes a confirmation of the reality of that object. For were such a change in experience *not* to occur in concert with the sense of moving one's body in such a way, the belief that one was indeed perceiving a physical, spatially located object would be undermined, and the original physical-thing-perception would 'explode' into the seeing of an after-image or some such non-objective phenomenon. So the fluctuations in Husserl's accounts of the present topic in different writings are wholly understandable. Even in the present text, where he distinguishes more carefully than elsewhere between self-evidence and self-evident confirmation, he can sum up his discussion by saying that it is 'self-evidence alone by virtue of which a really existing, true object, one that legitimately holds good for us, of whatever kind it may be, has sense for us' (95, my emphasis); and he goes on apparently to equate the two notions when he writes that 'every right stems from [self-evidence], . . . every imaginable adequation originates as our confirmation'.

Our notion of reality has a sense only in contrast with a sense of unreality. To believe that something is real is just to rule out all possible forms of deception, illusion, misapprehension, hallucination, and so forth. A subject whose experience of the world never featured any misperception, and who had no sense of the possibility of such misperception, could not have a sense of the reality of the things he or she perceives. Such a subject would be an epistemological naïf. And is not an appreciation of possible disharmony in our experience the only possible basis and content of our grasp of unreality? Confirmation is not some means for merely ascertaining the reality of a thing – something of which we already and independently have an understanding. Rather, confirming experience as such gives us to understand what reality is and means. What other basis could it have? After all, when we perceive a physical object, it is not as though we take what we are presented with as a sign, or other sort of indication, that a physical object is present behind the scenes – so that a concept of unreality might amount to the supposition that such a thing 'in itself' was perhaps not present despite our perceptual experience. Any such idea simply falsifies the phenomenology of perceptual consciousness. (See, e.g., Ideas I, 79.) When we move from considering an object simply as an object to considering it as a real thing, we do not shift our gaze from one type of thing to another, as if the former were merely a representation in consciousness of the latter. What we do, rather, is shift our gaze from what is a correlate of a limited phase of experience to what is a correlate of our experience taken in its totality. Hence, Husserl can say that 'all wrong interpretations of being [by which he surely has transcendental realism primarily in mind] come from naïve blindness to the horizons that join in determining the sense of being, and to the corresponding tasks of uncovering implicit intentionality' (118). Indeed, from where could a supposed object 'behind the scenes' derive its sense, given that all such 'empty' thinking points back to 'self-giving', intuitive experience? 'Where no physical thing is already experienced, even a God cannot hypothetically assume a physical thing', insists Husserl (B IV 6, 53b). Many philosophers have supposed that when we contrast seeing a real thing with merely hallucinating, we are dealing with two different kinds of thing as the objects of the two states: a physical thing in the first case, and something else – a sense-datum, or an array of visual sensations – in the second case. This is just what Husserl denies. If the two are phenomenologically identical, you will be aware of exactly the same kind of object in the two cases. It is just that in the one case the object is real – it really exists – and in the other case it isn't – it doesn't actually exist at all:

> Looking into the stereoscope, we say: this appearing pyramid is 'nothing', is mere 'appearance'. The appearing thing as such is the clear subject of the predication ... Here, as throughout phenomenology, one must have the courage just to accept what is really to be seen in the phenomenon, as it gives itself, and to describe it *honestly*, instead of re-interpreting it.
>
> (*Ideas I*, §108)

That is why, when you raise the question whether this book that you seem to see before you is at all real or not – i.e., raise the question whether you are hallucinating it or not – this question does *not* take the form: Is this (mentally focusing on a certain object) a merely hallucinatory object, or is there some physical thing out there, behind the scenes, causally controlling this visual appearance? It is, rather, one and the same thing that you focus on, and ask whether *it* is real or not. And although the answer to this question is determined by something other than the experience itself, it is not determined by the layout of the furniture in some world 'behind the scenes', but by the character of the rest of your experiencing life, of which it is a part.

At the very beginning of the Third Meditation Husserl states that he will treat the issue of reality and unreality 'under the titles "reason" and "unreason" '. Similarly, the fourth and concluding part of *Ideas I* had been entitled 'Reason and Reality'. Husserl understands the term 'reason' in a way that is influenced by Kant, who had influentially distinguished *reason* from *understanding*. Whereas the latter is concerned with 'judgements', the former is concerned with 'inferences'. Although the idea that reason is a matter of how we *follow things through* in our thinking and experiencing is fundamental for Husserl, he finds the notion of inference too narrow in this connection. Reason is not just concerned with inferences, which play a large but limited role in human life, and are commonly denied to 'irrational' animals: reason 'in a specific sense', as Husserl terms it (112). In a more general sense reason is *'not an accidental de facto ability,* not a title for possible accidental matters of fact, but rather a title for an *all-embracing essential structural form of transcendental subjectivity in general'* (92). For reason not only determines the principles in accordance with which we draw conclusions, revise our judgements in the light of further evidence, confirm our earlier suppositions, and so forth, but is at work in every phase of perceptual experience. 'Following through' is already to be found in the 'continuous synthesis' which is present in any extended perception of something.[2] Reason is, at root, a sensitivity to conflict or disharmony, and hence to accord and harmony. It is, more specifically, being motivated by the desire for such harmony within the domain of intentionality as a whole. For what is the drawing of an inference, but doing what we must in order to avoid a cognitive conflict, either 'logical' or 'inductive', being guided by the desire for cognitive harmony or 'coherence'? Inferences are not merely caused, *qua* mere 'subjective processes', but are *motivated*. They occur as they do, and are what they are, in virtue of the 'meanings' involved, and hence are essentially and primarily about *intentional* relations. But this is what is to be found even at the humble level of perceptual belief, where talk of inference is at best strained. The 'cancellations' and 'explosions' that occur when presumed courses of available perceptions are contradicted are, therefore, exercises or manifestations in our lives of reason in the widest sense. As Husserl says at one point, 'Thanks to self-evidence, the life of consciousness has an *all-pervasive teleological structure*, a pointedness toward "reason" and even a pervasive tendency toward it – that is: toward a discovery of correctness . . . and toward the cancelling of incorrectness' (*FTL*, 143, translation modified).

So, the topic of reality, far from being uncomfortably at home in a transcendental enquiry, is absolutely central to it. For what we have just explored is the fact that horizons are *horizons of validity* (as Husserl himself says in one manuscript: C 13 I, 15). They are horizons of what must *hold good* (or be 'valid': *gelten*) if our initial intentional act is to stand up as what it purports to be. Indeed, Husserl can characterize an object itself as 'a unity of a plurality of validities' (D 12 1, 6a). Given that the 'rightful content' of any act is its fulfilment content, the very notion of sense-explication, so central to phenomenology in its 'static' form, involves a reference to 'validity', to 'holding good', and therefore to reality. Hence, Husserl can explicitly characterize static phenomenology in these very terms: '*The idea of static phenomenology*: the universal structure of the holding-good of the world, the disclosure of the structure of holding-good in reference to the ontological structure of the world itself' (*Int III*, 615).

WORLD

What we have just been exploring is, in fact, but a further aspect of Husserl's rich notion of *world*. In Chapter 3 we saw the importance of habitualities for the constitution of a world. A world, at least with respect to its basic features, must have some degree of familiarity to it. Now, although such habitualities do indeed go towards the constitution of a world, it is the present account of reality that gives us the essential, pared-down core of the Husserlian notion of world. For although Husserl repeatedly stresses that a world is a familiar world, and that anything strange is merely something *un*familiar – i.e., is a 'modality' of familiarity, contrasting with and thereby presupposing it – he would nevertheless not deny that a repeatedly surprising world, even one that was unnervingly so, is thinkable – so long as such surprisingness did not undermine the very possibility of confirming anything at all. Nor would he deny that a very young child, for whom most things are unfamiliar, possesses a world. In fact, if a single 'external' object is real for a subject, that subject has a world in a minimal sense. For even a single such object implicitly contains infinite horizons; and as we have just seen, these horizons are horizons of confirmability. At its simplest, 'world' stands for *the horizonal structure of belief*. For to say that an object has a horizon is to say that it is presented in an essential wider context that is not actually being exhibited in my experience. This wider context, however, is so implicated as being *really there*. Horizons are not mere abstract possibilities of experience: they are *motivated* potentialities, ones I rely on and believe in. For such horizons are indicated by the empty intentions that are ingredient in any perception; and perception, at least in its original form, has the character of certainty. Seeing *is* believing (and so is perception generally), *except* when it is countermanded.[3] In its pristine form, unmodified by what may motivate a withholding of belief, it embodies what Husserl calls the *Urdoxa*: the primary 'position' of *certainty* that we hold in our experiential life. Now, Husserl saw early on that such certainty concerns the 'empty' components of perception. Simply in virtue of seeming to see this book, and having no intelligence to the contrary, you do – you *must* – believe it to be real. But believing *it* to be real – i.e., something of the form 'book', something having at least a certain material bulk and characteristic shape – is to believe that the anticipatory empty intentions that go into such a perceptual experience, that go towards making it an experience of the phenomenological character 'perception of a material thing', will not be contradicted when the horizons predelineated by those intentions are explored and realized: your hand won't go through it when you reach out for it, it will not track your gaze, it will not fail to offer up a hidden side for inspection, and so on and so forth. Moreover, if this book is real, you can avert your gaze from it and explore the environing spatial domain, in principle inexhaustibly. Even if, in so averting your gaze, you were to discover nothing but empty space, you must have a sense of perceptually traversing a *real* space: for otherwise the book would not appear *in* that space – as it must, if it is of the phenomenological type 'material object'. This is what it is for any object to be *in* or *of* a world. Note that in the exploration of an object's horizon, although confirmation and disconfirmation are both open possibilities, it is confirmation that has the upper hand, since an earlier empty intention can be contradicted only by something that you in turn take to be *real* – something which, therefore, has its own presumptive horizon of confirmation.

So, to say, phenomenologically, that there is a world – that a world at least *appears* to us to be there – is to say that experience is not a chaotic mess. It is to say, more particularly, that *confirmations that hold good are possible*. Without experience of and reliance on such confirmations, nothing would have for us the sense 'real' at all; and so there would be no sense of a world at all. Conversely, if anything other than what is 'really inherent' in consciousness itself is real, then there is an existing world. And to *take* any such thing to be real is to have a world-structured flow of experience – i.e., one in which individual experiences have the sense 'confirmation' and 'disconfirmation'. Husserl sometimes speaks in this connection of the world as a 'style' that the flow of experience exhibits: a 'unitary style' in which confirmations and disconfirmations hold good (e.g., *EP II*, 149). In an influential paper to which reference has been made in the Introduction, Ludwig Landgrebe suggested that Husserl discovered the true phenomenological sense of 'world' only in *Erste Philosophie II* – i.e., in the 1920s. In fact, the basic insight is already at least implicit in *Ideas I*, where Husserl presents the epoché, not as in essence the disconnecting of every worldly belief (though it does imply this), but as the disconnection of the 'general thesis of the world'. He already saw that what is to be disconnected is the general reliance on the possibility of confirming (and disconfirming) anything. That is why the only way in which Husserl ever illustrates the 'Cartesian thought' of the unreality of the world is by supposing that experience should degenerate into chaos. For by such chaos Husserl means a situation in which *nothing can be either confirmed or disconfirmed*. Where there are such possibilities, there is a world, at least in a minimal sense. In this sense, therefore, the world is *prior* to any individual real entity, since the assumption of a world is equivalent to reliance on the possibility of confirmation, and this latter is constitutive for perceptual experience in which anything real is *originally given*, thereby acquiring its 'sense'. Although Husserl can occasionally speak of the world in terms of a totality of entities, the fundamental phenomenological sense of 'world' is that of the horizonal structure of experience. And as we now know, horizons are not objects, but structures of experience without which no perceptual object can come to consciousness. The world is the ultimate horizon for any physical object: the horizon of all horizons, as it is sometimes said. We do not come by an appreciation of a world by perceiving this thing, and that thing, and many other things, and then synthesizing them together with indefinitely many other supposed and remembered things into one big thing called a 'world'. Phenomenologically speaking, the world is not a big thing. Indeed, it is not an 'object' at all – except for a reflective, theoretical attitude; and to explicate the world at *that* level would be to bring it in too late, and to miss its phenomenological origin, which is to be found in each individual perceptual experience. What we are primarily directed towards in perception is not some arbitrary set of individual objects, but *the world*, whose sense infuses every perceptual act. So Wittgenstein was wrong in the *Tractatus* – or at least did not penetrate deeply enough. The world is not 'all that is the case'. It is the precondition for anything being the case.

It should be said, however, that in thus distinguishing between a 'rich' notion of a world, grounded on specific habitualities, and a minimal notion of a world as involving nothing more than the possibility of confirmation, we are, once again, dealing with an artificial separation. For one thing, every confirmation itself presupposes some habituality, however minimal, as the ground for the presumption that is to be confirmed. Conversely, every new perception institutes some habituality on which we can rely in the future, and which fills out for us the material character of the world. The world is what you can rely on. I do not, every time I open the front door of my house, look to see that there is solid ground before me, and not a yawning chasm. Reality does not possess its full sense without such an element of stability. If I were convinced of anything's reality only while experiencing it, if I lacked any sense of the continuity of things when I closed my eyes, I should hardly have a sense of the reality of a world at all. My belief in the reality of the town in which I live, for example, would not be possible if I had no sense that I could go out and certify its existence by perceiving it itself. To exclude the possibility of such a thing *in principle* would be tantamount to denying the reality. As Husserl puts it, 'Without such possibilities there would be for us no fixed and abiding being, no ... world' (96). For in the absence of such possibilities, we should have but isolated, particular acts of confirmation, which would offer only an 'accidental being for me' of their objects, not that which exists 'in itself' as an 'abiding being' (*ibid.*). There is, then, but one notion of world, though it can be more or less richly realized in an experiencing life, depending on the genetic level that has been attained.

REALITY AS AN 'IDEA'

We may now have a fairly clear idea how Husserl thinks he can deal with the topic of reality within the transcendental reduction; but surely there is an obvious problem with it. For Husserl effectively equates reality with the noematic correlate of self-evident belief. But such belief can be *mistaken*, even when it arises as a result of a self-evident verification. For such verification amounts to the harmoniousness with which a course of experience unfolds, each subsequent phase of the experience conforming to the presumptive, empty intentions that are ingredient in the earlier phases. But, to take an extreme example, a 'coherent dream', as Husserl puts it, or a coherent hallucination, since it is specified to be coherent, will exhibit such harmoniousness. As a result, we shall attribute reality to the objects that continue to hold good for us during this experiencing, and no doubt do so justifiably; but we are still dealing with only a dream or hallucination. So, in short, is not Husserl simply confusing the 'objective' issue of reality itself with what we *take* to be reality? And could any more be expected from the attempt to address this issue from within such a 'subjective' perspective as the transcendental reduction? Husserl is, in fact, fully alert to this issue, and it is explicitly addressed in §28 of the *Cartesian Meditations*. Because of the necessary 'one-sidedness' of experience of worldly objects, every experience of such an object, even one that is self-evidently confirming in relation to earlier phases of experience, embodies 'contents of mere meaning, which refer us to corresponding potential self-evidences' (96). All such self-evidence is 'imperfect', or incomplete: it does not, and cannot, give us the *entirety* of the object and all that is intentionally implicated in it, however far the experience may be continued:

> This incompleteness of self-evidence becomes more complete in the actualizing synthetic transitions from self-evidence to self-evidence, but necessarily in such a manner that no imaginable synthesis of this kind terminates in an adequate self-evidence: any such synthesis repeatedly carries unfulfilled expectant and accompanying meanings with it. At the same time there always remains the open possibility that the prospective, anticipatory belief in existence will not be fulfilled, that what is appearing in the mode 'it itself' nevertheless does not exist or is different.
>
> (96–7)

The reality of the world, and, hence, of any thing in it, therefore transcends even the totality of my actual consciousness. All my confirmations are merely presumptive of the reality of things – which is why the Cartesian thought of the non-reality of the world, which got all these meditations started, is thinkable at all.

Since we have a sense of what it is for an object of the type 'material thing' to be real only because we have a sense of what it is for one to be unreal – one that itself arises through sense-experience when a harmonious course of experience breaks down – to believe in the reality of some worldly object is to presume that, ultimately, such a breakdown *cannot happen*. Not merely that it will not happen, for I may simply not realize possibilities of disconfirmation that are open to me. (I did not move my head just now; but if I had, I should clearly have seen that that wasn't a shadow, but a mere after-image.) When we thus bear in mind the relevance of *possible* experiences to the question of the reality of any individual worldly object, we find ourselves referred to infinity, to 'infinities of harmoniously combinable experiences' (97). The reality of anything worldly would noematically correspond to nothing short of an absolute, adequate, infinite consciousness of it, one that would embody all possible perceptions of it: ' "Really existent object" can have sense only as a unity meant and meanable in the nexus of consciousness, a unity that would be given as itself in a complete experiential self-evidence', a consciousness that would be 'a complete synthesis of possible experiences' (97). But such a total, all-encompassing experience, one combining all possible appearances at all times, is, of course, impossible – 'even for God', as Husserl sometimes says. And yet we have a concept of reality. The chief purpose of the present meditation is to understand how this is possible, given our situation as just described, and therefore to understand quite what our concept of reality amounts to. Now, the suggestion that with the notion of reality we are referred to an infinity that cannot possibly be encompassed in experience should remind us of something we have met before: an 'idea in the Kantian sense'. So, the reality of anything therefore emerges, in the only form in which it can have any sense for us, as an infinite 'idea'. Indeed, any real object is *itself* such an idea: 'A real object belonging to a world . . . is an infinite idea . . . *an idea that is the correlate of the idea of a perfect experiential self-evidence*, a complete synthesis of possible experiences' (97). For an object, as such, just *is* a unity in the flux of conscious life. Its reality, therefore, is such a unity *ideally holding good*, standing up, proving itself experientially *ad infinitum*. It is a 'holding good' *for me*, of course – as the solitary beginning philosopher – since I am explicating what has sense *for me*. But it is a holding good that outstrips my actual life.

In his numerous discussions of the nature of the infinite possibilities of experience that equate with the reality of a worldly object, Husserl is frequently not as careful as one would wish. In one typical passage, for example, he writes of our grasp of the idea of a real world as being the idea of whatever 'has been confirmed up to now in harmonious experience by the experiencing subject, would have been confirmed in different ways . . . had the subject conducted his life differently, and will also continue to be confirmed whatever the way in which I direct my future experiencing life' (*Int II*, 442). And elsewhere he claims that 'true being', or a 'real existent', is nothing other than 'the correlate of the legitimate, grounded conviction that the "entity", together with its being posited with certainty, will be continually confirmed, and previously could have been confirmed' (*Int II*, 247). It doesn't take much reflection to see that this is inadequate, since an experience may be only *apparently disconfirming* of an earlier presumed reality. For any disconfirming experience has its own horizon: it, too, only putatively indicates a *non-reality*, because something can be recognized as an unreality only in relation to something taken as a disconfirming reality, and the latter entails in its turn possibilities of confirmation. I may, for example, take a second look at some object, and, because of a perceived discordancy, discount its earlier appearance to me as illusory; but perhaps it is this second view that is illusory, and the object really was, and is, as it first appeared. Hence, it is not true that if an object is real, it will be constantly confirmed in experience. Such an object *could* be constantly confirmed, of course, in some *possible* course of experience; but then so could an unreal object, at least in any finite stretch of experience, for an aberrantly experiencing subject – as in the 'coherent dream'. Elsewhere, however, Husserl rejects the need for a uniformly concordant course of experience without setbacks, saying that the 'idea' that corresponds to the reality of an object is rather a matter of 'closer determination: that of the approximation to an ideal limit' (B IV 6, 26b). In this manuscript Husserl gives no further details; but elsewhere he writes that apparently disconfirming experiences, in relation to a real object, are 'the anomalous exception, which is harmoniously included again in a more general regulation of experience, and is included as a possible experiential occurrence belonging harmoniously to . . . the fully developed experience' (A VII 17, 34b).

This is closer to what we need – as is his claim elsewhere that all our experiences 'must be capable of being brought together in a synthetic unity of concordant experience' (B IV 6, 67b). Among Husserl's published works, the following is about the best expression of his considered view: 'Every illusion manifests a deeper truth, and . . . every conflict is, in its place, precisely what is demanded by more inclusive connections for the maintenance of total harmony' (*Ideas I*, 91, translation modified). If my second look at an object is but misleadingly disconfirming of the object's reality, this can only be because it is itself, in its turn, disconfirmable in a wider experience that is concordant with the original acceptance of the reality of the object. Suppose, for example, that some object looks red to me. I go over to take a closer look, and I see it to be black, apparently. I later discover, or can in principle discover, or seem to discover, that a sodium light has been turned on. This latest phase of my perceptual experience not only undermines the perception of the object as black, but harmonizes with and reinforces my original perception of it as red. If all experiences that apparently disconfirm the reality of something are themselves overturned in this way, I must believe that thing to be real. And if all *possible* disconfirming experiences (including mediately disconfirming experiences, inferentially related to the object in question) can be overturned in a way that harmonizes with the reality of the object, then the object *is* real. And, conversely, if an object of my experience is real, it must ultimately withstand 'cancellation' in the totality of possibilities that exist for my experiencing life. It is only experiences related to a *real* object and its *actual* properties that are *guaranteed* to be harmonizable in this way. Illusion ultimately conflicts with illusion. It is only reality that is *guaranteed* to be consistent.

The 'possible experiences' that have been in question throughout this discussion of reality are, of course, not simply 'logically possible' experiences. For just about any kind of experience is logically possible in any context. Such an untrammelled realm of possibilities will afford no constraint on reality at all. The possibilities in question are what Husserl calls 'real possibilities': facts about what would actually happen if . . . As Husserl puts it: 'If a thing exists in reality, there are not merely . . . logical, but real, possibilities [of cognition]; and this has no other sense than that they are motivated possibilities that have their motivation in actual cognizing consciousness' (B IV 6, 98b). During the last minute, for example, I didn't turn my head forty degrees to the right. But if I had, I should have come by a certain experience – one, in all likelihood, that I did not actually have. So the only possible experiences that are in question here are those that I could actually have, and would actually have had, if . . . And what ultimately provide the antecedents of these conditionals – what fill out the 'ifs' – are kinaestheses (see, e.g., D 3, 17). These, it will be recalled, are our experiences of our actively moving our bodies. So the possible experiences that are in question are, more precisely, those that are consequent upon all the possible ways in which we could sense our bodies moving. Kinaestheses, too, can be illusory, of course. So they, too, must be included in the ideal, harmonious experiential totality, and be judged accordingly. So, the idea to which Husserl's various remarks on reality point, but which he never precisely articulated, so far as I am aware, is as follows: A certain object is real, and really has such and such properties, if and only if a statement to that effect is part of the one and only complete physical description of the world that is compatible with all my actual and possible experiences – i.e., with all the experiences I have (including the kinaesthetic ones), and with all the experiences I would have, and have had, as a result of all the kinaestheses that are really possible for me, together with those kinaestheses. For ease of reference, I shall in future refer to this condition as that of the 'ideal harmonization' of my experience with respect to a certain object.[4]

REALITY AND OBJECTIVITY

But, it will be objected, the preceding account of reality is plainly inadequate. For nothing is easier than to conceive that this world I seem to experience is unreal even though my future course of experience continues swimmingly, and even if all factually *possible* courses of my experience should be ultimately harmonizable. All I have to do is to imagine that my whole conscious life is 'out of sync' with everyone else's: that I am, for example, a 'brain in a vat', whose experience is generated by an ideally knowledgeable neuro-surgeon who can anticipate the 'efferent output' of my brain that would in normal circumstances issue in bodily action, and who, being always one step ahead of me, ensures the continuing harmo-niousness of my experience. However harmonious and varied we suppose its experience to be, we shall not find within a single con-sciousness the wherewithal to constitute a real world. A solipsistic consciousness could indeed, if it contains experiences of illusions and other 'cancellations', have a use for a distinction between what is real and what is not. But its judgements on reality need not be *true*. For by a 'real world' we mean something that is intersub-jectively accessible and determinable. Such a world is 'public', as Russell put it. Husserl in fact completely agrees with this. No single subjectivity, whatever the nature of its conscious life, entails the existence of a real world. A real world corresponds to nothing less than a harmony *within consciousness as a whole*. Although phe-nomenology, for obvious and necessary reasons, starts out as 'egology' – as the solitary explication of *my* (or for you, *your*) transcendental ego – phenomenological research leads to the conclusion that no single transcendental life is that *absolute being* in reference to which all truth, sense and reality are to be explicated. This honour goes to *transcendental intersubjectivity*, or the *community of monads*: 'The intrinsically first being, the being that precedes and bears every worldly objectivity, is transcendental intersubjectivity' (182).

This reference to intersubjectivity brings us to the topic to which Husserl will devote the final, and by far the longest, of his medita-tions. As we are now beginning to appreciate, that final discussion of the constitution of 'other egos' is no merely illustrative example of constitutional analysis. Upon its success depends Husserl's account of reality, and, therefore, the viability of transcendental phenomenology as a whole. All of the first four meditations have been working with an *abstraction*: they have ignored the dimen-sion of objectivity, of intersubjectivity, that attaches to all our experience. Astonishing as it may be, the sense that all of us would naturally attach to the notion of a *really existing worldly object* –

namely, one that exists 'objectively' – is one that is not fully addressed in the first four meditations. Only with the dawning of the intersubjective dimension does there occur *'a universal super-addition of sense to my primordinal world,* whereby the latter becomes the appearance *of* a determinate *objective* world' (137). Omitting the intersubjective dimension has been a *crucial* omission. For it is not merely that I believe that the world I experience is also experienced by others, so that phenomenology must take account of this fact. It is, rather, that 'my world is, throughout, a world through others and their experiences etc.' (C 17 II, 30a). When I reflect, the 'superaddition of sense' has always already taken place. Even 'my' world is an essentially objective world, shot through with intersubjective meaning. Within a solipsistic perspective all objects, however harmoniously they are perceived, are but unities that are 'inseparable from my ego and therefore belong to its concreteness itself' (121). A solipsistically constituted world is but 'an "immanent" world' (*Int II*, 8), and its objects, even those legitimately posited as real, have but an 'immanent transcendency' (136). Genuinely worldly entities, however, are not mere unities of *my* possible experience. They are 'alien' to my consciousness, and hence are 'genuinely transcendent' (*Int II*, 442).

This seemingly enormous omission is, however, very simply remedied by appeal to the remaining meditation. For everything that has been said up till now about the relationship between reality and harmonious courses of experience simply needs to be transposed into the intersubjective register. For the alienness of worldly entities is dependent upon the only *ultimately* and *irreducibly* alien, genuinely transcendent type of entity that does or can exist: other transcendental egos. 'Where does pure consciousness that is solipsistic (*my* pure consciousness) transcend itself?' Husserl asks at one point; and the answer comes back, 'Only there where an alien consciousness is posited' (B IV 6, 62a). So, the ideal harmonization of experience that corresponds to a real world is now to be that of the experience of subjectivity *in general,* that of all the egos in the 'inter-monadic community': 'The constitution of the objective world essentially involves a *harmony* of the monads' (138). A real world is that world which alone is compatible with the totality of the experiences that are 'really possible' for the transcendental monadic community in its entirety. Although we have shifted from a solipsistic to an intersubjective perspective, the basic notion of the reality of an object has not changed. It remains an 'idea': that of an infinite, all-sided totality of experience in which the 'positing' of that object ultimately 'holds good'. It is just that it is now the universal totality of experience that we have to bear in mind. According to Husserl, it makes no *sense* to suppose that a world meeting this strong condition of ultimate, intersubjective confirmation should yet be unreal. To attempt to do so would be to try to uproot our notions of reality and unreality from their experiential basis in confirmations and disconfirmations, whence these notions derive all their sense and meaning.

HUSSERL'S IDEALISM

If the preceding account of reality is accepted, idealism is now but around the corner, though Husserl defers explicitly drawing this consequence until the last section of the Fourth Meditation. He there explicitly calls himself a 'transcendental idealist'. Although this is a perfectly reasonable term for him to have adopted – he is, after all, an idealist with a transcendental perspective – it is a potentially misleading label, since the term 'transcendental idealism' is most famously associated with Kant, so that Husserl's appropriation of it can easily be taken as indicating that he agreed with Kant's metaphysical account of the world, according to which, at least as traditionally interpreted, in addition to subjectivity and the 'transcendentally ideal', merely phenomenal world that such subjectivity sustains, there is a realm of 'things in themselves' which affect subjectivity from 'outside' – a view from which Husserl firmly distances himself (118). He goes beyond Kant in his idealism, since there is, for him, nothing 'outside' subjectivity. It may, therefore, be better to call Husserl an 'absolute idealist'. For he subscribed to the following simple, if extreme, idealist claim: *if consciousness did not exist, nothing would.*

I should perhaps say that quite a number of (mostly American) Husserlian scholars have denied that Husserl, even the mature

Husserl, was an idealist. I shall not be considering their more or less ingenious arguments on this score, but allow Husserl's own words to speak for themselves. For I attribute the foregoing extreme idealist view to him not only because all of his relevant writings after the early years of the twentieth century indicate that view, but also because he can himself enunciate it in so many words: 'If consciousness did not exist, not only would knowledge not be possible, but also nature itself would lose all its basis, its root, its *arché*, and thereby would be a nothingness' (B IV 6, 92b). And again: 'If there were no consciousness with appearances, there would also be no [physical] things' (B I 4, 21a). Over and above transcendental subjectivity there is, he says, 'nothing' (C 17 V 2, 88). Husserl can also sum up his position as follows:

> What we want to say is only this: that there is nothing at all other than 'spirits' in the widest sense, if 'there is' is understood in the absolute sense; and that bodies and other physical things exist only . . . as unities of experiential cognition. (B II 2, 17a)

These four passages come from still unpublished manuscripts of Husserl's; but the readily available works are hardly short of 'proof-texts'. We read, for example, that 'actual and possible consciousness, which contains all appearances in itself, thereby exhausts the physical world' (*Int I*, 7). Elsewhere we read that 'absolutely considered, the universe of what exists is a universe of subjectivity' (*Int II*, 278). Yet elsewhere he writes that nature is 'nothing other than "what appears", and what appears is a correlate of appearances, and is as little a something for itself as appearances are things for themselves' (*Int II*, 248). And in *Ideas I*, one of Husserl's most widely read works, we find the following, surely decisive, passage:

> Reality [*Realität*], the reality of the physical thing taken singly and the reality of the whole world, lacks self-sufficiency in virtue of its essence (in our strict sense of the word) . . . Reality is not something absolute which becomes tied secondarily to something else; rather, in the absolute sense, it is nothing at all; it has no 'absolute essence' whatever; it

has the essentiality of something which, of necessity, is *only* intentional, *only an object of consciousness.*

(Ideas I, 93–4).[5]

Hence, 'the existence of nature *cannot* condition the existence of consciousness, since nature itself turns out to be a correlate of consciousness: nature *is* only as being constituted in regular concatenations of consciousness' (*Ideas I*, 96).

Despite the fact that worldly objects are characterized by Husserl in terms of *'Realität'* (in the technical sense of being concretely spatio-temporal), since such objects – even real ones – are but ideal unities, intentional unities, within and for consciousness, their ultimate ontological status is that of 'idealities':

> A certain *ideality* lies in the sense of every experienceable object, including every physical object, over against the manifold 'psychic' processes . . . It is the *universal ideality of all intentional unities* against the *multiplicities* constituting them . . . [T]he *transcendence belonging to the Real [Reales], as such, is a particular form of 'ideality'* or, better, of a *psychic irreality.*

(FTL, 148, translation modified)

Hence, he can say that *'the transcendence of the world* has . . . no metaphysical secret. It is of a different type, but, in the most general terms, is of the same species as the *transcendence of numbers* and other irreal objectivities' (*EP II*, 180). Such idealities presuppose, are dependent upon, the actuality of conscious life: 'The constitution of an objective "Reality" [*Realität*] is the constitution of a certain sort of "ideal" unities, which have, that is to say, an analogy with other (e.g., eidetic) unities that as such presuppose real [*reell*] consciousness with its real contents' (*Int II*, 253). The 'transcendence' of any worldly object is not a transcendence of consciousness as such, but only a transcendence of any finite stretch of consciousness. It is the transcendence belonging to an infinite 'idea': the ideal harmonization of genuinely possible consciousness. I said earlier that, from the objective point of view, the physical objects that were 'real' for a solipsistic consciousness eventually emerge as merely 'immanent' unities of experience. But, on Husserl's final view, even fully real, objective physical objects remain immanent to consciousness. It is just that now they are immanent to consciousness as a whole: 'The objective world does not, in the proper sense, *transcend* that sphere [of inter-monadic subjectivity] or that sphere's own intersubjective essence, but rather inheres in it as an *immanent* transcendency' (137–8).

Physical entities are, therefore, 'transcendentally ideal' (B III 5, 5) – nature 'reduces' to consciousness (B II 2, 12) – for 'consciousness is absolute being, and . . . each [physical] thing is only an indicator of certain connections and motivations in absolute being' (B II 2, 3b–4a). There is no more to the reality of a world than the transcendental life in the community of monads unfolding in a certain harmonious way, since any real world is but the 'intentional correlate' of such intentionally performing life. To each possibly different history of transcendental subjectivity, within the set of those histories that are suitably harmonious, there will correspond a different possible world. The actual world is the one that is ontologically sustained by the actual life of monads. The very idea of anything beyond or distinct from consciousness and its ideal unities of experience is a '*nonsens*'. It is 'contrary to sense', Husserl says, to suppose that consciousness 'needs, or could possibly have, something outside itself, towards which it was directed' (*Int II*, 350). On the contrary, consciousness is 'a complex of *absolute being*, into which nothing can penetrate and out of which nothing can slip, to which nothing is spatiotemporally external and which cannot be within any spatiotemporal complex' (*Ideas I*, 93). There can be no spatio-temporal 'outside' of consciousness because space itself (and time) depend upon consciousness (e.g., B IV 6, 189). In particular, the idea of ' "explaining" any purely immanent data by a hypothetically assumable objective reality, causally connected with them', is 'a consummate absurdity' (*FTL*, 204).[6] It is because of this that any attempt, such as Descartes's, to justify our belief in a real world by relating what is really inherent in consciousness to something outside it, by reference to some causal principle, is nonsensical. It confounds causality (which holds only *within* a world) with constitution and intentional correlation (see, e.g., *FTL*, 223).

A HUSSERLIAN PROOF OF IDEALISM

It should now be fairly clear, I hope, what Husserl's idealism amounts to. But why should we believe any of it? Husserl himself clearly thought that idealism could be demonstrated to be true; but one will be disappointed in trawling through his extensive writings in search of a tidy proof. In one still unpublished manuscript from 1908 he announces a proof, but he indicates in the margin that it is not carried through (B IV 6, 143). (Husserl was not a great *arguer*.) In this section, I shall, therefore, construct a proof on his behalf, marshalling theses from his work that constitute his best case for idealism.

Husserl's idealism is the claim that physical facts and entities *supervene* upon consciousness. 'Supervenience' is a term philosophers use to express the intuitive notion of a certain type of entity or state of affairs being *nothing over and above* the existence of certain other types of entity or state of affairs. To take a simple example: a game of rugby is nothing over and above certain human beings – in a certain context, and with certain intentions – doing certain things with an egg-shaped ball. So rugby games are said to supervene on human activities of a certain sort. Supervenience in general amounts to the holding of three conditions.[7] A certain range of facts, S, supervenes on a range of facts A if and only if:

1 Certain facts of type A – 'relevant' A-type facts, let's call them – entail that certain facts of type S hold;
2 Any fact of type S holds only if some such relevant A-type fact holds;
3 Certain facts of type A – different from those in (1) and (2), hence 'non-relevant' facts – can hold without any relevant A-type facts holding, and therefore, by (2), without any facts of type S holding.

So, to return to our example: (1) if certain human beings are conducting themselves in a certain way, in a certain context, with certain intentions, with an egg-shaped ball, then *ipso facto* a game of rugby is being played. Nothing more is required for a game of rugby than such activity. (2) If a game of rugby is being played, then there must be people occupying their time in this sort of way. You can't have rugby games without people *playing* them. So far, however, we have not captured the idea of *dependence* – ontological dependence – that the idea of supervenience is intended to capture. For, so far, we only have it that there cannot be rugby games without a certain form of human behaviour, nor a certain form of human behaviour without rugby games: a purely symmetrical situation. The crucial element of dependence enters because it is only *a certain form* of human behaviour (and intention, context, etc.) that is relevant to rugby. There are plenty of other sorts of behaviour, intention and context that are irrelevant to the existence of rugby games: walking the dog, meaning to give up smoking, being on stage. And that people behave in a way that is relevant to rugby at all is entirely contingent. Hence, (3), certain types of human behaviour, intention, context, etc. can exist in the absence of any activity relevant to rugby, and hence without any game of rugby being played. Indeed, human behaviour in its totality might not have featured *any* 'rugby-relevant' behaviour; and so, by (2), there would then have been no games of rugby at all. This last condition is the crucial one, since it alone introduces the notion of the dependence of one sort of fact on another. 'Rugby facts' ontologically depend upon behavioural facts, and not conversely, because there can be behavioural facts of some sort without any rugby-facts – but no rugby facts of any sort without some behavioural facts.

Now, no one is going to be particularly excited by the claim that rugby games supervene on human behaviour, intentions, etc., because no one is even tempted to suppose that such games are a matter of anything else. Claims to supervenience are philosophically interesting and challenging when they hold that one sort of thing is 'nothing over and above' what we should all intuitively regard as a quite different sort of thing. This is the move that Husserl makes in relation to physical reality. For he believes that the above relation between human behaviour, intention and context on the one hand, and rugby games on the other is analogous to the relation that holds between experience and physical reality.

Physical facts are 'nothing over and above' experiential facts – facts concerning the occurrence of actual and possible experiences in consciousness as a whole: an initially counter-intuitive, not to say shocking, claim. And so Husserl needs to show that our three conditions for supervenience are met in this area. The first condition – that certain experiential facts entail certain physical facts – is embodied in the analysis of reality that we have already investigated. Inclusion of an object in an ideal harmonization of experience *entails* the reality of that object:

> Let us assume . . . that the pertinent regularities of consciousness are actually maintained, that, in the course of consciousness taken universally, nothing whatever is lacking which is requisite for the appearance of a unitary world and for the rational theoretical cognition of such a world. All that being assumed, we now ask: is it still *conceivable* and not rather a countersense that the corresponding transcendent world *does not exist?*
>
> (*Ideas I*, 92)

There can be no doubt about the rhetorical nature of this question. Husserl later added the following comment to a passage found just a few pages earlier in the same text: 'The physical thing *must* exist if the continuity [of experience] goes on harmoniously ad infinitum' (*Ideas I*, 86, note 229 [in *Appendix 44* of the German edition]). Consider the appearance of this book to you now. If, to take the simplest scenario, no course of your future experience, and no course that your future experience would take, given all the possible ways that you might exercise bodily agency in the future, and no course that your past experience would have taken if your kinaestheses had been different, casts doubt on the veridicality of your current perception, and hence on the present reality of this book; and if these facts chime in with the experiences, actual and possible, of every other conscious being in the universe; then (necessarily) your experience *is* veridical, and this book really does exist. The actual existence of this physical object is entailed by such a harmonious experiential totality. In fact, we have seen that, where physical entities that are *objects* of experience are concerned, the entailment goes both ways. Given that this book is an object of perception for you, necessarily it exists *only if* your present perception of it ideally harmonizes with all the possible courses that your experience may take and might have taken, and with the really possible experiences of all other conscious subjects. Indeed, this condition holds for all physical entities that are but *possible* objects of perception. You didn't turn your head forty degrees to the left just now. But if you had, you would have seen a wasp (let's suppose). Once again, applying the very same account of reality, we conclude that that perception would have been veridical if and only if it had been ultimately concordant with the actual course of experience among the totality of conscious subjects, and with all the courses that their experiences might take and might have taken. As far as objects of actual and possible experience are concerned, reality *equates with* the ideal harmonizability of the experiences in question in the totality of experience that is and was and will be possible.

So much for the first condition for supervenience: a certain form of transcendental life *entails* the existence of certain physical entities – entails that certain physical objects really exist. The second condition has it that *any* physical entity exists, and really has such and such properties, *only if* certain experiential facts hold. Once again, it is the totality of experiences that are really possible for all conscious subjects that is in question. It is at this stage that what we might call Husserl's 'ideal verificationism' comes into play. There is nothing, no possible entity, that is not in principle experienceable: 'What cannot be known cannot exist; existence is knowability' (*Int III*, 370). And again: 'Anything whatever that exists in reality but is not yet actually experienced can, in virtue of its essence, become given' (*Ideas I*, 89). Any worldly entity is indeed 'in itself' in the sense that it can exist if it is not actually perceived; but it is true of any such entity that 'it could have been perceived, or could be perceived' (*Int II*, 453). In short, 'all things are objects of possible perception' (*Int II*, 441). Anything else is, according to Husserl, *unthinkable*.[8] Although an entity radically inaccessible to consciousness is not 'logically impossible', since it involves no 'formal contradiction', it is 'materially countersensical' (*Ideas I*, §48).[9] We have already seen that for Husserl the reality of *possible objects* of experience amounts to the holding of certain experiential facts: namely, their ultimately uncancelled inclusion in a total harmonization of experience. With the present claim that all *entities* are possible objects of experience, that thesis now extends to encompass all such entities. So, not only does ideally harmonizable experience entail the reality of certain physical entities – those that are objects of possible experience – the reality of *every* physical entity entails such ideal harmonization. As earlier with the example of games of rugby, after these first two conditions for supervenience are in place we have a mutual entailment. In the present case it is between physical entities (all of them) and the experience of all monads being ultimately harmonious in a certain determinate fashion. As Husserl put it, 'If A exists, . . . the legitimate cognition of A must be possible. Conversely: if A does not exist, then it is impossible' (B IV 6, 6b).

The third and final condition on supervenience concerns the contingency of physical reality on only a *certain range* of experiential facts. This condition holds, because it is possible that consciousness could flow in such a way that it is *not* ideally harmonizable. The third condition, in other words, is delivered by the possible truth of the 'Cartesian thought' that got all of these meditations under way, though now applied to the totality of experiencing consciousness. If conscious experience were actually such as not to sustain the sort of ideal harmony that, by the first two conditions, is necessary for the existence of any physical entity, no such physical entity would exist: 'The possibility that the world should in truth be nothing signifies an idea: the idea, namely, of a disharmony that proceeds to infinity' (*EP II*, 392). Although in our actual experience we find, and continue to pursue, rational connections, there is no essential necessity here: 'The *rationality* made actual by the fact is not a rationality demanded by the essence' (*Ideas I*, 110). So Husserlian premises deliver all the three conditions necessary to show the supervenience of physical reality upon experiential facts, and hence the falsity of physical realism:

> All objective being and all truth has in transcendental subjectivity the ground for its being . . . Something objective is nothing other than the synthetic unity of actual and potential intentionality, a unity belonging to the proper essence of transcendental subjectivity. . . . This synthetic unity is relative to the universal community of the transcendental egos communicating with me and with one another. That is to say, it is a synthetic unity of the intentionalities belonging to this community as part of its own essence.
>
> (*FTL*, 242, translation modified)

THEORETICAL SCIENCE AND THE LIFE-WORLD

Although, by bringing in the intersubjective perspective, the first premise of the preceding argument for idealism – namely, Husserl's analysis of reality – has gained considerably in plausibility, it may be thought that the second premise – Husserl's ideal verificationism – is highly implausible. Such verificationism is the claim that anything that exists (or, at the very least, anything that exists in our world) is in principle experienceable, and, indeed, experienceable 'originally'. But what about atomic and sub-atomic particles that are simply too small to perceive? Or the centre of the sun – an environment that makes the presence of any perceiver impossible? Or magnetic fields and ultra-sonic sounds – phenomena to which we are not sensorily attuned? Or things located in the inaccessibly distant parts of the universe? These different examples raise different issues; but some of the problems for Husserl that are apparently involved here are at least ameliorated when the fully intersubjective dimension is borne in mind. For in order that something should be in principle experienceable, it is not required that it be experienceable *by me*, nor, indeed, by any other human being. The experienceability-in-principle that is in play in Husserl's philosophy is one that relates to any monad at all in the vast (possibly infinite) totality of transcendental subjectivity – a subjectivity that has objectified itself in many different life-forms, and could possibly objectify itself in countless others. Husserl freely admits that 'obviously there are physical things, and worlds of physical things, which do not admit of being definitely demonstrated in any *human* experience; but that has purely factual grounds which lie within the factual limits of such experience' (*Ideas I*, 91; compare *ibid.*, 84–5). Although, given such limits, it is impossible for us to get to know everything in the world, this only means, insists Husserl, that 'a higher spirit is thinkable, who can, with grounds, cognize what we could not cognize. And that is *no empty possibility.* For we *know* that there is infinitely much there that is unknown' (B IV 6, 72b). Again, in a discussion of a scenario in which we make an inference to the existence of some physical state of affairs that would be imperceptible to any human being, Husserl writes that 'if the unknown cause *existed* at all, it would have to be *essentially* perceivable and experienceable, if not by us then by other Egos who see better and further' (*Ideas I*, 98). To cope with magnetic fields and ultra-sound, we had better add 'other Egos who see (and hear – indeed, generally sense) *differently*'. Moreover, Husserl does not require that there actually now be creatures with such heightened, or differing, powers of perception – only that there could in principle be such. For on several occasions Husserl stresses the contingency of the specific organic forms in which consciousness finds itself embodied (e.g., D 3, 20). So there is an unimaginably large variety of *possible* life-forms that could experience the physical world. There are, to be sure, passages where Husserl says that any physical reality must be experienceable in principle by any and every actual subject (e.g., *Ideas I*, 90; B IV 6, 186). He cannot, however, mean that any such subject, *given its actual embodied state*, could experience any physical state of affairs whatever, but only, I take it, that any such subject could be organically transformed so as to be able to enjoy suitable perceptions. In a couple of passages in which Husserl discusses the possibility of perceiving the interior of the sun, for example, he speaks of the possibility of our bodies altering in such a way that the intense physical stimuli would allow that environment to appear to us (B I 4, 26; B II 2, 15). Similar considerations could also be employed to handle the existence of entities too small for us to see. (One is reminded here of Locke's idea that we could be equipped with 'microscopical eyes'.)

But could any *possible* embodied conscious subject even in principle perceive a photon, or, indeed, the centre of the sun? Husserl himself recognizes the limitations of the previous approach: 'We perfectly well feel that it is a mere construction when we speak of how things may perhaps "appear" on and in the sun under the photosphere; how the colossal temperature may be felt, etc.' (B II 2, 16a–b). And he says of atoms that they cannot show themselves in any possible experience (A VII 17, 11). When we imagine such things, we are, precisely, *imagining* them: engaging in imaginative, 'as-if' constructions that are merely illustrative for theoretical thought. We are dealing here with 'symbolic-analogical representations', with ' "invented" sensations' (B II 2, 15a). Such imaginative constructions are not mere fantasy, of course. They can, in their own way, be confirmed through being related, via some scientific theory, to our actual experience of the world (A VII 17, 7–8). What we must not do, however, is suppose that we could possibly be imagining how things 'really are out there'. For to imagine something is to represent how it would appear; and in a context that renders all appearance impossible, this 'would' fails to get any purchase. But, still, if there really are such things as the centre of the sun, and photons, what has Husserl to say about them? Two remarks of his indicate, I think, his considered position. The first is to the effect that *indirect* experience of certain objects is all that may be required: 'The existence of objects may presuppose the existence of appearances, but the existence of each object does not presuppose an appearance . . . that relates to *this object itself*, in the manner of a perceptual appearance' (B II 2, 11b). The second remark concerns the theoretically motivated, imaginative as-if constructions that we have just been considering. He says of them that they found 'the specific accomplishment of science' (A VII 17, 10b). He goes on to say that we must clarify the motivational relations between such representations and our actual experience of the world, so as to make the activity of theoretical science comprehensible to us. The indirect experiences to which the former remark refers are presumably those that connect our immediate experience of the world with the posits of scientific theory. So, the final test of Husserl's ideal verificationism is the nature of scientific cognition. Although Husserl does not discuss this topic in the *Cartesian Meditations*, he does mention the 'life-world' (165); and the issue we are now considering in fact concerns this crucially important concept of his. For all of the entities and environments that may seem to be in principle unperceivable are, precisely because of their imperceptibility, posited by some kind of *theory*. We need, therefore, to enquire into the sense that accrues to any such theorizing. And it is precisely the life-world that, according to Husserl, contains the source of all meaning for any such theorizing. The assertions of theoretical scientists need to be understood by relating their activity back to the life-world from which it arises and to which it points back in virtue of its very meaning.

Husserl seems first to have employed the term 'life-world' around 1917 in connection with his attempt to set out the relations between the physical sciences and the human sciences (the 'Geisteswissenschaften' as the Germans call them: the sciences of the human 'spirit'). This task is the principal subject of what is now published as *Ideas II*, and the manuscripts where he introduces the term 'life-world' are to be found there (e.g., Supplement XIII). The life-world – and Husserl has the same thing in mind when he speaks of the 'surrounding world' (160) – is 'the spatiotemporal world of things as we experience them in our pre- and extra-scientific life' (*Crisis*, 141 [138]). It is a world not only of sensuously perceivable objects, but of more or less valuable objects, beautiful objects, dangerous objects. It is the world in all its richness as it corresponds to our everyday awareness of and involvement in it. Theoretical science gets to work when we begin to *abstract* from this rich, immediately intuitable domain. In the interests of objectivity the world is stripped of all values and other predicates that relate to our affective lives. Sensuous qualities, such as colour and warmth, are also set aside, since these depend on the subjective constitution of our senses. For we can easily conceive of creatures who can perceive the same physical objects as we do, but who cannot reach any agreement with us about the things' colours, tastes, smells, etc. – or, more radically, who cannot even make sense of our reference to such qualities:

> The senses can also be completely different, provided they make possible a common understanding and constitute a common nature as

an appearing one. But in principle subjects cannot be blind as regards *all* the senses and consequently at once blind to space, to motion, to energy. Otherwise there would be no world of things there for them . . . Nature is an intersubjective reality and a reality not just for me and my companions of the moment but for us and for everyone who can have dealings with us and can come to a mutual understanding with us about things and about other people.

(*Ideas II*, 86)

All we are finally left with, therefore, is a spatio-temporal manifold and causal properties. In addition to such abstraction, the theoretical scientist engages in various *idealizations*. In place of the kind of straightness that we can perceive in, say, a taut string, the physicist will speak of *absolutely* straight lines, as he will of *absolutely* simultaneous events. Finally, the scientist will regard the causal properties of things as being absolutely quantifiable, so that he or she can engage in the manipulation of mathematically precise functional relationships between such properties in his 'laws of nature'. Various 'theoretical entities' are introduced as the bearers of these properties. So the theoretically postulated entities and states of affairs that we have been considering as presenting problems for Husserl's ideal verificationism are not imperceptible simply because they are impossible to get at. They are, rather, defined in such an abstract, idealized way that all talk of perceiving them as they are in themselves lacks any sense whatever.

As we know, Husserl believed that if we are to understand the 'sense' of positive science, we must trace it back and see how it arises as an accomplishment for transcendental subjectivity – since *everything* must be so clarified. He came, however, increasingly to feel the importance of leading us to what we may regard as an intermediate reduction: tracing theoretical science not in one blow all the way back to transcendental life, but initially to ordinary 'natural' life and the everyday world with which it deals. Although not *ultimately* satisfying, because not transcendental, Husserl thought that considerable light could be thrown on the nature of physical science by seeing how it is related to and arises out of our everyday, non-theoretical dealings with the world. For one thing

Husserl never doubted about science is that its ultimate subject-matter is the world of everyday experience: 'The physical thing which [the physicist] observes, with which he experiments, which he continually sees, takes in his hand, puts on the scale or in the melting furnace: that physical thing, and no other, becomes the subject of the predicates ascribed in physics' (*Ideas I*, 100). When physicists speak of electrical resistance, electron shells and so forth, they are not talking about things *other than* the perceivable objects of everyday experience. Rather, they are introducing a novel set of 'determinations', or properties, of the very things we are already familiar with:

> a wealth of causal properties belonging to the same physical thing [as we may perceive] which, as causal properties, make themselves known in phenomenal dependencies of familiar sorts . . . According to all this it is clear that *even the high transcendency characterizing the physical thing as determined by physics does not* signify *reaching out beyond the world which is for consciousness.*
>
> (*ibid.*)

Because of this, the sense that scientific statements possess must, in order to be clarified, be related to the experienced life-world, which is *founding* for the scientific world. To say that the world of everyday experience is founding for the world delineated by theoretical science is not simply to say that we must have the former if the latter is to be a possibility for us; nor is it simply to say that the latter is optional, whereas the former is unavoidable – though both of these things are true. For two other things are also true. First, our construction of scientific theories is parasitic upon everyday experience in such a way that the world as depicted by such theories can have 'existential validity' – i.e., can be rationally posited (and hence, ultimately, can exist) – only if the world of everyday experience has existential validity. Otherwise we should, cognitively, be sawing off the branch on which we are sitting. Second, since the entities referred to by theoretical science can, indeed, never be given in straightforward experience, their *sense* needs to be explicated and grounded in some other way. If such sense is not to be ultimately empty, it must be related to the intuitable, pre-scientific world.

Husserl says two sorts of thing about theoretical science, which may initially appear to be in tension with one another. On the one hand, there are passages in which he seems to relate theoretical constructions to the world of everyday experience in such a way as to amount to a form of *instrumentalism*: the view that the theoretical posits of science have the role simply of helping to deliver predictions about how the everyday world will be experienced, and that their sense and being is exhausted by such an inferential role. He can say, for example, that mathematical physics is a 'garb of ideas thrown over the world of immediate experience', and that scientific realists mistake 'for *true being* what is actually a *method*'; that they make 'a surreptitious substitution of the mathematically substructed world of idealities for the only real world, the one that is actually given through perception, that is ever experienced and experienceable – our everyday life-world'. What is accomplished by such a method, or 'technique', is 'nothing but *prediction* extended to infinity', a matter of 'improving, *in infinitum*, ... those rough predictions which are the only ones originally possible within the sphere of what is actually experienced' (all from *Crisis*, §9h and *EJ*, §10). Or, as he puts it elsewhere, 'The physical thing of the natural sciences has only a formal essence; it has only its *formula*, and for the rest this is its essence, that, according to this formula, it is a regulated intentional unity of an infinite variety of appearances "of all men"' (*Ideas II*, 376).

Even in relation to necessarily imperceptible theoretical entities, Husserl does not abandon his fundamental claim that all sense and meaning is ultimately constituted in self-giving intuition. 'Any consciousness, without exception,' he writes, 'either is itself already characterized as self-evidence (that is, as giving its intentional object itself, originally) or else is convertible into ones which give the object itself' (93). But how, it may be asked, can my thought about photons be possibly so convertible? The solution to this problem resides in recalling that 'intuitive', self-giving acts are not restricted to sense-perceptions. (As we saw in Chapter 3, there are also categorial intuitions and intuitions of essences, for example.) Within the realm of abstract thought there is a vital distinction to be drawn between 'authentic' and 'inauthentic' thinking. All thinking must be related to experience; but this relatedness may be highly theoretically mediated. Where it is, authentic thinking requires an understanding of that mediation. In one of Husserl's latest essays, for example, he investigates the way in which the science of geometry must have arisen out of the life-world (*Crisis*, Appendix 3 [6]). The ancient Greeks who 'instituted' geometry had an insight into the way that the meaning of their geometrical idealizations were rooted in the rough and ready everyday practices of measuring things, comparing shapes and sizes, and so forth. Since that time geometry has become 'sedimented', and has turned into a mere *technique* that we use without an appreciation of its 'original', 'authentic' meaning. The situation with the theoretical entities of physics is similar; and phenomenology must explain how it is that 'the philosophical-scientific striving for autonomy declines into methodically technical operation, how it sinks down into a secondary, blind impulsive activity' (E III 4, 10a–b). It is precisely in appreciating the role of talk about such things as photons in relation to our experimental practices, practices that are always oriented to perceivable events in the 'life-world', that we relate authentically to them. Since they are 'thought-objects', they are not given in sense-perception. They *are* given, however – in what Husserl calls 'insight'. Insight is an intellectual act, involving an exercise of reason (in the *narrow* sense), and is essentially 'the unity of a rational positing with that which essentially motivates the positing' (*Ideas I*, 284, translation modified). A (validly posited) theoretical entity is an '*einsichtige Vernunftsgegebenheit*' – something given to reason with insight (*Ideas I*, 101). What motivate the positing of such a theoretical entity are experimental results, or the legitimate expectation of such:

> The thinking pertaining to physics establishes itself on the foundation laid by natural experiencing (or by natural positings which it effects). Following the *rational motives* presented to it by the concatenations of experience, it is compelled to effect certain modes of conception,

certain intentional constructions required by reason, and to effect them for the *theoretical determination* of sensuously experienced things.

(Ideas I, 100)

Fully to appreciate how the positing of photons is motivated in this sort of way is for photons to be originally given to you. And, consistently with Husserl's general claims about meaningfulness, this is where all sense that 'photon' can have for you is to be located. Husserl of course recognizes that science can lead to the discovery of genuine empirical realities, mentioning the discovery of Neptune as an example. This, however, 'is something essentially different from an explanation in the sense of a determining of experienced physical things in the manner peculiar to physics – an explanation by such physical-scientific means as atoms, ions, and the like' (*Ideas I,* 98). The crucial difference, of course, is that something like Neptune is perceivable in principle. So Husserl would reject any appeal to photons, ions, and the like as an objection to his position; for he would present his opponent with a dilemma. *Either* such things are in principle experienceable (by which he means experienceable by any ego with whom we could possibly be in communication, in some possible embodiment); in which case no problem has been raised for Husserl's position. *Or* such things are not perceivable even in principle; but then talk of them is misconstrued if taken as referring to peculiarly inaccessible entities in our world. For it is sense-perception, with its adumbrations and its functional dependencies of kinaestheses and sensory contents, which fixes the sense that 'physical object' can possibly have for us: 'If anything runs counter to that sense it is countersensical in the strictest signification of the word' (*Ideas I,* 98). When we speak of atoms or photons, we almost ineluctably imagine them as very, very small billiard balls or points of light. If they really are like this, however, then they are in principle perceivable ('if not by us, then . . . '), since imagination, as a 'non-original' mode of experience, essentially points towards possible fulfilment in self-giving intuition. If, on the other hand, such imaginings are entirely out of place, or serve a merely propaedeutic function in relation to theoretical concepts, the latter are but a 'garb of ideas' cast over the life-world in the service of prediction in relation to things experienceable within that life-world.

On the other hand, Husserl repeatedly says that it is the task of theoretical, mathematical science to strive for the *truth* of the physical world – a truth that would be 'truer' than the truths of the life-world. If we are interested in the kind of knowledge that, as we recall from the Introduction, Husserl has above all prized – universally acceptable, justified knowledge – then scientific knowledge beats everyday knowledge hands down. Theoretical science alone gives us a truly objective picture of the world. For one thing, there is not just one life-world, but several – corresponding to the different cultures or 'forms of life' that are not only possible, but actual. In the *Cartesian Meditations* Husserl briefly speaks of the surrounding world that different communities have, and the *restricted* objectivity that attaches to them because of the limited accessibility that is to be had from one to another (160). Elsewhere he is even more explicit: 'We do not share the same life-world with all human beings. Not all human beings "in the world" have in common with us all the objects that make up our life-world' (*PP*, 496). Husserl does emphasize that all such life-worlds will have a common structural core determined by the essence of perceptual experience – on which they are all grounded, of course (160). All such worlds will, for example, contain more or less persistent material objects in an unbounded spatial realm. But even such a common core, since it is an object of experience, will possess various 'secondary qualities' that noematically answer to various sensory features of experience; and all such qualities ultimately fail of objectivity, since, as I have already mentioned, we can easily imagine beings with quite different senses from ourselves:

> Nowhere is there a final truth as the truth of intuition, an intuitive descriptive world that must be the final norm for all thinkable beings . . . No one, no species, can say *a priori* that in their system of experience they have the optimal experience, in which *all* physical properties are represented.
>
> (*Int II*, 134–5)

Hence, the theoretical recognition of what Husserl calls the 'physicalistic thing', stripped of all relative determinations, is *forced* on us in our quest for objective truth:

> When we are thrown into an alien social sphere, that of the Negroes in the Congo, Chinese peasants, etc., we discover that their truths, the facts that are settled for them, generally verified or verifiable, are by no means ours. But if we set up the goal of a truth about the objects which is unconditionally valid for all subjects, . . . then we are on the way to objective science. When we set up this objectivity as a goal (the goal of a 'truth in itself') we make a set of hypotheses through which the pure life-world is surpassed.
>
> (*Crisis* 141–2 [139], translation modified)

Since it is precisely theoretical science that abstracts away from 'subjective', contingent differences between subjects and their life-worlds, Husserl can say that 'speaking generally, the rationality of nature consists in the fact that a mathematical science of nature is possible' (B II 2, 23b). By contrast, he can go as far as to say that the life-world is constituted for us in so far as we 'live passively, in the manner of animals' (*Ideas II*, 99).

So, on the one hand, we have the life-world as 'the only real world', and the world of physics as a 'garb of ideas', a method mistaken for a reality; and on the other hand the world of physics as alone objective and oriented towards reason and 'truth in itself' in relation to nature. Now, it may well be that Husserl's ideas on this matter wavered, or developed; but there is no necessary inconsistency in what he says. There might be if Husserl were any sort of physical realist. For one sort of realist would hold that the empirical, experienced world is absolutely real, and scientific theories but 'useful fictions' for predicting experienceable realities. And another sort of realist would hold that scientific theories alone are in the running for describing the physical world in itself, and the phenomenal world is but an 'appearance' of this genuine reality. For Husserl, however, *only* transcendental monads ultimately exist, and all physical objects – solid chairs as well as energy waves – are but ideal poles of identity in relation to experience. He is thus in a position to recognize *both* scientific and everyday statements as true and as dealing with realities. (See, for example, *Ideas II*, 179–80.) Even if to talk of ions and photons is to manipulate a 'garb of ideas', such ideas may be *true*. The only issue for Husserl is to understand the *sense* in which they are true. For recall that in fashioning their 'constructions', physicists are 'following rational motives', and are doing what is 'required by reason' (*Ideas I*, 100). Hence, given Husserl's account of reality, such entities are *real* – or at least must be deemed such until disconfirmed. I should mention, however, that Husserl can on occasion question the 'idea' of a definitive, objective truth, valid for all subjects, that drives the scientific spirit. Perhaps, he says at one point, the idea of a nature 'in itself' has but a 'relative validity' (*Int II*, 293, note 1) – of the kind found in any particular life-world, rather than a validity that amounts to that world being uniquely singled out by all the possibilities of experience in the monadic totality. 'There is no fixed world for us,' he writes elsewhere, 'though a world other than the world for us, with all its vague subjective and intersubjective horizons, has for us not the least sense' (*Int III*, 212). Indeed, we should not, Husserl counsels, be over-impressed by the universal objectivity and exactness that guides the theoretical scientist:

> The trader in the market has his market-truth. In the relationship in which it stands, is his truth not a good one, and the best that a trader can use? Is it a pseudo-truth, merely because the scientist, involved in a different relativity and judging with other aims and ideas, looks for other truths – with which a great many things can be done, but not the one thing that has to be done in the market? It is high time people got over being dazzled, particularly in philosophy and logic, by the ideal and regulative ideas and methods of the 'exact' sciences – as though the In-itself of such sciences were actually the absolute norm for the being of objects and for truth.
>
> (*FTL*, 245, translation modified)

So, although, as we saw in the Introduction, Husserl allies himself with the original Greek philosophical impetus to reject all mere opinion ('*doxa*') in the quest for true science and fully grounded knowledge ('*epistémé*'), transcendental phenomenology finally emerges as 'a peculiar science . . . , since it concerns the disparaged *doxa*, which now suddenly claims the dignity of a foundation for science, *epistémé*' (*Crisis*, 158 [155–6]).

HUSSERL'S METAPHYSICS

Husserl's metaphysics is a topic seldom broached by commentators. This is not surprising. Husserl's main claim on our attention is as the creator of phenomenology, and phenomenology is, as such, constitutional and genetic analysis, not metaphysics. Nevertheless, that Husserl had a metaphysical picture of the world, one, moreover, that he believed followed from the method of transcendental phenomenology, is unignorable. (The heading of §60 of the *Cartesian Meditations* speaks of the 'metaphysical results' of phenomenological analysis). I shall, therefore, end this chapter with a brief sketch of ultimate reality as Husserl viewed it, since there are still significant aspects of it that we have not yet touched on.

The metaphysics that is closest to Husserl's in the history of philosophy is that of Leibniz, for whom the world ultimately consists only of an infinite number of 'monads' – more or less rudimentary minds – independently living out their lives in harmony with one another thanks to the arrangement of God. It is not for nothing that Husserl calls a transcendental ego together with its concrete transcendental life a 'monad'. In the *Cartesian Meditations* he speaks, indeed, of his 'deliberate suggestions of Leibniz's metaphysics' (176). To be sure, earlier in the text Husserl had rejected the accusation that in the final meditation he escapes solipsism only by 'an unacknowledged metaphysics, a concealed adoption of Leibnizian traditions' (174). According to Husserl himself, however, this accusation fails to stick, not because his own final position fails to be discernibly Leibnizian in character (otherwise, why the 'deliberate suggestions'?), but because his is not simply an 'adopted' metaphysics, but one that 'draws its content purely from phenomenological explication of the transcendental experience laid open by transcendental reduction' (176–7). The Leibnizian metaphysics has, Husserl believes, been *earned* phenomenologically. Indeed, he says elsewhere that 'phenomeno-logy leads to the monadology that Leibniz anticipated with an *aperçu* of genius' (*EP II*, 190). He can also raise as a genuine question whether Leibniz's specific suggestions that there are an infinite number of monads, and that there are infinite hierarchies of monads corresponding to (ultimately: ontologically sustaining) the increasingly basic levels of physical reality all the way down to elementary particles, are correct (*Int III*, 609). The enormous agreement between the two is only underlined by Husserl's one insistent departure from Leibniz: monads 'have windows' (e.g., *Int II*, 260), the windows being those of 'empathy' – the topic of the next and final meditation. In other words, it is not enough to say that a world is constituted thanks to a plurality of monads living out their separate, private lives in a way that is harmoni-ous. For Husserl, monads *communicate* with each other. Although there is ultimately no physical causality of course – since this, indeed anything physical, is merely an ideal correlate of conscious-ness – the ontological sustaining of a physical world presupposes a transcendental 'causality' between monads that are 'directed' towards one another (*Int II*, 266–8). We shall have to await the final meditation to see what such inter-monadic causality precisely amounts to.

So here, in brief, is how things ultimately stand according to Husserl. There is a vast number of subjects of consciousness. Each such subject, as we saw in Chapter 2, is without beginning and without end, and its subjective life is continuous. Indeed, each such subject is, at root, an 'absolute flow' of consciousness, a 'standing-streaming present' in which time itself is constituted, and so is itself 'super-temporal'. There is 'a standing, original liveliness (the primal present, that is not a mode of time), that of the monadic totality. The absolute itself is this primal present; in it "lies" all time and world in every sense' (*Int III*, 668). Hence, it ultimately makes no sense to locate pure consciousness in time:

> A time before all consciousness can only mean a time in which no animal was alive. That has a sense. But a time and no absolute con-sciousness: that has no sense. *Absolute* consciousness is 'before'

objective time, and is the non-temporal ground for the constitution of
infinite time and of a world infinitely stretching out in time.

(*Int I*, 16)

Thanks to the most basic of all processes of passive synthesis, however, absolute consciousness temporalizes itself, so that it is constituted as having a *history*. As we saw in Chapter 2, in the section on
time, this history is indefinitely extended into the past and the
future. No monad is, however, 'awake' throughout this infinite
time. Each monad was initially 'asleep', or 'dull' (*dumpf*), or – bor-
rowing a term from Leibniz – 'involuted' (e.g., B II 2, 14). Typically
it then 'awakes' – which means that it begins to be affected by *hylé* –
and for a finite period begins to live a 'conscious' life in which a
world is constituted, and in which it objectivates itself as a part of
that world. The central aspect of such self-mundanization is that
during this period the monad has a *body*. For the striving that
affection by *hylé* arouses necessarily involves the kinaestheses,
which in any case are required for the constitution of a world of
objects 'over and against' the subject. Husserl can speak, indeed, of
the onset of affection by *hylé* as the *acquisition of a body* on the
part of a monad (B II 2, 14; 16). Because of the way in which
sensory data are tied up with the kinaestheses, 'the constitution of
nature . . . is from the start indissolubly interwoven with the constitution of a body' (C 17 II, 45b). So, to be a perceiver of a world, it
is a phenomenological necessity that one be embodied (e.g., *ST*,
154, 160, 176; *Ideas II*, §18(a); *APS*, 13–15). After this period, the
monad returns to an involuted state – the transition at the transcendental level that corresponds to the death of the organism at
the empirical, constituted level (B IV 6, 16). Although at one point
Husserl says that there is no essential necessity that an originally
sleeping monad should awake – though the possibility of waking is
an *essential* possibility (*Ideas II*, 108) – he elsewhere says that such
monads cannot be permanently in this condition – for then they
would be unknowable, and *nothing* is in principle unknowable (*Int
II*, 157). Indeed, although there is no 'essential necessity' here – i.e.,
one arising from the sheer essence of consciousness – Husserl
eventually came to see a sort of necessity – or at least a non-

contingency – in the teleological development of absolute consciousness. For awake monads are at various stages of development, as determined by the greater or lesser complexity that is to be found in their conscious lives, and by the more or less complex objects that are thereby constituted in them. Not all such monads have reached the level of person that we find among those egos who have been constituted in the world as human beings. Below us there are the non-human animals, who are also 'conscious' in the usual sense, and hence correspond to awake monads – all the way down to jellyfish at least (B IV 6, 44). In fact, on many occasions Husserl correlates the waking of monads, not with the beginning of 'conscious' life, but, more widely, with the beginning of life as such – with the evolution of *organic nature* as a whole (e.g., B II 2, 12). There may also be monads who are developmentally higher than human monads. Husserl discerns here not only a hierarchy, but a *development* from lower to higher levels of consciousness. It is not necessary that at every point there be egos who have reached the level of personhood, but there is a necessary development in monadic life towards that level (*Int II*, 130–6). Sleeping monads are involved in this evolutionary process. For not only is it the case that each monad was initially asleep; there was a time when *all* monads were asleep – a condition of the inter-monadic community corresponding to the time before the emergence of organic life in the world. Absolute consciousness as it exists at the moment has *evolved* from such a totally involuted condition (e.g., B II 2, 14).

The status of the physical world in this period before the emergence of life presents Husserl with something of a problem. For we have every reason to believe that there *was* a physical world before the emergence of animal life, and hence of any life that was 'conscious' in the usual sense. It would be absurd, Husserl firmly holds, to deny the findings of geology. But what, then, are the processes in absolute consciousness that ontologically sustain such a world? Husserl rejects the idea that our past as transcendental monads is just a 'necessary construction' motivated by present experience (B II 2, 11–12). But could the past of the physical world be just such a retrospective construction? He generally rejects this suggestion also, and holds to the view that at all points a physical world requires 'contemporaneous' transcendental constitution on the part of absolute consciousness. At a time before the arising of organic life, however, the totality of transcendental consciousness was 'asleep'. So Husserl concludes that such an early state of the world corresponds to a *regulation of the totality of sleeping monads* (B II 2, 12; 16). Indeed, on one occasion Husserl makes reference to such a thing even in relation to the constitution of the *present* world, saying that this involves 'monads that are awake, and at the same time those that are yet unwoken, being law-governed' (B II 2, 12b). This, however, presents something of a problem, because we have seen in Chapter 2 the sort of wholly monotonous subjective life that Husserl takes such involuted monads to possess. So it is difficult to see how, in some distant geological period, they alone could then have been constituting an actual world. To what 'connections of consciousness' in them could a then-actual physical world 'reduce'? It is this general problem that Husserl is wrestling with in the following passage:

> The existence of subjects, laden with harmonious rules of experience corresponding to the constitution of things, is, according to idealism, equivalent to the existence of things themselves and of the world of things. The constitution of things is only potential. But what sort of potentiality is that? The course of consciousness is not arbitrary, but is predelineated by the existence of nature even when it is not actually constituting (where no actual apperceptions of things have developed). But how, since such a thing as wholly dull consciousness is possible?
>
> (B IV 6, 5a–b)

At one point Husserl says that sleeping monads are in 'instinctive communication' with each other (*Int III*, 609). But that is equally difficult to understand. The problem is not so much that involuted monads, being wholly 'dull', lack any differentiation; for that is not true. Involuted monads possess various 'transcendental dispositions' (B IV 6, 87). This should come as no surprise, since, as we saw in the previous chapter, we awake to the world equipped with a

variety of innate tendencies and dispositions. And different creatures have quite different innate dispositions. I awake to the world
differently disposed from the way a newly born frog is, for
example. As Husserl puts it, 'Each organic being is a "begetter" of
new ones that are immediately (or in a swift development) taken
up to the same level (of clarity) as the parents' (B II 2, 12b). And so
we can recognize a whole range of ways in which sleeping monads
can be differently disposed. Indeed, each sleeping monad *must* be
differently disposed from every other, for otherwise there would be
no way of differentiating them (B IV 6, 15–16). The real problem is,
rather, in understanding what *changes* could take place in sleeping
monads that might be rule-governed. The only possibility I can
think of is that such changes should be in the unexercised 'transcendental dispositions' of the monads. Husserl certainly thinks
that when we die, although we shall fall into an 'absolute sleep', we
shall retain a 'heritage' from our awake life and will *still function* in
some fashion in the monadic totality (*ibid.*) Elsewhere he expresses
himself in a more qualified way, though in a similar vein: although
a 'deceased' monad does not actually 'function' (*fungieren*), it is
'functionally existent' (*funktionell-seiend*). Although in a sense a
'non-being', it is 'a "non-being" . . . that helps make being possible'
(C 17 V 2, 88b). On occasion, when Husserl is closest to espousing
the full monadology of Leibniz, he can identify *all* physical entities
with the bodies of monads – organic bodies with those of awake
monads, inorganic things with the bodies of sleeping monads. On
one occasion, for example, and despite the conflict with the earlier
passage concerning the acquisition of a body, he says that the
nonsense of a physical world without consciousness would be
countered by the thesis

> that every physical thing is, in a certain way, the body of a conscious-
> ness, *even if it be only a dull consciousness*; that the being of nature
> leads back to the being of sheer consciousness, eternal conscious-
> ness, divided into monads and assemblages of monads; and that
> when we speak of a nature without consciousness, it is merely a mat-
> ter of stages of lower consciousness.
>
> (B IV 6, 72b, my emphasis)

At about the time of the writing of the *Cartesian Meditations*, Husserl entertains the picture of less and less complex assemblages of less and less awake monads corresponding to all the levels of nature, 'from humans to animals, to plants, to the lowest life-forms, to the atomic constitution of the new physics' (*Int III*, 609).

One important issue that Husserl never properly addresses, as far as I can tell, is why conscious experience actually takes the course that it does. He repeatedly says that we are here dealing with a brute fact: 'Primal sensibility, sensation, etc., *does not arise out of immanent grounds*, out of psychic tendencies; it is simply there, it emerges' (*Ideas II*, 335). In particular, to focus on one specific aspect of this issue, Husserl never properly answers the question why there are just the actual *hyletic data* that there are and not others. 'Past *hylé* prescribes no essential necessities in the monad for the occurrence of determinate, future *hylé*', he writes. '*Hylé* comes accidentally' (*Int II*, 14). However, for a world to exist of which monads have perceptual experience, there must be a harmony between the sensory experiences of these monads, and hence between their hyletic data – 'a harmony between the collective factical subjects with respect to the irrational content of consciousness, . . . and hence a harmony of factical sensory data' (*Int II*, 290– 1). When we bear in mind, especially, that the harmony in question also governs the *possible* experiences of monads, the idea that which sensory data a monad experiences is simply a brute fact, or a matter of chance, is wholly unacceptable. We need to know what grounds the possibilities of experience that play such an important role in Husserl's account of reality. Otherwise put: we need to know what makes a 'real possibility' more than a merely logical, or 'empty', possibility. On one occasion Husserl explicitly raises the problem:

> The flow of consciousness in a monad. At first a contingent one. It could have proceeded differently. Can we ask why it proceeded just as it did? What *ground* it has? All talk of ground and fathoming leads back to motivational connections in consciousness.
>
> (B II 2, 25a)

But when I suddenly hear a car backfire, that is hardly something that is *motivated* by my previous experience – as Husserl clearly recognizes when he says that *hylé* comes 'accidentally'. Perhaps, however, although the ground for the course of my experience is not to be found within my experience itself, it is to be found within consciousness taken more broadly. For Husserl continues the last quoted passage by referring to 'this teleology'. If he saw the occurrence of sense-experiences as but one feature of the working out of this teleology, then we have a possible answer to our question – for he *does* explicitly and repeatedly state the ground of the teleology that is to be found in the world.

When Husserl speaks of teleology, what he has principally in mind is the evolutionary directedness of nature, one that 'leads from blind physical nature up to psycho-physical nature, where consciousness opens its mental eye, and further up to human nature' (B II 2, 13a) – an evolution that is matched by, because grounded upon, a development in pure consciousness from a state of total involution to one that includes fully conscious, 'spiritual' monads. It is a development towards (or, perhaps better, a development *of*) reason. It is a *teleological* development because there are definite goals towards which the overall process is inwardly directed: 'All absolute being is a stream of teleologically concordant becoming that is directed towards ideal goals' (B I 4, 23b). These goals are 'ideal values', which at one point Husserl sums up in the medieval triad *unum, verum, bonum*: unity, truth, goodness (E III 4, 36). What, however, he most consistently presents as the ultimate value to which reality is directed, and of which all other values are but particular expressions, is *harmony* – complete, unified harmony. He speaks of a 'will to harmony, to unity' that is at work throughout monadic reality (A VI 34, 36b). In relation to spiritual beings like us, this 'will' is fully conscious – '*A spirit* loves completeness, . . . strives to realise it' (B II 2, 26a) – and at this level the teleology takes on a specifically moral accent. For we, as spiritual beings, are directed towards an ultimate spiritual harmony – an 'absolute "state"', a 'realm of absolute harmony' in which each subject is responsible for each, and each shapes each in an 'intersubjective genuineness' (e.g., C 17 V 2, 82–3; E III 3, 6). We must strive to develop a 'higher self' that is fit to be a member of such a community, a self that will be fundamentally motivated not, as are all lower monadic forms of life, by pleasure and the desire to possess, but solely by love – the ultimate source from which all spiritual values flow. For in love alone can we be united, in harmony, with one another (e.g., *Int III*, 406; C 17 V 2, 83; E II 2, 39).

We, however, are at present interested in this teleology in relation to perceptual experiences. Here it manifests itself in the harmoniousness of our experience – a harmoniousness that is necessary for the stable intentional objects of experience that fulfil the striving for satisfying unities that, as we saw in the previous chapter, is fundamental to monadic life. It is because such harmony is not demanded by the *essence* of consciousness as such, that Husserl discerns here a 'wonderful teleology'. So the occurrence of particular sensory experiences is at the very least severely constrained by the teleological nature of reality. He says that 'to every monad there belongs a law-governedness that controls the course of its experiences' (B II 2, 14a). And again: 'From a certain point of time onwards the streams of consciousness developed, in accordance with the law-governedness that controls all of monadic reality, in such a way that differentiated sensations and feelings arose' (B II 2, 14b). Although Husserl frequently characterizes both the development of consciousness towards ever higher levels and the harmony between monads that sustains each stage of this development as a '*Faktum*', a sheer given fact, he will also freely use the language of necessity here: 'Phenomenology must . . . show how transcendental intersubjectivity *can only exist*, first, as constituting a world in a passive constitution through instincts . . . ; how it then *must* "awake" as a result of inner motivation, out of primal predispositions toward reason' (E III 4, 16b, my emphasis). He speaks of each stage of the development of monadic reality being 'prescribed' – a development that is 'possible only in so far as a world is constituted in it as objective, only in so far as an objective biological development takes place' (*Int II*, 271). Again, although it is easy for us to imagine that our course of experience could have been different from what it was, are we here, asks Husserl, not simply engaging in sheer speculation, rather than considering real possibilities concerning what can succeed what in our experience? He does, indeed, speak in this passage of such real possibilities in terms of what can enter consciousness either as what is demanded or as what is *left open* (D 3, 5). But perhaps things are left open only if we focus on a single stream of consciousness. Perhaps when we bear in mind the totally interconnected universe of teleologically ordered monadic life, nothing will be left open, or left to chance. *'If a nature exists, the stream of experiences cannot be arbitrary'* (B IV 6, 16b). Husserl also writes of nature as a 'rule under which all monads ... stand ... Which changes in sensory constitution are possible is prescribed for all eternity' (B II 2, 17a). This must be so, for we should recall that hyletic data correspond to 'psychological' sensations in a 'soul' in the constituted world; and these are causally determined by states of our bodies – which in turn are constituted by intersubjective consciousness in its totality. The non-arbitrariness of experience is entailed by the harmonious interconnection of monads. Still, it is one thing to show that monadic experience cannot be arbitrary; it is quite another to give a reason for precisely that course of experience that has actually unfolded. In other words, we have as yet been given no reason to think that the constraints on monadic experience that Husserl has mentioned are of such a nature as to narrow down all the abstractly possible courses of experience that consciousness might have followed down to just one – the actual one.

In fact, he came increasingly to feel the inadequacy of the contrast between the necessary and the contingent at this level of ultimate reality:

> Do humans and animals exist 'by chance'? The world is as it is. But it is contrary to sense to say 'by chance', for chance comprises a horizon of possibilities, and the chance thing itself signifies one of these possibilities – precisely the one that has actually entered upon the scene. 'Absolute fact': the word 'fact', in virtue of its meaning, is misapplied here ... It is precisely the absolute – which cannot be called 'necessary' either – that is at the basis of all possibilities ... , giving them sense and being.

> (*Int III*, 668–9)

It still remains the case, however, that any necessity that we can find in the flow of absolute consciousness is predicated upon such consciousness being teleologically ordered. And given that a teleological harmony among monads is not demanded by their very essence, such teleology must have a ground – though not one that is to be understood in terms of 'causality', which holds only within the constituted world (*Ideas I*, 111). That ground is God, who is 'not the monadic totality itself, but its indwelling entelechy' (*Int III*, 610). Teleology is 'an ideal value that is realised' (B II 2, 26a); and it is God who is the realizer. The evolution of the monadic community – from sleeping monads to waking ones, from irrational to rational ones, on to ever higher levels of humanity, indeed to 'super-humanity' – is but 'the process of self-realisation of the Godhead' (*Int III*, 610). Indeed, 'All experiential reality and all finite mentality is an objectivation of God, a deployment of divine activity' (B II 2, 27b). This divine activity is 'God's willing-to-be-real [*real*]', a will to realize in the monadic totality his own life of infinite love. Indeed, the flow of divine action *is* absolute consciousness in the form of monads (*ibid.*).

I do not pretend to be able to explain how Husserl thought he could derive all of this from his transcendental phenomenology. And perhaps he himself did not believe that *all* the facets of this grand metaphysical picture of the world – one which will strike most readers as somewhat speculative, not to say baroque, in character – could be so derived. But he certainly did think that phenomenology led to a position with at least the broad outlines of this system. Otherwise he could not have written, as he did, of phenomenology as a 'non-confessional path to God' (E III 10, 14a).

NOTES

1 See the Note on Translations and Citations above (pp. xiv–xvi).
2 Indeed, as we saw in Chapter 3, Husserl sees reason at work in the play of our instinctive drives that are in operation at a deeper, more 'primal' level even than simple sense-perception.
3 I have defended and expanded this view with reference to Husserl at some length in Smith 2001.

4 That there is one and only one total physical description of the world compatible with such an experiential totality is, of course, not self-evident. Perhaps there could be a number of such. That is one issue we shall need to bear in mind in what follows. The issue is in fact addressed by Husserl's recourse to 'ideal verificationism', which we shall be exploring shortly.

5 Some who deny that Husserl was an idealist have claimed that he uses the term 'absolute' only in a highly technical sense that has no metaphysical implications. According to this view, to say that something is not absolute is simply to say that it is given to consciousness in 'adumbrations'. This is not true. Husserl can speak of a thing being absolute 'in the sense that it is what it is whether consciousness in general exists or not' (B IV 6, 81a) .

6 As we saw in the previous chapter, Husserl allows that sensations (though not intentional acts) have physical causes in the body. This is only true, however, of sensations understood as constituted, 'psychological' states within the world. It is not true of monadic *hylé*, which is 'pre-worldly' .

7 My account of supervenience, especially the reference to entailment, is not entirely uncontroversial. For more details and defence, see Smith 1993, §iii.

8 I should perhaps mention that Husserl does, on occasion, admit an *absolute* limit to experienceability. He writes, for example, of 'what is in principle "unrepresentable": the unconscious, death, birth' (A VII 17, 5a).

9 I am not entirely sure what Husserl means by this, but perhaps he had the following in mind. Either we attach some minimal content to this 'object' or we do not. If we do, it has a sense that must be explicable in relation to possible experience. If we do not, then Hegel's point applies: *wholly* indeterminate being is effectively equivalent to non-being – to *nothing*.

5

FIFTH MEDITATION

§§42–62

A cursory glance at this last, and by far the longest, of the *Cartesian Meditations* indicates that Husserl is much preoccupied in these pages with subjects of experience other than himself, the 'solitary, meditating philosopher'. It does not take much attention, however, to discern that this is not yet another essay concerning the 'Problem of Other Minds' as that has been traditionally conceived. One reason for this is that this traditional problem typically takes it for granted that we at least have a conception of the possibility of other 'minds' existing; the only issue is to prove that there actually are any such things around. Husserl's problem is much deeper than this: it is how we can come by so much as even a conception of another subject of consciousness in the first place. As he says, his task is to 'discover in what intentionalities, syntheses, motivations, *the sense* "other ego" becomes fashioned in me' (122, my emphasis). As is usual in Husserl, however, questions of sense and of confirmation are not ultimately separable, so that he is, indeed, also concerned with showing how our belief in the actual existence of others is justified and grounded in our experience. Hence, the passage just quoted continues 'and [how], under the title, harmonious experience of someone else, [the sense "other ego"] becomes verified as existing'. Indeed, the whole meditation is introduced as being concerned to gain 'insight into the explicit and implicit intentionality wherein the alter ego becomes evinced *and verified* in the realm of our transcendental ego' (122, my emphasis). Nevertheless, the fact that Husserl addresses the problem of how the very sense of another subject can become constituted by me at all, and indeed expends much of his effort in wrestling with this question, indicates that he is concerned with a much more ramified and fundamental issue than that of the 'Other Minds Problem'. So our initial concern will be with his account of how another self is even thinkable. Or rather, since all thought is a high-level, founded, cognitive accomplishment, which implicitly refers to first-hand experience, the real question is how another self can be at least putatively *experienced*. How can an object of my experience even so much as appear as another subject, whether veridically or not? Husserl commonly employs the term 'empathy' for this (putative) experiential awareness of another subject. Let us not hesitate over the word itself. Husserl himself expresses reservations about the corresponding German term ('*Einfühlung*'), its very first appearance in these pages being 'so-called "empathy"' (124). And in any case, he is not trying to explain our awareness of others by appeal to empathy: the term is but a label for the accomplishment. So, a substantial part of the present meditation is concerned to explain how empathy is possible as an intentional achievement.

There is, however, far more to this final meditation than this – i.e., than just one more example of 'constitutional analysis' in action, one simply directed to a new type of object. In fact, the ultimate purpose of this meditation is not to analyse the sense 'other subject': that is but one step on the path to the final goal. An indication of this is to be found in a second way in which Husserl's concern differs from that of someone addressing the Other Minds Problem. For Husserl is not principally concerned with *minds* in the traditional sense. Traditionally, such 'minds' are conceived as being the consciousnesses of other human beings, or other sentient animals, and the question is: We see various animal bodies around us, but are they conscious? In other words, such minds, if they exist, would be minds *existing in the world*. Such minds, in other words, would be 'psychological' entities. Husserl makes it quite clear that this is not his primary concern: 'The sense "other subjects" that is in question here cannot as yet be the sense: "objective subjects, subjects existing in a world"' (124). Elsewhere he speaks of 'the *pure* others (who as yet have no worldly sense)' (137). Again, he says that his concern is with 'the transcendental clarification of experiencing "someone alien" – in the sense in which the other has not yet attained the sense "man"' (138). The reason for this is that the ultimate concern of this final meditation is with *objectivity*, or the sense of something – anything – existing in a way that does not reduce to facts concerning *my* consciousness. Other minds themselves clearly transcend my own consciousness in this way, but they are not alone in this. Cultural objects and artefacts, for example, clearly implicate a sense of other conscious subjects. To take something to be a screwdriver, or a concert-hall, is to take it as something fashioned by someone for a purpose – one probably directed at still more others. And in fact the whole world, and everything in it, is laden with this sense of objectivity, as we saw in Chapter 4. The merest physical object presents itself to me with the sense of being perceptible, and hence determinable, by others. '*Thereness-for-everyone*', Husserl says, 'is always co-intended wherever we speak of objective reality' (124). Even after the epoché, it is an *objective* world that I consider within the 'brackets': 'Within the limits of my transcendentally reduced pure conscious life, I experience the world . . . not as (so to speak) my private synthetic formation, but as alien to me, as *intersubjective*' (123). As we saw in the previous chapter, the bulk of Husserl's analyses in the *Cartesian Meditations* abstract from such a sense of objectivity. Now, finally, it is time to make good this shortcoming. That this is indeed the true purpose of this final meditation is made clear by Husserl on its very first page, where he says that he proposes to address a 'grave objection' that any attempt to treat of 'the objective world' from within a transcendental perspective may be thought to face (121). The analysis of the sense 'other ego' is, he later says, but the 'first step' in addressing this objection (138) – though, of course, a crucial one. With the constitution of the sense of other subjects of experience 'there occurs a *universal super-addition of sense to my primordinal world* [i.e., the world abstractively dealt with in the earlier meditations], whereby the latter becomes the appearance *of* a determinate *objective* world, as the identical world for everyone, myself included' (137). Husserl refers to anything that genuinely transcends my own consciousness as *alien* (sometimes translated by Cairns as 'other'). Although 'the intrinsically first alien thing (the first Not-I) is the other I', this notion of what is alien comes to embrace the whole world, for this first alien object 'makes constitutionally possible a new infinite domain of what is alien, an objective nature and a whole objective world' (*ibid.*). It is because this 'superaddition of sense' is the real topic of this final meditation that Husserl would not be content with establishing the existence of at least one conscious subject other than himself – something that would meet the Other Minds Problem as usually conceived. Because of his ultimate interest, Husserl can be satisfied with nothing less than establishing a *community* of other conscious subjects who can together constitute an objective realm. So even the sheer existence of a plurality of other subjects would not meet the task at hand. What Husserl requires is that these subjects should *intercommunicate*, that they should *affect* one another, so as to establish *transcendental intersubjectivity*. More on this later. For the moment it is enough that we have discerned the ultimate purpose of this last meditation as a necessary superaddition to what has preceded.

THE SPHERE OF OWNNESS

One reason for the difficulty that Husserl finds in giving an account of the constitution of other subjects arises from the radicality with which he pursues his philosophical analysis. For it is one that must be given without employing any notion of objectivity at all (since the analysis is itself to be used to explicate this). In particular, Husserl wishes to trace the constitution of others back to what he calls a sphere of *Eigenheit* – of 'ownness' (or of what is 'peculiar' to an ego, as Cairns also renders it). He sets out the problem of intersubjectivity by introducing a 'peculiar kind of epoché', which is distinct from the one we are familiar with because it is effected 'inside the transcendental sphere' (125), rather than serving to induct us into that sphere in the first place. This novel bracketing gives us the 'sphere of ownness'. Now, as a matter of fact, Husserl's employment of this notion of ownness is confusing, if not confused. For, on the one hand, it introduces us to just what we should expect of a constitutional analysis of a form of consciousness that is *founded*. What we should expect is to be given a description of a level of consciousness that is to be founding in relation to the higher, founded level – a description that need make no reference to the higher constituted unities, since the higher level emerges only when the lower level of experience happens to follow a certain synthetically unified course. Consider, as an analogy, the constitution of space: how, that is, we come to be aware of objects as spatially arrayed around us. This, too, is a founded intentional accomplishment. It presupposes that we experience various 'sensory data' and various 'kinaestheses', and these need not necessarily be such that our experience is as of spatially located objects. As we saw in Chapter 3, this would be the case, according to Husserl, if there were not certain specific functional dependencies between these two types of experience. When, for example, I have the kinaesthetic experience as of moving my head to one side with eyes open, my visual data are displaced in a characteristic manner; and as I have the kinaesthetic experience as of moving forward with eyes open, the original visual data come to occupy a greater expanse of my visual field. Only because of such if–then relationships do we take ourselves to see objects as located in a space – i.e., as reachable through self-movement. It is conceivable that such dependencies should be absent. Because of this, talk of visual and kinaesthetic experience does not of itself entail that the subject's experience is of objects arrayed in space. We make spatial perception intelligible to ourselves, as an intentional accomplishment, by showing how it becomes constituted as a result of certain possible, but not necessary, syntheses at this founding level of sensory data and kinaesthesis – a level which, as such, is therefore pre-spatial. Whenever

we are presented with a founded phenomenon, the phenomenological task is adequately carried out only when we dip below the
level of what is uniquely characteristic of the phenomenon in question, and tell our constitutional story. Only then will the phenomenon have been exhibited as an intelligible accomplishment of consciousness. Now, our experience of others, and hence of an objective
realm, is also founded. So 'it must be made understandable how, at
the founded higher level, the sense-bestowing pertaining to transcendency proper, to constitutionally secondary *objective transcendency*, comes about – and does so as an *experience*' (136). We
must, therefore, dip below the level at which anything at all is
taken to be another self, or to be at all objective, and concern ourselves, abstractively, with a level of experience which is capable in
principle of being 'solipsistic' or 'solitary'. We then need to explain
how, at this founding level, certain syntheses are possible that
result in, or motivate, the constitution of all objects that in any way
implicate other subjects. As Husserl says, 'This unitary stratum is
further distinguished by being essentially the founding stratum –
that is to say: I obviously cannot have what is *alien* as experience,
and therefore cannot have the sense "objective world" as an
experiential sense, without having this stratum in actual experience; whereas the reverse is not the case' (127). Without this
'bracketing' of what is alien the question of the constitution of the
other as a possible object of consciousness would simply be begged.
In Husserl's view, no other writer had sufficiently appreciated how
much in our ordinary picture of the world presupposes a notion of
objectivity, and hence an appreciation of an alien subject's perspective on the world. In the next section we shall see how little Husserl
thinks we are really entitled to if we rigorously enforce the solipsistic epoché, and hence how extensive and problematic our constitutional story must be.

When, however, Husserl explicitly defines 'ownness' in the present text, what emerges is a somewhat different notion from the
above. For according to the previous 'solipsistic' bracketing, we
must restrict our attention to modes of consciousness that can in
principle unfold without our having any inkling of even the possibility of there being other subjects. The task is then to specify those

syntheses that can (and, of course, do) happen in relation to such experiences, as a result of which other subjects are constituted for us. When, however, Husserl speaks of the 'sphere of ownness' in the Fifth Meditation, he usually takes it to include *everything* in our conscious life, including all the objects that are constituted therein, *except* for other subjects and whatever presupposes such subjects. The sphere of ownness therefore includes 'the intentionality directed to what is alien' (125) In other words, although the sphere of ownness excludes the noematic side of intentionality directed to others, it includes the noetic side – those forms of synthesizing consciousness in which others are constituted as objects. It includes, as he says elsewhere, 'even the modes of empathy' (*Int III*, 559). This is puzzling, since the noetic and the noematic are absolutely inseparable for Husserl. So the 'restriction' to such a sphere of ownness is no real restriction at all. It poses no challenge to constitutional analysis, since the sought-after forms of synthetic consciousness are *included* in the sphere in question. It is particularly puzzling when Husserl goes on to speak of this level of ownness as *motivating* the constitution of other selves (139), and as forming a 'unitarily coherent stratum' of experience that is founding in relation to our experience of others (127). This is puzzling, since the relation between noesis and noema is never that of founding or of motivation; and a noesis without its noema is not 'unitarily coherent'. So, where the stratum of ownness in this second sense is at issue, it is mistaken of Husserl to say that 'I obviously cannot have what is *alien* as experience ... without having this stratum in actual experience; whereas the reverse is not the case' (127). This is true, rather, of the stratum of solipsistic experience discussed above. The 'reverse' *is* true of any stratum that includes the noetic acts directed to others.

After writing the *Cartesian Meditations*, Husserl recognized that his notion of ownness (or of 'primordiality' – sometimes 'primordinality', as he also calls it) was ambiguous (*Int III*, 51; 635). I shall, therefore, refer to the first notion just discussed as the 'solipsistic' sphere or stratum, and reserve the expression 'sphere of ownness' for the second notion – that which includes the intentional acts directed towards others, but not their objects. For

Husserl does have a use for both these notions. Although the solip-sistic sphere is, given Husserl's general phenomenological approach, the obvious place to start a constitutional investigation of intersubjectivity as a founded accomplishment of consciousness, a sphere of ownness is also relevant to the discussion, since the issue before us is essentially that of how a *foreign sphere of ownness* can be constituted in our experience. Although Husserl can define a sphere of ownness negatively as that which excludes any object that in any way relates to other subjects, and hence to objectivity, he also defines it positively as that which we experience 'originally' (§§46–7). The fundamental contrast here is between *my* experience (and what is inseparable from it), and the irreducibly 'alien' experi-ence of any other self. For example, I can experience only *my own* pain 'originally'; I can enjoy only *my* perceptual experiences 'ori-ginally'. Similarly, only you can stand in this original relationship to your own experiences. That is what makes them *mine* and *yours* respectively. As Husserl says,

> Neither the other Ego himself, nor his subjective processes or his appearances themselves, nor anything else belonging to what is essentially his own, becomes given in our experience originally. If it were, if what belongs to what is essentially the other's ownness were directly accessible, it would be merely a moment of my own essence.
>
> (139)

The essential point, now, is that for certain objects – even objects that exist 'for me' – their constitution involves experiences other than mine. This is true not only of other selves, but of anything that is objective. By contrast, there are certain objects for which only my experiences need be mentioned in the constitutional account. This is true, for example, of everything that is reflectively recognized as 'really inherent' in my conscious life. Equally sig-nificantly, there are certain abstractly specifiable strata of objects available in non-introspective experience for which only my ex-periences need be mentioned. Here are to be found all those objects dealt with in the first four meditations, before the question of objectivity was raised. In this final meditation Husserl makes it clear that those earlier meditations were dealing with an abstraction from the fullness of our experience. Indeed, he can now start referring to what, in those earlier meditations, counted as the world, as but 'a kind of "world"', something that is not a world 'in the natural sense' (129). The first thing to make sense of, in order to remove this abstraction and to account for the constitution of the world in all its fullness and objectivity, is an alien sphere of ownness. We are then impelled to explore the nature of the *interrelatedness* of all the individual spheres of ownness, for the objective world will emerge as what is *jointly* constituted by all subjectivities: 'Transcendental intersubjectivity has an intersubjective sphere of ownness in which it intersubjectively constitutes the objective world' (137). In fact, even without being thus led by the sense of what it is for something to be objective, Husserl regards it as obvious that to 'apperceive' an object as a person, or indeed as a non-human animal (at least of the higher sort), is to apperceive it as a centre of consciousness distinct from mine. To take something other than oneself to be a sentient subject is to take there to be a '*there too*' (139).

THE BODY

We become aware of other subjects by perceiving their bodies. Indeed, as we shall soon see, the fundamental recognition of another subject just is the recognition of something *as a body*. In this connection Husserl employs the handy distinction that exists in German between '*Leib*' and '*Körper*'. The former, which I shall render simply as 'body', refers to an animate, living (or, as it is often put, 'lived') body. It is usually rendered as 'organism' by Cairns. The latter, by contrast, refers to any 'material body' in the philosophical sense. I shall render it as 'material body' or 'material thing'. (It is often simply 'body' in Cairns.) The central problem of the Fifth Meditation is that of explaining how any material thing, constitutable within solipsistic experience, could come to be perceived *as a body*, and as an *alien* body. That deep problems lurk here soon becomes evident when one reflects on how such a thing as a body is originally constituted in one's experience. For the first, the original, body is *one's own*, and its constitution is quite different from that of any mere material object.

There are three dimensions to the original constitution of our bodies, all of which are lacking in any other object of possible awareness. First, my body is the 'null centre' of my orientation towards the world. My body is how I am where I am; it constitutes my 'here'. And this location is constituted, not by my placing myself within some objective map of the world, but by virtue of its being the place *from where I perceive the world*. Any other worldly object is (necessarily) perceived as more or less near or far, as up to the left or down to the right, and so on; and all such positions are egocentrically specified. This first dimension of the constitution of the body is, in a sense, perceptual; it is not, however, the constitution of any perceptual *object*, but rather of a perceptual *origin*. Second, my body is what I can move 'without further ado'; it is that by and with which I move any other object. Once again, I do not originally appreciate this movement perceptually, through observation, but as a result of kinaesthesia. I have a primitive sense of an 'I can', the exercise of which is accompanied by my feeling my body, or a part of it, move, and sensing that I have moved it. Third, the body is the locus of feelings. My body is not only the locus of 'emotional' feelings and 'bodily' sensations, it is a *sensitive* body: when I am touched, I typically feel it. An awareness of my body in these three ways is primary and is presupposed by any 'external' perception of it (e.g., *Int II*, 61). It is only in virtue of such an awareness that anything I might perceive externally – catching sight of my hand, for example – could possibly count as a part of *me*, or of my body. And I can, of course, have no such awareness of anything else in the world: 'In this nature and this world my body is the only material thing that is or can be constituted originally as a body (a functioning organ)' (140). Husserl refers to this intimate and original relation between myself and my body in terms of the ego 'governing' or 'holding sway' in the body. The first task of the Fifth Meditation is to explain how *another* body can be constituted in my experience: hence, how I can perceive an external material object as sensitive, as active, and as the null-centre of perspectives on the world. This ultimately involves the question of how I can recognize another body *as something that is originally constituted in an alien sphere of ownness* in the way in which my own body is constituted for me within my sphere of ownness.

Husserl claims that taking an external material thing to be a body is founded upon a perceived *likeness* between that thing and my own body. It is such a likeness that motivates a 'transfer of sense' from my own body to the external thing, whereby the latter is apperceived as a living body. There is an 'analogizing apprehension whereby a material thing in my primordinal sphere, being similar to my own body, becomes apprehended likewise as a body' (141). The likeness that is in question here must, of course, be a physical likeness, one that is recognizable at the solipsistic level 'before' other living bodies have been constituted. Now, a problem arises here, because Husserl's description of our original relation to our own bodies was entirely 'from the inside': no mention was made of our *perceiving* our bodies as external objects. Indeed, no mention was made of the materiality of our bodies at all. It is, however, of course necessary that our bodies should be taken by us to have such a material nature, and one which is similar to certain external material objects, if the transfer of the sense 'body' from ourselves to others is to be effected by a perceived similarity. Hence, in one of his last manuscripts on this topic, Husserl writes of 'the apperception of my body as a material thing as the first presupposition of empathy' (*Int III*, 660).

Although the relation of 'holding sway' is what is fundamental about our relation to our bodies, it may be thought to be hardly problematic that our bodies can be taken within solipsistic experience as having a physical nature of sorts. We can, after all, simply *see* our own hands, for example, and touch them, and observe them moving in space, and even observe them being mechanically moved by external physical objects. There is a serious worry for Husserl, however, over how far a solipsistic constitution of our own bodies as material objects can go, and in particular whether it can go far enough to sustain a perception of likeness between our own body and any external material object. For the kind of world that he has been describing in the previous four solipsistic meditations has a restricted nature that we have even yet not fully appreciated. It is easy to suppose, when reading those meditations, that the world Husserl is explicating is just like the world of everyday experience – only minus other streams of consciousness. The problem, however, is in determining how much of this familiar world is lost if any alien perspective on it is excluded. For example, we all have a picture of ourselves as being, or having, a typical human body: a material thing in space, and to that extent at least similar to any other material thing. But would this picture of ourselves as having a characteristic three-dimensional shape and as moving about in a homogeneous space be available in a solipsistic world? Perhaps it would; but the constitutional story needs to be told, and Husserl devotes page after page of his manuscripts to wrestling with this issue. Here are two problems that particularly worried him. A material thing is constituted in perceptual experience that gives many-sided views of the object. By contrast, my own body is but imperfectly constituted through external perception. I cannot, for example, see my eyes or the middle of my back. I can touch them of course; but in contrast to the situation involving standard material objects, here I cannot see what it is that I am touching. It would be to little point to bring in the possibility of seeing oneself in a mirror, or a pond: not only because such things are clearly unnecessary for the everyday conception that we have of ourselves, but also because recognizing ourselves in a reflection is an intentional accomplishment that itself involves empathy, as Husserl himself points out (*Ideas II*, 148; *Int II*, 509). The second problem concerns the radically different ways in which we experience the movement of our own body through space on the one hand, and that of any other material thing on the other. We cannot, for example, see our own body disappearing into the distance. If the very conception of ourselves as coherent three-dimensional objects that can move through space like any other material object is problematic in the solipsistic sphere, then so will be the possibility of the recognition of any similarity between my own body and that of anyone else – for the latter certainly *is* constituted in my experience as having a spatio-material nature like any other physical thing.

There are certain texts in which Husserl suggests that my own body cannot be sufficiently 'physicalized' in solipsistic experience to stand on a par with any other sort of worldly object, and that one function of other subjects is precisely to effect this physicalization – by virtue of these others being apperceived as having an entirely external perspective on me. Were this the case, however, Husserl's account of empathy as we have it in the present meditation could not get off the ground, for the theory as a whole would involve a vicious circle: awareness of others and their perspectives on the world presupposing recognition by me of a physical likeness between my body and theirs, and recognition of myself as physically like them presupposing their external perspective on me. Fortunately, Husserl elsewhere expresses optimism that such problems can be resolved – that, within the solipsistic sphere, I *can* come by a conception of my own body as possessing a physical stratum that it shares with merely material things. And in the present text he simply assumes this optimistic view, saying that 'my material body can be, and is, apprehended as a natural material body existing and movable in space like any other' (146). Or, as he puts it later, a certain 'self-objectivation' (what I have been calling a self-physicalization) of a transcendental monad takes place within its solipsistic sphere, 'the different levels of which are essential necessities, if others are possibly to exist for the monad' (159).[1]

EMPATHY

Assuming that you have managed to appreciate your own body as having a material, spatial nature like 'external' material things generally, it is possible that such an external thing should appear *like* your own body, materially conceived, in a way that goes beyond merely sharing a material nature. It is possible, in other words, that you should perceive a *specific* material likeness between some external thing and your own body. It is such a perceived similarity, according to Husserl, which serves as 'the motivational basis for the *analogizing* apprehension of [a material thing] *as another body*' (140). He refers to a perceived similarity between simultaneously perceived objects in general as a 'pairing', which is one of the most primitive forms of passive synthesis. If two things are perceived as similar, then they are *associated* for us. As associated, they form a certain phenomenological unity, which we call 'a pair' of things. If there are more than two objects involved, they form what we call 'a group'. What is of particular importance to Husserl is what such phenomenal pairing gives rise to genetically: namely, a certain 'intentional overreaching . . . , a living mutual awakening and an overlay of each with the object-sense of the other' (142). To take an example, suppose I see a durian for the first time. On investigating it, I perceive it to have a peculiar smell. Then another durian, visually similar to the first, presents itself. I will immediately take this second one to have that distinct smell. That which, over and above its visual appearance, was constituted as part of the 'object-sense' pertaining to the first durian – its smell – will be transferred to the second. If I have not tasted the first fruit, but do taste the second, an 'apperceptive transfer' will occur in the reverse direction. 'Intentional overreaching' is, hence, bidirectional. Whatever intellectualist scruples one might have about such an operation, this is, as Hume stressed, how our minds work. However, such a genesis is not for Husserl, as it was for Hume, a matter of mere psychological law, but of intentional, indeed eidetic, necessity. There is an intrinsic intelligibility about this operation, which needs no further explanation. It is not a matter of mere psychological causation, but of meaningful appurtenance. Applied to the case of others' bodies, the suggestion is that when I perceive a material object as similar to my own body, materially conceived, the sense that pertains to my body over and above its physical appearance – being a sensitive organ that is the null-centre of perceptual orientation and action – will be transferred to the similar material thing, which will thereby be apperceived as a *body*.

This is not the end of the story, however. For even if I have a sense of my physical appearance, there is yet a marked dissimilarity between my own body and any other material thing that I might outwardly perceive, however physically similar to my body it may intrinsically be. For the latter is necessarily always more or less *over there*, while I am constantly *here*. The actual appearances of the two are therefore at any time considerably different. Because of this, Husserl says that a suitably fashioned external material body is not immediately grasped as similar to 'the manner of appearance actually belonging at the time to my body (in the mode *here*); rather it awakens reproductively a similar appearance included in the system of my body as a material thing in space' (147). This 'system' is everything I have come to associate essentially with my own body: not only what is involved in my 'holding sway', and what I have at any time perceived of my body, but also all the representations ('presentifications') I can have of my body as a material object locatable anywhere in space. One of the elements in this system is how I would outwardly appear *if I were over there* where I perceive some bodily-shaped material thing. Husserl in fact expends considerable effort in his manuscripts making sense of this counterfactual, and in particular answering the objection that if I were over there, the appearance of my body would be just as it is now – for I would have taken my 'null-centre' with me. We need not spend time over this worry, however, since it is but one aspect of the general problem of 'self-physicalization' within the primordial sphere, which we are, following the present meditation, treating as soluble. So, what perceiving a suitably shaped material object 'awakens' is 'the way my body would look *if I were there*' (147). This is the relevant 'appearance included in the system of my body'. So it is this outward presentification of myself that is 'paired' with the suitably shaped material thing that I am perceiving over there. This initial pairing then allows an associative synthesis to pass through the rest of the 'system' of my own body, and thus to connect with my 'holding sway'. As a result, this latter is apperceptively transferred to the appearing material thing, which is therefore constituted as a body – i.e., as a locus in which a self is holding sway.

I shall shortly return to the motivation involved in this 'apperceptive transfer'; but for the moment let us get a little clearer on what precisely it effects. As we know, the ultimate effect of empathy is that universal superaddition of sense whereby my primordial 'world' becomes a truly objective world that transcends my sphere of ownness. The *first* objective item to be constituted by me is, however, the other's body, 'which is, so to speak, the intrinsically first objective thing [*Objekt*], just as the alien man is constitutionally the intrinsically first man' (153).[2] This is so because the other's body is the first thing that essentially involves two different 'perspectives', in that it is essentially constituted in two spheres of ownness. For the other's body is originally constituted in my sphere of ownness as a certain material thing. To apperceive that very thing as a body, however, is to take it as being *originally* constituted as a body in an *alien* sphere of ownness. For recall that my body receives its sense 'body' as a result of my 'holding sway' in it: I immediately feel it, move it and perceive the world from it as origin. That is what it *means* to be a body. So if I take a certain perceived material thing to be a body, that can only be because I take it that it is inwardly constituted in this very way in some other consciousness: 'If [a certain material body] functions appresentatively, then, in union with it, the *Other* becomes an object of my consciousness – and primarily with his body, as given to him in the manner of appearance pertaining to his *absolute here*' (150). That the consciousness which thus holds sway must be an alien one, and not my own, is determined by the fact, recently mentioned, that the other's eventual body, originally perceived by me as a certain material object, is not immediately paired with my own body as it now is, but with a certain *presentification* of my body: namely, as it would appear if it were over there but seen from here. It is because of this that the transfer of sense resulting from this pairing does not result in my apperceiving some external object as a *second* body of mine. For this pairing leads me to invest a material thing with experiences of a body and perspectives on the world that I would have *if I were there*. Since I am necessarily not anywhere but 'here', these experiences and perspectives must be different from and incompatible with mine: 'My own ego however, the ego given in constant self-perception, is actual now with the present content belonging to its Here. Therefore an ego is appresented as other than mine. That which is primordinally incompatible, in simultaneous co-existence, becomes compatible' (148). Since one and the same thing – the other's body – thus receives a *double* constitution, an *intersubjective* constitution, it transcends any single sphere of ownness, and has attained the status of an objective entity.

The other ego and his experiences are not, of course, *originally presented* to me, since they are alien to my sphere of ownness. Technically they are 'presentified'. So the analogizing transfer of sense consequent upon pairing involves one presentation and two presentifications, and one of the latter fuses with the presentation to constitute an appresentation or apperception. The presentation is of the other's body as a material thing in my sphere of ownness. One presentification is of my own objectivated body as it would appear if seen where the presented material object is. This presentification is awakened because of the similarity of the material object to this presentified 'view' of myself. Because these two are similar, a pairing takes place, which, running through the whole 'system' of my body, leads me finally to presentify another ego as governing in the presented material object – which latter therefore acquires the sense 'alien body'. This last presentification is but an instance of that apperceptive transfer of sense that is consequent upon any pairing; and so, as apperceptive, it is, unlike the former presentification, fused with the presentation of the material object:

> Appresentation as such presupposes a core of presentation. It is a presentification combined by association with presentation, with perception proper, but a presentification that is fused with the latter in the particular function of 'co-perception'. In other words, the two are so fused that they stand within the functional community of *one* perception, which simultaneously presents and appresents, and yet furnishes for the total a consciousness of its being itself there.

(150)

It is important, therefore, that the other is from the first *perceived* as a governing, embodied ego. We are not dealing here with any mere inference (141), and the material body which appresents the other's ego is no mere 'indication' of an alien subjectivity (151). Every perception, after all, involves some apperceptive 'surplus' over and above what is properly exhibited in consciousness. To take the simplest case: when I perceive a material object, only one side is properly seen, one which appresents other sides that are not currently visible (141). Similarly, in the present case, a certain type of perceived material object appresents another ego. The only difference in the present case is that, whereas the merely appresented sides of a perceived physical object can in principle become presented, through perceptual exploration, this is impossible in relation to the appresented ego of the other, which necessarily falls outside my sphere of ownness. Alien egos can only ever be at best presentified. But this is how it should be, of course; for we are here dealing with the radically new level of intentionality that relates to what is alien.

INTERSUBJECTIVITY

So far we have been concerned with the constitution of the mere sense of another ego. The question of the actual *existence* of such egos – or, equivalently for Husserl, the question of the confirmation of this sense in experience – has not yet been broached. And Husserl recognizes that there may well be felt to be a difficulty here. After all, since I am in principle denied any immediate, original access to the conscious life of another, why must not any alien apperceptions I may engage in 'be annulled forthwith' (143)? This problem is related to another limitation of the account so far given: namely, that the object of empathy has so far emerged as nothing more than an undifferentiated alien consciousness as such. In contrast to this, 'the first determinate content obviously must be formed by the understanding of the other's bodiliness and his specifically bodily conduct: the understanding of the members as hands groping or functioning in pushing, as feet functioning in walking, as eyes functioning in seeing, and so forth' (148). All of this is comprehensible to me, however, because the other is an 'intentional modification' (144) of my own self: all of this is governed by the apperceptive transfer 'as I would be functioning if I appeared over there moving thus'. It is precisely such *behaviour* which allows the existence of another to be confirmed or disconfirmed in our experience, for such behaviour may be harmonious or not: 'The experienced alien body continues to prove itself as really a body solely in its changing but incessantly harmonious *behaviour* ... The body becomes experienced as a pseudo-body precisely if there is something discordant about its behaviour' (144). Such harmoniousness, here as elsewhere, is a matter of certain empty intentions – specifically anticipations – being fulfilled. To be sure, there is in the present case a certain mediateness of confirmation, since the subjective life of another is never given 'originally' to us. As Husserl points out, however, this is a situation not without parallel. For we are in the same situation in relation to the past phases of our own stream of consciousness. I can never confirm that my experiential past was really as I recollectively take it to have been by *reliving* that past. Here, too, we are limited to a harmoniousness of mere presentifications – specifically, in this case, of memories.

I shall not discuss how, on the empathic basis already established, contents belonging to the 'higher psychic sphere' of the other (149), as well as higher-order 'spiritual', cultural products, may be constituted – if only because Husserl himself spends little time on such issues in these pages. It is more important for us, given the overall purpose of this final meditation, to understand how an objective world can be constituted at all. In order to understand this, we need to see how a *community* of egos can be established – for 'the first community' is 'in the form of a common world' (150). We have already noted where objectivity begins: with the body of the other, 'the intrinsically first objective thing'. What we need to understand now is how this first alien object can transmute my primordial world into an alien world – one that does not supervene on my consciousness alone, or, as Husserl usually puts it, one that is not 'inseparable' from me. Before that, however, we need to become a little clearer about what exactly is involved in the objectivity of this first alien body. What is fundamental here is a certain *identity*. The result of the apperceptive transfer of sense consequent upon pairing is not just the sense of some alien ego or other, but of such an ego *over there holding sway in that body*. What is required for objectivity to arise is that the material thing that is the eventual body of the other, constituted in my primordial world, should acquire the sense of being *the very same as* a living body constituted in another ego's primordial world. The other's sphere of ownness and mine will then *intentionally intersect* at this common, and therefore objective, point. The problem of objectivity therefore effectively boils down to the challenge to answer the following question: 'How can it at all come about that the material body belonging to my original sphere and the material body constituted, after all, quite separately in the other ego *become identified* and are called the identical body of someone else?' (150, my emphasis). And what is central to securing the needed identity here is, as we have seen, that the accomplishment in question is a perception – an act that involves the uniting of what is presented and of what is appresented in a single object. In the present case, the appresented alien ego is fused with a presented bodily shaped thing in the unity of a single perceptual object. What is important now is that this alien ego is not fused with the appearing material thing as a mere 'annex', but is apperceived by me *as governing* that material body: the other's material body 'appresents *first of all* the other Ego's *governing* in this material thing over there' (151, my emphasis). This means, of course, that the other ego is appresented *as constituting a lived body for itself*. But, simply in virtue of the appearing material body appresenting a governing ego, it is constituted *for me* as a body. So one and the same thing is constituted by *both* of us as a body. If empathy in this way supplements an experience of a material body, 'I have appresentationally, and as coinciding synthetically with the presentational stratum, the *same body* as it is given to the other Ego himself' (153, my emphasis). Although the two primordial spheres of ownness are necessarily separate as noetic and hyletic streams of consciousness, there can be an intentional, noematic identity – which is to say, an intersubjective co-constitution. The universal 'superaddition of sense' whereby my primordial 'world' becomes a genuine, objective world is a matter of such possible intentional identities being omnipresent.

Although Husserl speaks of the other's body as the first – and hence, so far, the only – objective entity, the 'superaddition' of the sense of objectivity cannot stop here. For the other is not only apperceived as feeling and moving his body, but also as perceiving his environment from his own null-point of orientation. The

other's material body 'appresents first of all the other Ego's governing in that material object over there, and mediately his governing
in the *nature* that appears to him perceptually – identically the
nature to which the material object over there belongs, identically
the nature that is my primordinal nature' (151–2). In short, as a
result of the other's 'insertion' into my world I perceive the other
as perceiving (or, at the very least, as being able to perceive) the
very things that I perceive. So, throughout the world, we have
possible intentional intersections between my sphere of ownness
and another's. Every object perceivable by me is open to alien perspectives that I, given my actual situation, cannot have. In this way
the alienness of the other at one stroke transforms my 'world' into
a truly objective world. Or, more precisely, my former 'world' now
acquires the sense of being but one perspective on, one possibly
distorted appearance of, the one common world. Furthermore, I
myself acquire a superaddition of sense whereby I, indeed my very
consciousness, become *part* of that world: I become a 'psychological' and 'psycho-physical' subject. Although within my solipsistic sphere I can constitute myself as partly 'physicalized' – since
this means merely that I can appreciate that my body has a
material stratum to it, and is to that extent comparable with any
mere material thing – what the other achieves is that I am *mundan-
ized*. I am thrown into a world by glimpsing the other. The other
ejects me from 'my' world. I am now equalized with any other
possible subject and hold no privileged position as regards the
constitution of reality – undergoing what Husserl calls an 'objectivating equalization of my existence with that of all others' (158).

Husserl's account of intersubjectivity closes with explicitly
metaphysical conclusions. What now, at the conclusion of this
work, emerges as absolute reality is not my transcendental ego, but
transcendental intersubjectivity. This is, concretely, 'an open
community of monads' (158), and it is this that constitutes the
objective, only truly real, world. The notion of a *community* is of
the utmost importance to Husserl, and he stresses it repeatedly in
these pages. Although he freely admits that his metaphysical
scheme of things is strikingly close to Leibniz's monadology,
Husserl points out that his monads, unlike Leibniz's, have

windows – 'windows of empathy' that allow monads 'to receive alien influences' (*Int II*, 295). For other monads to exist in community with me is, Husserl says, for them to be 'in connection with me' (157). On the same page he even speaks of a 'reaching of the other into my primordinality'. None of this, of course, amounts to any 'real relation' of a causal nature holding between monads.[3] Indeed, at the constituted level of the world the spatial separation of embodied subjects serves as an image of the real separation between transcendental subjects. No: the connectedness in question here is 'irreal' or intentional. I am affected by the other in virtue of the *sense* of another and of his particular achievements being constituted in my transcendental ego *as* something *co*-constituted. Although the transcendental community is constituted in me, it is constituted 'as a community constituted also in every other monad' (158):

> As a transcendental ego (as living in the absolute attitude), I find myself as determined from the outside – now, however, not as a spatio-temporal reality determined by an external reality. What do 'external to me' and 'being determined by something external' signify now? It is obvious that, transcendentally speaking, I can be conditioned by something 'external', by something that goes beyond my self-contained ownness, only if it has the sense 'someone else', and, in a thoroughly understandable manner, gains and legitimates in me its acceptance as being another transcendental ego. Starting from here, the possibility and the sense, not only of a plurality of *co-existing* absolute subjects ('monads'), but also of subjects who *affect one another* transcendentally . . . becomes clear.
>
> (*FTL*, 243–4)

I can be affected 'from outside' *transcendentally speaking* only through a 'sense', since to speak transcendentally of myself is to speak of myself *as constituting sense*. And only the sense of another can take me 'outside' senses that are purely my 'own'. Moreover, I am *passive* in relation to this. The constituted and confirmed 'unities of validity' that are other subjects are no mere fantasy, or even theory, of mine: I *experience* them. I do not actually experience *all* of them, of course, for the inter-monadic community is indefinitely, perhaps infinitely, large – an 'open plurality' mirroring the 'openly endless nature' that it constitutes within itself. (158). But all are in *possible* communication with each other, and hence with me (167).

Since others are only thinkable thanks to the sense of another that is constituted only in empathy, and since empathy involves a body and entails objectivization, transcendental intercommunion can take place *only in a world*. Transcendental intersubjectivity 'spatializes, temporalizes, realizes itself (psychophysically, and in particular, as human beings) within the world' (166). Moreover, it *must* do this: Husserl prefaces the passage just quoted with the words 'I cannot conceive a plurality of monads otherwise.' A little later he says that an objective nature, and hence, by implication, the self-mundanizing intersubjectivity that constitutes such a nature, '*must* exist, if there are any structures in me that involve the existence along with me of other monads' (167). Moreover, monads necessarily form but *one* community, and hence constitute a *single* objective world. Although there may be several communities of monads that are actually isolated from one another, and that have quite different physicalizations, since every monad can in principle communicate with any other, the various 'worlds' that would be constituted by these several communities would be but 'mere *surrounding worlds . . .*, mere aspects of a single objective world which is common to them' (167). As is characteristic of Husserl's metaphysical writings, such claims to necessity are frequently ambiguous. Sometimes – as, perhaps, in the last-quoted passage – Husserl may be saying only that a self-incarnating intersubjective community of monads must exist *given that* my transcendental ego enjoys harmonious empathic experience. More precisely: that the *sense* of such a community is implicit in my experiencing a world with an objective sense, and that the actual *existence* of such a community is conditionally apodictic – being inconsistent with an ultimately harmonious experience. Sometimes, however, Husserl seems to claim that the mundanization and communalization of transcendental subjectivity is an unconditional metaphysical necessity. Bearing in mind his views on the divine entelechy of the world and the aseity of transcendental monads, I believe that at least most of these statements should be taken in the stronger sense. After all, as we saw in Chapter 4, the harmonious integration of each monad in the transcendental community is, for Husserl, 'a part of the process of the self-realization of the godhead' (*Int III*, 610).

EMPATHY: THE WIDER PICTURE

Although the principal topic of this final meditation is objectivity, most critical attention has been directed specifically to Husserl's account of empathy. In fact, it is widely held that this is one of the least satisfactory elements in his whole philosophy. Although I have, perforce, generally abstained from detailed assessment of Husserl's views in this work, since empathy is the one concrete problem to which he devotes extended discussion in the *Cartesian Meditations*, and also because this discussion is commonly taken as his definitive treatment of the topic, some assessment is perhaps in order. As I cannot discuss all the multifarious criticisms that have been levelled against the account, I shall focus on just two that I regard as the most fundamental and apparently conclusive.

Although Husserl's account of empathy will no doubt be agreed to be both subtle and searching, it may well be felt that, however one might quibble over the details, even the general picture that he provides of empathy is extremely implausible. His account would seem to imply, for example, that in order to recognize anyone else as an animate organism, I must possess a mental picture of my own outward physical appearance – at least are far as concerns those bodily parts that are significant in my perception of another's body. But is this really absolutely necessary? Surely someone who paid scant attention to his or her own bodily appearance could yet recognize another live human being? The account is especially implausible from a genetic point of view. For although Husserl says in the Fifth Meditation that he is concerned with a 'static analysis' of intersubjectivity, one that 'is not a matter of uncovering a genesis going on in time' (136), such a separation cannot ultimately hold for Husserl. For him, at least as far as basic types of object are concerned, whatever is foundationally prior is genetically prior, as we saw in Chapter 3. Indeed, Husserl himself, in the midst of his supposedly static analysis, tells us that all apperception points back to a *primal instituting* in which the sense of the apperception 'became constituted for the first time' (141). And is not his account of empathy in the Fifth Meditation an account of its motivational genesis, and hence of this 'primal institution'? If it is not, what would such an account look like? And how would the account offered in this meditation be made compatible with such an account? Husserl needs, at the very least, to offer us *some* genetic account of empathy, because a phenomenological analysis of an object that leaves genetic questions wholly out of the picture will not possess that ultimate clarity that he always sought. At one point Husserl speaks of the greatness of Hume as a philosopher, a greatness that, he claims, is still insufficiently appreciated, and which he characterizes as follows:

> In the concreteness of purely egological internality, as he saw, every-thing objective becomes intended (and, in favourable cases, per-ceived) thanks to a subjective genesis. Hume was the first to see the necessity, in relation to that concreteness, of investigating precisely what is thus objective *as a formation of its genesis, in order to make the legitimate being-sense of everything that exists for us intelligible through its ultimate origins.*
>
> (*FTL*, 226–7, my emphasis, translation modified)

If the account in the Fifth Meditation is supposed itself to be an account of the originally instituting genesis of empathy, then, it would seem, the wonderfully intricate motivation that Husserl describes in these pages must, implausibly, be attributed to the very young infant who shows any appreciation of the existence of others. Most implausibly of all, the suggestion would seem to be that the infant attains the ability to engage in empathy in essential part as a result of scrutinizing his or her own body! Again, although Husserl treats other human beings as the central cases of other bodies, he certainly intends his account to cover our recogni-tion of animals in general. Indeed, the earlier and briefer discussion of empathy in *Ideas II* was explicitly presented as, in part, introducing the constitutional issues pertaining to the realm of '*animalia*' as such (*Ideas II*, §§43–7). But an ostrich, for example, does not resemble me to any great extent – far less so, in many respects, than a statue of a human being, which evokes no empathy at all.

A second apparent problem with Husserl's account is the following. Not only in the present text, but in the bulk of his writings on this subject, Husserl seems to assume two things: that what is to be constituted is a self *like mine*, and that my original appreciation of what it is to be a self is gained in relation to myself – through 'self-perception' or 'self-experience', as he often calls it. The picture that therefore emerges is that of subjects interpreting others in terms of a mentality that they have first grasped *in foro interno*. We have already seen that, despite Husserl's claim that he is doing only static phenomenology in this meditation, he makes reference to the genetic notion of 'primal institution'. What is particularly worrying in the present connection is his claim that *I* am the primally instituting original in relation to empathy. For this would indeed seem to imply a 'self-experience' that is genetically prior to the awareness of others. A much more plausible view, however, one that seems first to have emerged with post-Kantian German idealism, is that there is no self-consciousness without intersubjectivity. The idea is not that we are supposed to have here a swift answer to the 'Problem of Other Minds' – i.e., that sheer self-consciousness, the Cartesian *Cogito*, entails the existence of others. The idea is, rather, that such self-consciousness is impossible without some *conception*, or some (perhaps merely putative) *experience*, of another subject. The usual philosophical solipsist certainly does not lack such a conception: he must have it in order to deny that anything actually answers to it in reality. So the question is: How plausible is the suggestion that it is possible that a self-conscious subject should exist, one who is not only aware of a 'primordial' world but who is capable of reflection and self-awareness, who yet has no conception of other subjects of experience – even as mere possibilities – at all, but has to await courses of experience that will 'motivate' such a sense? Could it not be, conversely, that the latter is a transcendental condition of the possibility of the former? Or, more plausibly, that the two are reciprocally conditioning, the constitution of others going hand in hand with the constitution of ourselves as self-conscious beings? Certainly, on the empirical level, we find no indication of self-awareness or of reflection in very young children before the age when they start relating to others in a 'personal' way. And feral children, despite being biologically identical to us, never attain self-conscious personhood without the intervention of other persons. The more one thinks about it, the more intelligible it becomes than an 'I' can emerge only as correlate to a 'You'.

In the remainder of this chapter I shall be suggesting how the above criticisms may be significantly blunted, if not dissolved, by bearing two things in mind. The first is the *level* at which Husserl's theory of empathy, at least as presented in the *Cartesian Meditations*, is supposed to operate. For empathy is relevant to the constitutional story of all of the following: animal life in general, the 'soul' and its 'psychological states', other persons as intentionally directed to a meaningful 'surrounding world', and transcendental monads. We need to pay careful attention to how these various sorts of 'others', and the constitutions that make them possible as objects, are related to one another. That will be the topic of the final section of this chapter. The second thing to bear in mind is the extensive writings by Husserl on empathy other than the present meditation. For although this text is commonly taken as being Husserl's definitive statement on the subject, there are now available in the *Husserliana* series three large volumes devoted in great part to this topic, the third (and largest) of which postdates the present discussion. The issue of intersubjectivity is one to which Husserl returned over and over again, repeatedly finding problems with his earlier attempts at a 'solution'. The open-ended and tentative nature of Husserl's treatment of this subject is matched only by his treatment of the ultimate constitution of time – the most difficult of all constitutional problems, according to him. To those whose only knowledge of Husserl's views on empathy come from the *Cartesian Meditations*, much of this other material may come as something of a surprise. In this section we shall briefly explore this material.

One thing that a reading of Husserl's other writings on empathy quickly reveals is that he was indeed much exercised by the question of its genesis. Here is just one telling passage (in the somewhat telegraphic style not uncommon in the manuscripts):

> The mother as a visual and tactual unity ... The child desires the mother in her normal 'aspect', in which the original needs of the child are fulfilled. He cries involuntarily; sometimes it 'works'. Very late the child first has a space with spatial material things, and the mother as a material thing in his spatial field. The first mother as something identical, recognizable – as a 'premise' for the satisfaction of desire: when she comes and is there, then satisfaction occurs. Nothing yet of empathy.
>
> (*Int III*, 605)

We shall be looking at the succeeding critical stages of this developmental story shortly; but Husserl claims that empathy occurs shortly after these elementary stages of infant development. The apparently over-intellectualized account of the Fifth Meditation notwithstanding, Husserl can place the onset of empathy at such an early stage because he sees it as the expression of *innate instincts*. The connection between mother and child, he tells us, 'originally develops instinctively' (*Int III*, 582). And there are, in general, 'intersubjective instincts' (*PP*, 486). Elsewhere Husserl states that 'the instinctive life of drives can produce an intersubjective relationship' (*Int II*, 405), citing sexual instincts as an example. Given, as we have seen over the last two chapters, the quite fundamental role that 'instinct-intentionality' plays in Husserl's metaphysical system, this should come as no surprise. But nor should we expect him simply to postulate innate 'empty representations' and apperceptive horizons that experience will simply serve to trigger. Here, as generally with instincts, all that Husserl is willing to recognize as innate is a certain predisposition. Recall, also, that even the 'disclosure' of instincts, through their satisfaction, falls short of the constitution of objects proper – and hence, in the present connection, falls short of an awareness of other subjects. The satisfaction of the sexual instinct, for example, although it involves a 'reaching into another "soul" ', is not yet, as such, a case of empathy for Husserl (*Int III*, 596). There is more of a developmental story to be told.

Returning to our first problem, concerning the fact that an appreciation of our outward appearances is implausibly seen as absolutely necessary for empathy, there are many passages where Husserl places primary emphasis not on similarity of outward appearance, but on similarity of *behaviour* – solipsistically apperceived as but a certain kind of physical movement, of course (e.g., *Int II*, 284). In the present meditation such 'behaviour' tends to be relegated to the role of *confirming* an empathic appresentation that has already taken place (e.g., 148–9). But Husserl's writings in general do not suggest such a separation – one that in Chapter 4 we in any case saw to be somewhat artificial. So the suggestion now is, not that certain movements are taken as behaviour because performed by a suitably shaped material object, but that certain types of *movement* immediately motivate the empathic 'pairing'. What kind of movement, however, among the many that we do ordinarily take to be expressive of 'governance' in a body, might be fundamental here? Well, movement is taken as behaviour when it appears *guided* – perceptually guided – in virtue of being movement of a kind not in the style of general physical causality. In one manuscript Husserl writes of 'an opposition. Natural causality and I-causality as the causality of the body, in which the I governs as one who deploys energy' (*Int II*, 427). It may be difficult abstractly to specify, spatio-temporally, the class of movements in question, but we know from experience that they are perceptually all but unmistakable. Indeed, in one psychological experiment twelve lights in an otherwise dark room were immediately taken by subjects to be attached to a human body (which they were) as soon as the wearer began to move (Johansson, 1975). Such an emphasis on behaviour also helps with the related problem that we immediately apperceive at least the higher animals as co-perceivers of the world, despite the fact that they have a quite different appearance from ourselves. Although an ostrich may physically look very different from me, its movements are not so dissimilar. Indeed, it is more similar in its movements to my behaviour than anything I do not apperceive as conscious. We see it not only running, and crouching, but also as scanning, as peering at things, and so on. This 'as' implies some considerable degree of similarity between its movements and those I exhibit.

Is there not, however, still the problem that even an emphasis on the movement of perceived objects, if it is supposed to be recognized as similar to my own, also requires a greater degree of awareness of how my own moving body appears from an external perspective than is plausibly necessary for empathy to occur? Now, although I am not aware of Husserl having explored the possibility – though, as we shall see shortly, he does at least allude to it – we can surely make out a case for a recognizable similarity between others' movements and our own in the absence of any appreciation of how our own movements appear to an external view. Since the other's body is clearly registered by us in perception, Husserl tends to assume that any experiential similarity such a body may bear to our own must likewise be a *perceptual* similarity. Perhaps, however, what we are empathically attuned to are the similarities between certain types of movements as such – some being perceived externally, but some being 'internally' perceived through kinaesthesis and our changing perspectives on the world. For we know 'from the inside', without having to imagine how we look to others, that and how our bodies move through space, that and how our eyes sweep across a scene, fixate objects and so forth. Perhaps similarities between the *purely kinematic* properties of such movements and of those perceived in certain external bodies can be detected in the absence of a sense of any *material* similarity. In fact, it now appears that an ability to appreciate certain equivalences between perceived external movements and unperceived, but felt and executed, bodily movements is innate. There is, for example, evidence that babies on their first day of life imitate various externally perceived facial movements, such as sticking out one's tongue (Meltzoff and Moore, 1983). There is no chance that such a baby would have an appreciation of the fact that its own face is visually similar to the one seen. Indeed, given that there is also evidence that young babies can even imitate externally perceived *non-bodily* movements – such as the protrusion of a pencil – material similarity can hardly be what is crucial here.

Even if there are such innate 'inter-modal' equivalences, however, we still need to understand what sort of behaviour is critical for the genesis of empathy in the baby, and why. After all, the behaviour of adults is not in general that much like a baby's: we do not spend most of the day on our backs, jerkily moving our limbs! In certain of his writings Husserl makes a suggestion that is remarkable for its prescience. For he suggests that both others' *verbal and facial expressions*, and also behaviour *directed towards us*, are what are of paramount importance for the genesis of empathy. Although he sometimes treats the last as if it were relevant only to an appreciation of the 'personality' of another, and to confirming our assessment of the other's mentality, both of which presuppose that empathy is already in place, after one such passage Husserl also suggests that such an appreciation of behaviour directed to us plays a special role in the 'most original genetic continuity of child and mother' (*Int II*, 504). He also suggests, in relation to the voice, that

> in the child the self-produced voice, and then, analogously, the heard voice, serves as the first bridge for the objectification of the Ego or for the formation of the '*alter*', i.e., before the child already has or can have a sensory analogy between his visual body and that of the 'other'.
>
> (*Ideas II*, 96n)

I think it fruitful to put these thoughts together with a very late passage in which Husserl discusses the early interactions between mother and child, and which underlines the importance of the expressive, speaking face. The passage in question is in fact the continuation of the story of the infant's development towards intersubjectivity cited earlier, which was interrupted before the emergence of empathy. He continues by writing of

> that which is instinctive in the relation of [the child's] own body – of his own already constituted organs, of the lips in talking, of the eyes

and eye-movements etc. – to the lip movements and the speaking of the mother. *An alien body as body, and empathy.*

(*Int III*, 605, my emphasis)[4]

He goes on to wonder about the role in the development of empathy that could be played by the mutually imitative pre-linguistic interactions that mother and child playfully engage in – 'proto-conversations', as they are sometimes called. If we put these two passages together, what emerges is the idea that what is fundamental to the apperception of a material thing as a body is that it *respond* to you in a way that merely material things do not. In particular, an attunement to a certain *reciprocity* in movements, indicating that certain movements are both elicited by you and responsively directed to you, is what emerges from these passages as critical. Here, perhaps, we have the materials for a sense of similarity that is neither merely 'material', nor even merely 'kinematic', but one that concerns the *guidedness* and *directedness* of 'behaviour'. I say that these remarks of Husserl's are astonishingly prescient because it is only quite recently that child psychologists have come to realize that an infant's development into intersubjectivity features two qualitative changes – at around two and nine months – and the first of these, the emergence of what, following Colwyn Trevarthen, is now commonly termed 'primary intersubjectivity', features just the kinds of interactive behaviour mentioned by Husserl (see Trevarthen 1993, and his earlier writings cited therein). In these 'proto-conversations' the baby is focused on the face of the mother; the latter directs facial expressions and 'baby-talk' to the child; and the child itself responds – in terms of limb movements, vocal responses, and facial expressions – in a way that it does to no other thing in its environment. The mother responds in turn, and the interaction is fully under way. What is crucial in this process is the temporal sequencing of the partners' actions, the mother's responses – usually, at this stage, imitative in nature – being contingent upon and immediately following action by the baby. Trevarthen likens the interchange to a musical duet. But what, in this kind of interchange, is being exchanged? Bodily actions, of course; but what motivates them, and what is their significance? It is now generally recognized that what is essentially being exchanged here is *emotion*. Trevarthen writes that the 'duet' becomes 'a coherent and satisfying narrative of feelings' (1993, p. 139). This is hardly surprising, given that the mother's actions are clearly influenced by the perceived enjoyment that the baby derives from the interaction. Communication is characteristically born in affectivity – indeed affection, joy. If the mother's face remains impassive, the baby either looks away or shows signs of distress. Here we clearly have some sort of appreciation on the part of the developing infant of a vital responsiveness in the other; and in the passage recently quoted Husserl regards this as already an indication of the onset of empathy. We are still far, however, from an appreciation of the *subjectivity* of the other, which, throughout his writings, Husserl regards as the central achievement of empathy. And elsewhere in his writings he demands more, even of the young child. In order to approach this further issue, it will be helpful to turn to a consideration of our second problem.

Although there are passages in Husserl's writings that may give the impression that he regarded self-conscious egoity as the most basic form that subjectivity can take, so that all constitution pre-supposes such self-consciousness as background and foundation, this is, in fact, far from being his opinion – something that has, indeed, already emerged in the course of our investigation. For not only does Husserl's talk of 'passive synthesis' indicate a level of constitution prior to the attentive activity of the ego, and hence of self-awareness; in my brief sketch of Husserl's metaphysics I mentioned his grand picture of the teleological development of subjectivity from a fairly primitive beginning up to self-conscious personhood. In one passage he speaks of 'the pre-I that is not yet living' because it has not yet been affected by *hylé*. Such a monad, which has but an 'implicit "world"', needs to be inducted into reality by us who are the living carriers of the evolution of reason: 'The living waken the unliving' (*Int III*, 604). So it should come as no surprise that Husserl explicitly raises the issue of the genesis of the self-conscious ego in the context of intersubjectivity. He speaks, for example, of the *'Urkind'* – the 'primal child' – who must *develop* into a personal, self-conscious being, a development that starts with a primitive awareness that is 'without reflection'. It is in this connection that he raises the issue of 'the first' occurrence of empathy, and says that for the young child 'the I is hidden, in so far as it is not thematic as an I' (*Int III*, 604–5). It can hardly have been Husserl's view that empathy is possible only if we are already in 'primordial' self-possession of ourselves as self-conscious beings if he also thinks that we initially have ourselves to be inducted into personhood and self-awareness through coming to appreciate the 'personal' significance of others. Indeed, Husserl can say explicitly that it is a priori that 'self-consciousness and consciousness of others are inseparable' (*Crisis*, 256 [253]). Elsewhere he writes that 'the primal generative development of man in which he first grows into self-consciousness and consciousness of an environment, into the first "I and environment", produces this first I already as an I of a We' (*Int III*, 182). And in another passage Husserl can say quite bluntly that, where no 'you' has been constituted, 'there is also no I in opposition to it' (*Int I*, 6). Finally, Husserl claims that the 'necessarily present pole of all affections and actions' in a solipsistic subject

> *becomes an I* and thereby *a personal subject*, gaining thereby *personal 'self-consciousness'*, in the I–Thou relation . . . In empathy the I is already aware of itself as a subject of its life and subject of its environment, and it is conscious of the foreign I as 'another I' . . . thanks to a reference back to the reflecting subject that is one's own.
>
> (*Int II*, 171)

This last statement in particular may suggest that Husserl sees both self-consciousness and consciousness of others as arising together in empathy. Here we are clearly at a higher level than that of the 'primary intersubjectivity' discussed above, and have arrived at empathy in the true sense.

Husserl shows yet more prescience in his discussion of this stage of development. He speaks, for example, of the importance of an almost Gricean responsiveness to the intentions of others: 'I do something with the intention that the other should notice it, and in the expectation . . . that the other, noticing that I have this intention, should do [such and such]' (*Int II* 167; compare Grice, 1957). He then goes on to refer specifically to the intention to *communicate something*, albeit prelinguistically, giving as an example the way gypsies lay twigs at a cross-roads so that their fellow travellers, recognizing a certain intention behind the presence of the twigs, will know which road to take. This leads him to speak of 'immediate communications – or better, a *touching*, establishing *an original connection between I and You* in originally experiencing empathy', saying that here we have 'the original experience of standing-over-against-one-another'. I say that this too is prescient, because at the second critical stage of infant development into intersubjectivity at around nine months of age – the emergence of 'secondary intersubjectivity' – this is just the kind of thing we find. In the intervening period babies have developed a more discriminating sensitivity to the emotions evinced by others. But as one leading researcher in the field puts it,

> In the younger infant the empathic *process* itself goes unnoticed, and only the empathic *response* is registered. It is quite another thing for the infant to sense that an empathic process bridging the two minds has been created. The caregiver's empathy . . . now becomes a direct object of the infant's experience.
>
> (Stern 1998, p. 126)

It is at this second stage that 'third-party' objects are brought into the mother–child interaction. It is only now, for example, that infants begin to follow the gaze of another and look at what the other is looking at. They also begin to understand the pointing gesture. They themselves also bring such objects into the interaction, by pointing or gesturing towards objects, and they look to see how the other reacts to such third-party objects and events. The gesturing, in particular, expresses an appreciation that others have perceptual attention, and manifests an intention to direct that attention. Furthermore, when the infant follows the other's gesture, it sometimes looks back for confirmation that it has read the other's intention aright. Indeed, when the infant itself points towards something, its own gaze typically alternates between the indicated object and the other's face to see if the other is read-ing its own intentions aright. All of this, as well as the following of the other's gaze, clearly evinces an appreciation on the part of the child that others have a perspective on the world. Here we have the first true appreciation of another's subjectivity. It is just such inter-actions as these that Husserl surely had in mind when he wrote of the genesis of the 'I–You relation' in the following terms:

> I experience a fact and, it being in any case in the other's immediate experiential domain, I make him notice it through an 'indication'. A certain movement of hand or finger . . . etc., makes him attend, 'dir-ects' his attention, 'leads' it in this direction in which there is some-thing of interest to the other (as it was already for me).
>
> (*Int II*, 167)

THE STATUS AND SCOPE OF HUSSERL'S ACCOUNT OF EMPATHY

I hope to have shown both that Husserl was keenly interested in the issue of the genesis of empathy, and that his remarks contain remarkable insights (especially for the time) into the truth of the matter. There are, however, two problems that we now face. The first is: What is the status of these remarks of Husserl's? Many of them appear to have the nature of empirical hypotheses. For example, he prefaces his remark about the vital importance of the voice in the development of intersubjectivity with the words: 'It seems, from my observation, that . . . ' (*Ideas II*, 96n). But what place can such casual observation have in an eidetic transcendental phenomenology? Clearly none; nor, I am sure, did Husserl suppose that it could. The passages I have recently been citing come from working notes that he never intended for publication, notes in which he is painfully working out his own views with any help that may come to hand. Nevertheless, I believe that he eventually hoped for a fairly abstract set of conditions for the genesis of empathy that would indeed be true with eidetic necessity. The abstraction would, to be sure, have to be considerable. The voice of our mother may well have been of huge practical importance for most of us; but deaf people also attain empathy. And so do blind people, despite Husserl's typical emphasis on what sight delivers. Nor is one or the other of these senses essential, as is shown by the case of Helen Keller – someone who was restricted to touch as her only access to the world and to others. The only thing that can be *essential* in this area is something that can be embodied in *all* the forms of inter-action that we know can lead to empathy. Hence it can be no *material* factor at all. I have been suggesting, in harmony with some of Husserl's own thoughts, that what lies at the origin of the development of empathy is an appreciation of the *responsiveness* of the body of another to one's own actions, and that the motivation for such an appreciation is the temporal sequencing of the behaviour of the two actors in the interchange – something that is itself regulated by emotional responses. It is not wholly implaus-ible to suppose that the more one thinks about this, and bears in mind the primitive level of mental development of the subjects we are concerned with, it may come to be recognized as having the status of an essential necessity. However, even if light has been shed on these genetic matters, it cannot be said that we have gained Husserl's always final goal of absolute transparency or intelligibil-ity in relation to the genesis of intersubjectivity (or self-consciousness) as such. That remains a mystery, and doubtless always will.

The second problem is, perhaps, even more serious. Why, if Hus-serl was so concerned with the genetic aspect of empathy, does it barely surface in the present meditation, and not at all constrain the account of motivation presented there? Although the genetic material I have cited comes from a period after the writing of the *Cartesian Meditations*, I do not think that the answer to this ques-tion is that Husserl changed his mind after the writing of the pres-ent meditation – if only because his later writings also feature passages where he persists in developing the approach to empathy found in this final meditation. So what *did* he think he was doing when he propounded these genetically implausible accounts of empathy? In particular, why does he insist that *self-consciousness* must be in place first if empathy is to be possible? I think the answer to this is to be found by paying close attention to *whose* empathic performances Husserl is concerned to analyse in these pages. The answer to this question is not difficult to find: what he is primarily concerned with is how empathy is possible for *the transcendentally meditating philosopher*. The whole meditation, after all, gets under way with the following question: 'When I, the meditating I, reduce myself to my absolute transcendental ego by phenomenological epoché, do I not become *solus ipse . . .?*' (121). It is this problem, arising within the transcendental attitude, that Husserl is trying to address; and he eventually concludes by claiming to have clarified the sense of 'the existing other for me *in the transcendental attitude*' (175, my emphasis). Correlatively, the 'other' that Husserl is primarily interested in is the *transcendental* other, or, as he repeatedly says, the other as a *monad*. His task is to show how 'another monad becomes constituted appresentatively in mine' (144). And as he says in a later note, 'The question after all concerns not other men! But rather how it comes about that the ego, as transcendentally experienced by the transcendental onlooker, constitutes within itself the distinction between Ego and other Ego' (124, note 1). This is easy to overlook, because, as this note continues, the distinction in question 'presents itself first of all in the phenomenon "world"; as the difference between my human ego (my Ego in the usual sense) and the other human Ego' (124). This 'first' phenomenon, however, is precisely what we have to make sense of transcendentally. For the Fifth Meditation is ultimately devoted to analysing the sense of objectivity. Husserl is primarily interested in *transcendental co-constitution,* and hence in other transcendental subjects. Other 'human egos' cannot be our primary concern, since they will emerge as the *product* of such constitution, being members of a common world. That is why Husserl says that the target of empathy is 'the *pure* others (who as yet have no worldly sense)' (137). They are transcendental egos, apperceived as such. Transference of sense in empathy can achieve this recognition, since I, as the primally instituting original, am myself a transcendentally meditating monad recognized as such. Part of what is 'apperceptively transferred' in empathy *is my status as transcendental.* That nothing less than this is required by the Fifth Meditation should be evident from its purpose, which is to trace the sense of the objectivity and the reality of the world back to transcendental intersubjectivity, the absolute ground of being.

If, however, Husserl is solely interested in the constitution of other transcendental subjects by a meditating philosopher who also recognizes him- or herself as a transcendental subject, then it would hardly be immediately to the point to delve into the issue of the genesis of self-consciousness in a monad, since a transcendental philosopher will already, of course, be in possession of this. Even if a nine-month-old child has begun to attain some sort of empathy, it will hardly have a full appreciation of itself as a centre of consciousness, let alone as a constituting monad. But it is *as the latter* that I must recognize other subjects if the project of transcendental phenomenology is to be carried out. I must recognize the other as *doing the same as I do*: namely, constituting a world in a sphere of ownness. For only when I have so constituted them in my own sphere of ownness will I have constituted an objective world for myself (and for them). It is not that the motivations that are of such genetic importance, and that may be available for a child, will be inadequate to the intentional accomplishments at issue here: *any* behaviour that suffices to incite primitive empathy in a child will certainly be sufficient to motivate empathic awareness of another transcendental subject in a self-conscious, meditating adult with a transcendental perspective. It is, rather, that what is of such genetic importance is *unnecessary* in relation to the latter subject. Actions directed at the subject, for example, may well be of crucial genetic importance for empathy; but they are not in adult life, where, indeed, the simple appearance of a human body typically does suffice for an empathic appresentation. For we all have, as a matter of fact, a fairly good sense of our own outward appearance. *Anything* that suffices for empathy in the adult will satisfy Husserl's requirements in the present context: he can cast his net as widely as the adult primordial sphere is rich. Even in adult life there is an everyday empathic awareness of, or reckoning with, others that stops short of explicitly positing the other's stream of consciousness: we do not explicitly think '*alter ego*' every time we see someone. Husserl fully recognizes this fact, and refers to it, as we should by now expect, as 'inauthentic' or 'improper' empathy

(*Int I*, 478–9). This, however, constitutes no criticism of Husserl's account, which is not meant to be one of such everyday consciousness. The important point is, rather, that given the right intellectual equipment and focus of interest, we *can* 'authentically' posit the other as a conscious subject, indeed as a transcendental ego, and that we *must* do so if we are transcendental phenomenologists. It is the possibility of this latter intentional accomplishment alone that is Husserl's concern in the present text.

NOTES

1 Cairns's capitalization of 'objectivation' in this passage is misleading – as if a notion of objectivity were in play here. It is a pre-objective physicalization, or objectivation, of the body that is in question. Otherwise Husserl's account would be circular.

2 '*Objekt*' here, for once, does imply objectivity – for Husserl immediately goes on to refer to 'this primal phenomenon of objectivity'. (See 'Note on Translations and Citations' above (pp. xiv–xvi).)

3 Since the term has a wide sense that expresses no more than an 'if–then', Husserl can, however, occasionally speak of inter-monadic 'causality': e.g., *Int II*, 268; *Int III*, 376.

4 Note the reference to what is 'instinctive': presumably acknowledgement of the innate inter-modal equivalences recently mentioned.

CONCLUSION

(§§63–64)

Husserl's *Cartesian Meditations* ends with the Delphic motto, 'Know thyself!', and with a quotation from St Augustine: 'Do not go outside. Return into yourself. Truth dwells in the inner man.' In case the reader has been wondering where we now stand in relation to the epistemological concerns with which we began – and, in particular, how transcendental phenomenology stands in relation to the philosophic ideal of universal knowledge produced through insight – these quotations may serve to return us to that inaugural, 'primally instituting' idea. For Husserl's contention is that *transcendental reflection alone* can match up to this ideal of knowledge. By contrast, all 'positive sciences', both actual and possible, as well as all everyday beliefs, are 'naïve' and based on 'prejudice', because they are not grounded in 'ultimate insight'. When Husserl characterizes such naïveté, as he frequently does, as its being a matter of presupposing that a real world actually exists, many readers are likely to be unimpressed by the accusation, thinking that such a prejudice is one that we can fairly safely allow ourselves. What, however, has emerged in the course of our exploration of Husserl's thought is that naïveté here is a matter of an obliviousness to the processes in consciousness that are the preconditions for any belief in any matter of worldly fact at all. 'Daily practical living', writes Husserl, 'is naïve. It is immersion in the already-given world, whether it be experiencing, or thinking, or valuing. Meanwhile all those productive intentional functions of experiencing, because of which physical things are simply there, go on anonymously' (179). As we have seen, this is even true when we are concerned not with 'physical things' but, in 'psychological', reflective mode, with our own minds and their contents. In concerning ourselves with objects in the world, whether mental or physical, we overlook the nature of the constituting processes of consciousness that allow such objects to appear to us. Even 'positive' science is characterized by such naïveté, the 'naïveté through which objectivist science takes what it calls the objective world for the universe of all that is, without noticing that no objective science can do justice to the subjectivity which accomplishes science' (*Crisis* 342 [294–5]). Since all objects are grounded in transcendental constitution, the original philosophical 'idea' of ultimately grounding and grounded knowledge must be transcendental in character: 'Transcendental subjectivity, constituting life, . . . remains anonymous. Fully developed science must be a science also of transcendental origins' (*EP II*, 356). Only such a truly scientific philosophy, 'through such a regressive enquiry back into the last conceivable ground in the transcendental ego, can fulfil the meaning which is inborn in philosophy from its primal establishment' (*Crisis* 195 [192]). For this primal establishment was that of an ideal of knowledge that would be finally justified through insight. But any possible knowledge that we may have is such *thanks to* rational processes of constitution in consciousness. Final grounding in insight therefore requires insight into this relation of constitution: 'Without insight into the nature of rational accomplishment as such, no formation of reason, no truth, no theory, no science has a final justification' (*EP II*, 356).

Although in the early pages of the *Meditations* the ultimate goal of absolutely apodictic knowledge was used to draw us along, the promise of phenomenology to offer us such knowledge has been indefinitely deferred. Here, in the final sections of the *Meditations*, 'indubitability' is again implicitly renounced. For Husserl says that these meditations have demonstrated 'a necessary and indubitable beginning and an equally necessary and always employable method' (178). Although necessary and employable, the phenomenological method is not itself claimed to involve indubitable steps: only the 'beginning' – the 'I think' – is indubitable. What has emerged, rather, as the immediately realizable goal of phenomenological enquiry is a kind of knowledge that has a certain *priority* in relation to all cognition conducted in the 'natural attitude'. This issue of priority is re-emphasized by Husserl in this concluding section – the word 'Apriori', in particular, being used repeatedly. Phenomenology is concerned with 'the constitutional Apriori' (180), with '*the all-embracing Apriori* that is *innate* in the essence of a transcendental subjectivity' (181). For all objects are constituted objects; and transcendental phenomenology is the enquiry into the processes by and in which anything at all is constituted: the *pre*conditions in consciousness in virtue of which anything is an object for us. Because the constitution of an object is either *our own* activity, or is a passive process in *our* consciousness, transcendental phenomenology is 'radical self-investigation, . . . intentional self-explication of the transcendental ego' (179). Hence the references to Delphi and St Augustine. And in virtue of its character as self-explication, phenomenological enquiry not only has a priority in relation to all other forms of human investigation, it also has an intrinsic intelligibility that no positive science, and no set of everyday beliefs, can have. In understanding that, and how, objects are constituted in and for consciousness, we have 'the *living truth from the living source, which is our absolute life*' (*FTL*, 246).

Husserl also claims that transcendental phenomenology alone is authentic science because it alone properly makes sense of 'the ideal of the grounding of knowledge in absolute presuppositionlessness' (*FTL*, 279). This lack of 'prejudice' is meant to be embodied in the actual practice of phenomenological enquiry, since this is rooted in a straightforward 'looking' at the 'things themselves' given in intuitive experience, as well as a 'looking' at the experiences themselves, given in reflexive awareness, that 'originally give', or 'constitute', such things. 'I seek not to instruct,' Husserl can write, 'but only to lead, to point out and describe what I see' (*Crisis* 17 [18]). This can easily make phenomenological enquiry sound simple. But of course it is not; nor did Husserl himself find it so. But he saw the primary effort involved here as ultimately one that is ethical in character. For he continues the passage just cited by saying that 'I claim no other right than that of speaking according to my best lights, principally before myself but in the same manner also before others, as one who has lived in all its seriousness the fate of a philosophical existence.' Such existence is that of final *self-responsibility*. For philosophy is the life of reason, and reason lives in such self-responsibility alone:

> *Reason* is the specific characteristic of man, as a being living in personal activities and habitualities. This life, as a personal life, is a constant becoming through a constant intentionality of development. What becomes, in this life, is the person himself . . . Human personal life proceeds in stages of self-reflection and self-responsibility from isolated occasional acts of this form to the stage of universal self-reflection and self-responsibility, up to the point of seizing in consciousness the idea of autonomy, the idea of a resolve of the will to shape one's whole personal life into the synthetic unity of a life of universal self-responsibility and, correlatively, to shape oneself into the true 'I,' the free, autonomous 'I' which seeks to realize his innate reason, the striving to be true to himself, to be able to remain identical with himself as a reasonable 'I' . . . The universally, apodictically grounded and grounding science arises now as the necessarily highest function of mankind, as I said, namely, as making possible mankind's development into a personal autonomy and into an all-encompassing autonomy for mankind – the idea which represents the driving force of life for the highest stage of mankind. Thus philosophy is nothing other than . . . *ratio* in the constant movement of self-elucidation.
>
> (*Crisis* 272–3 [338])

Even such dedication, however, by itself would doubtless not warrant our continued interest in what Husserl 'sees'. That warrant finally lies in the simple fact that Husserl was a philosopher of genius, whose extensive analyses of consciousness, pursued with unparalleled pertinacity, repeatedly throw up insights. No philosopher with a true interest in the 'mind' can afford to ignore these. This fact is indicated by a growing interest in his work that is to be found in a most unexpected quarter: namely, cognitive science. (See, for example, Petitot *et al.*, 1999.) In the 'analytical tradition', the 'philosophy of mind' was derailed early in the twentieth century by behaviourism – about which the less said, the better. When, in this tradition, cognitive science finally got round to realizing that, even where we are concerned only with explaining behaviour, we cannot forgo specifying various 'contents' in the mind that underlie such behaviour, it found little that could shed light on this enterprise in the philosophy of mind that lay before it within its own tradition. Even though cognitive science is ultimately interested in discovering the physical processes in the brain that supposedly 'realize' mental states and processes, this search needs to be guided by a proper account of mentality itself – whose 'realization' cognitive scientists are seeking. It is hardly surprising, therefore, that they should be turning to Husserl's extensive researches into the complex structures of consciousness – researches that, as I have been stressing, are of an unparalleled acuity.

Husserl himself would not, of course, have been satisfied with only such a legacy. The most important thing for him about his phenomenology was its *transcendental* character – its insight into the fact that we alone are the ultimate sources of meaning and of the sense that anything can possibly have for us. Any object at all is an 'accomplishment' of consciousness. A failure to appreciate this constitutes the naïveté of 'positivism' and 'objectivism'. Even worse than its naïveté, however, is the ultimate meaninglessness of the world that, according to Husserl, results from any such nontranscendental approach to the world. The world and its objects appear alien to the subject on such an approach, especially where the depiction of reality by theoretical science is concerned. And ultimately, as a result of trying to understand human beings in terms of objectivistic categories, we become alien even to ourselves. Husserl would, I feel, see in our own age – one in which the most culturally and economically influential nation in the world is given over, philosophically, to the most extreme form of materialistic 'objectivism' that the world has ever seen (according to which we are supposed to understand ourselves along the same lines as we understand computers and robots); and one in which the principal 'continental' alternative to this is an enchantment with 'post-modern' anomie – the descent into a new Dark Ages of the human spirit.

APPENDIX

Here are the original passages from Husserl's still unpublished manuscripts that I have quoted and translated.

CHAPTER 2

'eine Gefühlseinheit, die allem Erscheinenden eine Farbe verleiht' (M III 3 II 1, 29; p. 74).

'Jedes unserer hyletischen Daten schon ein "Entwicklungsprodukt" ist, also eine verborgene Intentionalität hat, die zurückweist auf eine Synthesis' (F I 24, 41a; p. 86).

'absolutes *Entstehen* von Bewußtsein aus Unbewußtsein ist Unsinn' (B II 2, 4b; p. 95).

'Freilich sagen wir, ein hyletisches Datum sei ichfremd, aber dieses Ichfremde hat das eigene, daß es nur eignem einzigen Subjekte zu eignen kann . . . Das hat das Hyletische mit jedem Erlebnis gemein' (D 3, 11; p. 100).

CHAPTER 3

'Jedes transzendentale Ich hat sein Eingeborenes' (A VII 17, 46a; p. 122).

'Intentionalität, die zur ursprünglichen Wesensstruktur des seelischen Seins gehört' (C 8 II, 16a; p. 122).

'instinktiv auf Welt gerichtet' (E III 3, 5a; p. 122).

' "Erbmasse" ohne Erinnerung und doch eine Art "Erfüllung" von Weckungen etc.' (K III 11, 4a; p. 123).

'erfüllende Explikation des universalen Instinkthorizontes' (E III 9, 3a; p. 124).

'Am "Anfang" instinktives Streben' (C 13 I, 6a; p. 149).

'Alles Leben ist unaufhörliches Streben' (A VI 26, 42a; p. 149).

'Transzendentaler Instinkt – in einem Sinne die durch die Totalität der Intentionalität des Ego hindurchgehende universale Tendenz' (C 13 I, 13b; pp. 149–50).

'Das System der Intentionalität ist ein System von assoziativ verflochtenen Trieben' (A VII 13, 24a; p. 150).

'die Uranlage des Ich vorausgesetzt für alle Konstitution' (E III 9, 4a; p. 150).

'Das Streben ist aber instinktives und instinktiv, also zunächst unenthüllt "gerichtet" auf die sich "künftig" erst enthüllt konstituierenden weltlichen Einheiten' (A VI 34, 34b; p. 150).

'Etwa der Geruch allein weckt ein Weiteres . . . die doch kein "bewußtes" Ziel hat' (C 16, IV, 36b; p. 150).

'Interesse an Sinnesdaten und Sinnesfeldern – vor der Objektivierung Sinnesdaten' (C 13 I, 11b; p. 151).

'Das Erste der Weltkonstitution in der Primordialität ist die Konstitution der "Natur" aus . . . dem dreifachen Urmaterial: sinnlicher Kern, sinnliches Gefühl, sinnliche Kinästhese. Dem entspricht der "Urinstinkt" ' (B III 9, 67a; p. 151).

'Die Instinktintentionalität der Monaden gehört zu ihrem weltlichen Sein und Leben, ihre Erfüllung ist weltlich gerichtet' (C 8 II, 16a; pp. 151–2).

'Im Spiel der Instinkte: das Wiedererkennen, Identifizieren, Unterscheiden – vor einer schon konstituierten "Objektivität" aus Erscheinungen. Wiedererkennen eines Datums als Inhalt eines Genusses, während man satt ist' (C 13 I, 10b; p. 152).

'Die instinktive Affektion führt auf Zuwendung und Erfassung, das ist noch nicht Konstitution von Seiendem; Seiendes ist erworbene Habe, das ist, wozu ich immer wieder Zugang habe als etwas, das bleibend für mich da ist' (A VI 34, 35a; p. 152).

'Alle Befriedigung ist Durchgangsbefriedigung' (A VI 26, 42a; p. 152).

'die instinktive Freude am Sehen ist ein Prozeß instinktiver Intentionen und Erfüllungen, und die Erfüllungen lassen immer noch etwas offen: der Instinkthorizont geht weiter' (A VI 34, 36a; p. 152).

'Das Ich . . . von Erfüllungen zu neuen Erfüllungen fortstrebend; jede Erfüllung relativ, jede mit einem Horizont der unerfüllten Leere. Konstruktion der Genesis der Fundierungen im entwickelten Ich' (C 13 1, 10a; p. 152).

'Jede höhere Stufe beginnt mit dem Versuch, das Bessere . . . zu verwirklichen' (A VI 34, 36b; p. 153).

'optisch ist das Gefälligste immer das Optimum' (A VI 34, 34b; p. 153).

'die ständig allgemeine "Freude oder Unlust an der Sinnes-wahrnehmung", ein allgemeines "Interesse" im Mitgezogen-sein, das vermöge der mitgehenden Kinästhesen instinktiv auf Konstitution vom Optima, auf Konstitution von Dingerfahrungen, auf Dingkenntis gerichtet ist' (B III 9, 67; p. 153).

'Leben ist Streben in mannigfaltigen Formen und Gestalten der Intention und Erfüllung; in der Erfüllung im weitesten Sinne Lust, in der Unerfülltheit Hintendieren auf Lust als rein begehrendes Streben' (A VI 26, 42b; p. 153).

'Die angeborenen Instinkte als eine Intentionalität, die zur ursprünglichen Wesensstruktur des seelischen Seins gehört' (C 8 II, 16a; p. 154).

'Bloße Empfindungsdaten und in höherer Stufe sinnliche Gegenstände, wie Dinge, die für das Subjekt da sind, aber "wertfrei" da sind, sind Abstraktionen. Es kann nichts geben, was nicht das Gemüt berührt' (A VI 26, 42a; p. 154).

'bei jedem Inhalt . . . ist das Ich fühlendes' (C 16 V, 68a; p. 154).

'das Irrationale, das Rationalität möglich macht' (E III 9, 4b; p. 154).

CHAPTER 4

'wo nicht ein Ding schon erfahren ist, kann kein Gott ein Ding hypothetisch annehmen' (B IV 6, 53b; p. 165).

'Einheit einer Mannigfaltigkeit von Geltungen' (D 12 1, 6a; p. 167).

'Näherbestimmung: die der Approximation an ideale *limites*' (B IV 6, 26b; p. 174).

'die abnorme Ausnahme, die sich in eine allgemeinerer Erfahrungsregel wieder stimmend einfügt und in der vollentwickelten Erfahrung schon als stimmend dazugehöriges mögliches Erfahrungsvorkommnis . . . eingefügt ist' (A VII 17, 34b; p. 174).

'zu einer synthetischen Einheit zusammenstimmender Erfahrung zusammenfügbar sein müssen' (B IV 6, 67b; p. 175).

'Ist in Wirklichkeit ein Ding, so bestehen *nicht bloß . . . logische Möglichkeiten, sondern reale Möglichkeiten*, und das hat keinen anderen Sinn als den, daß es motivierte Möglichkeiten sind, die ihre Motivation in einem aktuellen Erkenntnisbewußtsein haben' (B IV 6, 98b; pp. 175–6).

'meine Welt ist Welt durch die Anderen und ihre Erfahrungen etc. hindurch' (C 17 II, 30a; p. 178).

'Wo transzendiert das reine Bewußtsein, das solipsistische (mein reines Bewußtsein) sich selbst? Nur da, wo es fremdes Bewußtsein setzt' (B IV 6, 62a; p. 178).

'wenn Bewußtsein nicht wäre, nicht nur Erkenntnis nicht möglich wäre, sondern auch Natur selbst jeden Anhalt, ihre Wurzel, ihre *arché* verlieren würde und damit ein Nichts wäre' (B IV 6, 92b; p. 180).

'Gäbe es nicht Bewußtsein mit Erscheinungen, so gäbe es auch keine Dinge' (B I 4, 21a; p. 180).

'Was wir sagen wollen, ist nur dies, daß es gar nichts anderes gibt als "Geister" im weitesten Sinn, wenn nur das "gibt" im absoluten Sinn verstehen, und daß Leiber und sonstige physische Dinge nur sind . . . als Einheiten der Erfahrungserkenntnis' (B II 2, 17a; p. 180).

'absolut ist in dem Sinn, daß sie ist, was sie ist, ob Bewußtsein überhaupt ist oder nicht' (B IV 6, 81a; p. 211, note 5).

'Bewußtsein absolutes Sein ist und . . . jedes Ding nur Anzeige ist für gewisse Zusammenhänge und Motivationen im absoluten Sein' (B II 2, 3b–4a; p. 182).

'das prinzipiell "Unvorstellbare": das Unbewußte, Tod, Geburt' (A VII 17, 5a; p. 211, note 8).

'Existiert A, so muß die . . . rechtmäßige Erkenntnis von A möglich sein. Andererseits: Existiert A nicht, so ist sie unmöglich' (B IV 6, 6b; p. 187).

'*Ein höherer Geist ist denkbar, der mit Grund das erkennen kann, was wir nicht erkennen können. Und das ist keine leere Möglichkeit.* Denn das *wissen* wir, daß unendlich viel Unerkanntes da ist' (B IV 6, 72b; p. 189).

'Wir fühlen sehr wohl, daß es eine bloße Konstruktion ist, wenn wir davon sprechen, wie es wohl auf der Sonne und in der Sonne unter der Photosphär "aussehen" mag, wie sich die ungeheuere Temperatur empfinden mag etc.' (B II 2, 16a–b; p. 190).

'symbolisch-analogischen Vorstellungen . . . "erfundene" Empfindungen' (BII 2, 15a; p. 190).

'*Existenz von Objekten mag Existenz von Erscheinungen voraussetzen, aber es setzt nicht die Existenz jedes Objektes die Existenz einer Erscheinung . . . voraus,* die sich auf *dieses selbe* bezieht in der Weise der Wahrnehmungserscheinung' (B II 2, 11b; p. 190).

'die spezifische Leistung der Wissenschaft' (A VII 17, 10b; p. 190).

'[wie] das philosophisch-wissenschaftliche Streben nach Autonomie im methodisch technischen Betrieb verfält, wie es herabsinkt zur sekundären blinden Triebhaftigkeit' (E III 4, 10a–b; p. 195).

'Allgemein gesagt besteht die Rationalität der Natur darin, daß für sie eine matematische Naturwissenschaft möglich ist' (B II 2, 23b; p. 198).

'Die Konstitution der Natur ist ... von vornherein untrennbar verflochten mit der Konstitution der Leiblichkeit'(C 17 II, 45b; p. 202).

'eine Gesetzmäßigkeit der erwachten und zugleich noch unerwachten Monaden' (B II 2, 12b; p. 204).

'Die Existenz von Subjekten, die in Akkord behaftet sind mit Erlebnisregeln, die der dinglichen Konstitution entsprechen, sind im Sinn des Idealismus äquivalent mit der Existenz von Dingen selbst und der Dingwelt. Die Dingkonstitution ist nur potentiell. Aber was ist das für eine Potentialität? Der Buwußtseinslauf ist nicht beliebig, sondern auch, wo er nicht wirklich konstitutiv ist (wo keine wirklichen Dingapperzeptionen entwickelt sind), durch die Existenz der Natur vorgezeichnet. Aber wie, da doch so etwas wie völlig dumpfes Bewußtsein möglich ist?' (B IV 6, 5a–b; p. 204).

'jedes organische Wesen ist "Erzeuger" für neue, die alsbald (oder in schneller Entwicklung) auf dieselbe Höhe emporgehoben werden (der Klarheit) wie die Eltern' (B II 2, 12b; p. 205).

'ein "nicht-seiend", das . . . Sein mit ermöglicht' (C 17 V 2, 88b; p. 205).

'*daß jedes Ding in gewisser Weise Leib zu einem Bewußtsein ist, wenn auch zu einem dumpfen Bewußtsein,* daß das Sein der Natur zurückführt auf *Sein von lauter Bewußtsein, ewigem Bewußtsein, sich verteilend auf Monaden und Monadenverbände,* und daß, wenn von einer bewußtlosen Natur die Rede ist, es sich um *bloße Stadien niederen Bewußtseins handelt*' (B IV 6, 72b; p. 205).

'Der Fluß des Bewußtsein in einer Monade. Ein Faktisches zunächst. Es könnte auch anders ablaufen. Kann man fragen: warum läuft er gerade so ab? welcher *Grund* hat das? Alle Rede von Grund und Ergründing führt auf Motivationszusammenhänge im Bewußtsein zurück' (B II 2, 25a; p. 206).

'von der physischen blinden Natur emporleitet zur psychophysischen Natur, wo das Bewußtsein sein Geistesauge aufschlägt, und weiter empor zur menschlichen Natur' (B II 2, 13a; p. 207).

'Alles absolute Sein ist ein Strom teleologisch zusammenstimmenden und auf ideale Ziele gerichteten Werdens' (B I 4, 23b; p. 207).

'Wille zur Einstimmigkeit, zur Einheit' (A VI 34, 36b; p. 207).

'*Ein Geist* liebt Vollkommenheit, . . . strebt sie zu realisieren' (B II 2, 26a; p. 207).

'Zu jede Monade gehört eine den Verlauf ihrer Erlebnisse beherrschende Gesetzmässigkeit' (B II 2, 14a; p. 208).

'Erst von einem gewissem Zeitpunkt ab entwickelten sich nach der Gesetzmäßigkeit, die alle monadische Wirklichkeit beherrscht, die Bewußtseinsflüsse so, daß . . . differenzierte Empfindungen und Gefühle auftraten' (B II 2, 14b; p. 208).

'Die Phänomenologie muß . . . zeigen, wie die transzendentale Intersubjektivität nur sein kann, zunächst Welt in passiver Konstitution aus Instinkten konstituierend . . . , wie sie dann "erwachen" muß aus innerer Motivation, aus ursprünglichen Anlagen zur Vernuft' (E III 4, 16b; p. 208).

'*wenn eine Natur existert, kann der Erlebnisstrom nicht beliebig sein*' (B IV 6, 16b; p. 209).

'als Regel, unter der alle Monaden . . . stehen . . . Welche Änderungen in der Empfindungskonstitution möglich sind, dies ist für alle Ewigkeit vorgezeichnet' (B II 2, 17a; p. 209).

'ein idealer Wert, der realisiert ist' (B II 2, 26a; p. 210).

'Alle Erfahrungswirklichkeit und alle endliche Geistigkeit ist Objektivation Gottes, Entfaltung der göttlichen Tätigkeit' (B II 2, 27b; p. 210).

'das Real-sein-Wollen Gottes' (B II 2, 27b; p. 210).

'inkonfessioneller Weg zu Gott' (E III 10, 14a; p. 210).

BIBLIOGRAPHY

Burge, Tyler (1979) 'Individualism and the Mental'. *Midwest Studies in Philosophy*, 4, 73–121.

Cairns, Dorion (1973) *Guide for Translating Husserl*. Dordrecht: Kluwer.

Cairns, Dorion (1975) *Conversations with Husserl and Fink*. Dordrecht: Kluwer.

Davidson, Donald (1980) 'Mental Events', *Essays on Action and Events*. Oxford: Oxford University Press, 207–225.

Drummond, John J. (1975) 'Husserl on the Ways to the Performance of the Reduction'. *Man and World*, 8, 47–69.

Fink, Eugen (1988) *VI. Cartesianische Meditation*, 2 vols. Dordrecht: Kluwer. The first volume of this work has been translated into English by Ronald Bruzina as *Sixth Cartesian Meditation* (Bloomington: Indiana University Press, 1995).

Grice, H. P. (1957) 'Meaning'. *The Philosophical Review*, 66, 377–388.

Heidegger, Martin (1977) 'Der Ursprung des Kunstwerkes'. In *Holzwege*, *Gesamtausgabe*, Frankfurt am Main: Vittorio Klostermann, vol. 5. 1–74. ['The Origin of the Work of Art', tr. David Farrell Krell, *Martin Heidegger: Basic Writings* (New York: Harper & Row, 1977), 149–187, with omissions].

Heidegger, Martin (1993) *Sein und Zeit*. Tübingen: Max Niemeyer. Originally published 1927. [*Being and Time*, trs John Macquarrie and Edward Robinson (Oxford: Blackwell, 1973)].

Hume, David (1978) *A Treatise of Human Nature*, eds L. A. Selby-Bigge and P. H. Nidditch, 2nd edn, Oxford: Clarendon Press. Originally published 1739/40.

James, William (1950) *The Principles of Psychology*, 2 vols. New York: Dover. Originally published 1890.

Johannson, G. (1975) 'Visual Motion Perception'. *Scientific American*, 232, 76–88.

Kern, I. (1964) *Husserl und Kant*. The Hague: Martinus Nijhoff.

Kern, I. (1977) 'The Three Ways to the Transcendental Phenomenological Reduction in the Philosophy of Edmund Husserl'. In Frederick Elliston and Peter McCormick (eds) *Husserl: Expositions and Appraisals*. Notre Dame, Ind.: University of Notre Dame Press.

Kripke, Saul (1980) *Naming and Necessity*. Oxford: Blackwell.

Landgrebe, L. (1981) 'Husserl's Departure from Cartesianism', in his *The Phenomenology of Husserl*. Ithaca, NY and London: Cornell University Press.

McDowell, John (1986) 'Singular Thought and Inner Space'. In Philip Pettit and John McDowell (eds) *Subject, Thought, and Context*. Oxford: Clarendon Press.

Meltzoff, Andrew M. and Moore, M. Keith (1983) 'Newborn Infants Imitate Adult Facial Gestures'. *Child Development*, 54, 702–9.

Moore, G. E. (1922) *Philosophical Studies*. London: Routledge and Kegan Paul.

Moore, G. E. (1953) *Some Main Problems of Philosophy*. London: George Allen and Unwin.

Petitot, Jean, Varela, Francisco J., Pachoud, Bernard and Roy, Jean-Michel (eds) (1999) *Naturalizing Phenomenology*. Stanford: Stanford University Press.

Putnam, Hilary (1975) 'The Meaning of Meaning', in his *Philosophical Papers*, vol. 2. Cambridge: Cambridge University Press, 215–271.

Russell, Bertrand (1984) *Theory of Knowledge: The 1913 Manuscript*, in *The Collected Papers of Bertrand Russell*, vol. 7. London: George Allen and Unwin.

Sartre, Jean-Paul (1992) *La Transcendance de l'Ego*. Paris: J. Vrin. [*The Transcendence of the Ego*, trs Forrest Williams and Robert Kirkpatrick (New York: Octagon Books, 1972)].

Schumann, Karl (1977) *Husserl-Chronik*, Husserliana Dokumente vol. 1. The Hague: Martinus Nijhoff.

Smith, A. D. (1993) 'Non-Reductive Physicalism?' In Howard Robinson (ed.) *Objections to Physicalism*. Oxford: Clarendon Press, 225–250.

Smith, A. D. (2000) 'Space and Sight'. *Mind*, 109, 481–518.

Smith, A. D. (2001) 'Perception and Belief'. *Philosophy and Phenomenological Research*, 62, 283–310.

Stern, Daniel M. (1998) *The Interpersonal World of the Infant*. London: Karnac Books.

Trevarthen, Colwyn (1993) 'The Self Born in Intersubjectivity: The Psychology of an Infant Communicating'. In Ulric Neisser (ed.) *The Self Perceived*. Cambridge: Cambridge University Press, 121–173.

INDEX